MONETARISM OR PROSPERITY?

Also by Bryan Gould

CHARTER FOR THE DISABLED (*with Eda Topliss*)

Also by John Mills

GROWTH AND WELFARE: A New Policy for Britain

MONETARISM OR PROSPERITY?

Bryan Gould, John Mills and
Shaun Stewart

Foreword by
Rt Hon Peter Shore, PC, MP

First published 1981 by
THE MACMILLAN PRESS LTD
London and Basingstoke
Companies and representatives
throughout the world

ISBN 0 333 30782 8 (hardcover)
ISBN 0 333 31973 7 (paperback)

Photoset in Great Britain by
ROWLAND PHOTOTYPESETTING LTD
Bury St Edmunds, Suffolk
and printed and bound by
BILLING AND SONS LTD
Guildford, London, Oxford, Worcester

Contents

List of Tables and Figures

TABLES

FIGURES

Note References to 'us', 'our country' and so on throughout refer
to the UK.

Foreword
by Rt Hon Peter Shore, PC, MP

I believe this book will be widely read and that it deserves to be. That British economic policy has lost its way in a Hampton Court Maze of monetarist dogma and half-truth, few will dispute; nor that to find the way out is the essential precondition for a new start.

But escape from our present follies will not be enough. Once we have regained some measure of sanity and realism, we must look afresh at the central and abiding objectives of economic strategy and how we can best achieve them. Above all we have to arrest the continuing decline in our fortunes – a trend clearly established long before the present Government took office and took leave of its senses.

Both these tasks, the short-term rescue and the long-term revival, are vigorously engaged in this book. And it begins with a refreshing candour and simplicity in addressing itself to the central purpose of economic policy: the expansion of national wealth, the growth of the economy. Of course there may come a time when we would consciously wish to give lower priority to the creation of wealth. But, as the authors point out, with so many unsatisfied demands, that is certainly not the case now: and the attempt to present other goals (while they should not be neglected, particularly in the environmental field) is mainly a rationalisation of the past and present failure.

Low growth in the 1950s and 1960s; nil growth in much of the 1970s and now minus growth in the 1980s both record and stress what has been the great problem of our country. Its cause should be the main focus of serious enquiry and its remedy the main objective of economic policy. Economic expansion, not inflation, not the exchange rate, not the size of the public sector borrowing requirement, not the level of public expenditure and certainly not the fulfilment of paper targets for the growth of the money supply, should be the central purpose of economic policy.

For, with growth, comes higher productivity, more employment, the stimulus to investment and a weakening of all those social and psychological obstacles to progress that fear of job loss and an increasingly defeatist attitude have intensified.

How to achieve this central objective is the closing theme of this excellent study. I share the authors' belief that a competitive exchange rate is the key and further that the weight of financial opinion, emanating from the financial institutions of the City and given great authority by the Bank of England, has been the particular incubus on Britain's postwar economic policy.

Without a positive policy for the exchange rate, nothing will come right: and the great flow of North Sea Oil, which perversely is impoverishing rather than enriching us, makes this all the more urgent.

Whether the authors have given enough weight to counter-inflation policy or to the supply side of the economy is open to argument. But no one in their senses would dispute that these policies cannot possibly succeed unless policies for competitiveness and expansion are at the centre of national policy.

Much has been said in recent years about '*the* alternative strategy'. The truth is that there are a number of alternative strategies and they all need careful study. But this, in my judgement, is the most thoughtful and persuasive that has yet been published.

The authors deserve a vote of thanks from all who wish to reverse and revive the economic fortunes of this country.

17 November 1980

1 Growth and Productivity

INTRODUCTION: THE BRITISH FAILURE

The decline of the British economy, and with it, of British influence in the world, is perhaps a century old, but has been gathering pace over the last decade or two. It has been marked by a massive fall in the British share of world trade in manufactures, while Britain's rate of economic growth has been only about half that of other industrialised countries. The 30 per cent share of world trade in manufactures which Britain enjoyed at the turn of the century, after dipping to 22 per cent just before the Second World War and recovering to 25 per cent in 1950, has fallen almost continuously since then to its present level of 8 per cent–9 per cent. Even that figure is misleadingly favourable, since it owes much to the reduction in tariffs on UK exports to the EEC and is more than offset by the rapid rise in our imports from the same area.

The Germans, who had first overtaken our share of world trade in 1938, again overtook us in 1958 and their share has settled down substantially above ours at 20 per cent–22 per cent. In 1970 Japan pushed us into fourth place – behind the United States and Germany – and in 1973 France overtook us as well. We may soon be overtaken by Italy, at least in terms of volume, and we are in danger of being relegated to the same league as much smaller countries like Belgium and Holland in the foreseeable future.

There seems no prospect of an early recovery. Manufacturing output is already 10 per cent lower than in 1973 and the impact of North Sea oil will, with present policies, lead to a further and substantial contraction. Our traditional surplus of exports over imports of manufactures has almost disappeared and only a fall in domestic demand as a result of rising unemployment has saved us, for the first time in at least two centuries, from becoming a net importer of manufactured goods. What happened to the British textile, shipbuilding and motor cycle industries in the 1960s and 1970s is now threatening such other bastions of our former manufacturing strength as the motor car, machine tools and carpet industries.

It is one thing to live with a rate of growth only half that of one's major competitors; a growing disparity in living standards, both in terms of private consumption and public services, and a corresponding loss of political power and influence in favour of more powerful economies can be tolerated for a time, since it happens almost imperceptibly and its results are not seen directly by the majority of the population. Nil, or even negative growth, however, with all that this will mean for living standards and employment, will be much more difficult to bear. We shall be moving into uncharted territory. We shall be the first major industrial country to suffer such a decline, and to confront the social and political strains which will inevitably ensue.

This grim prospect has not arisen by design. A rate of economic growth comparable to that achieved by most other industrialised countries has been the goal of every British government since the Second World War. The failure to achieve this goal is largely responsible for our increasing loss of national self-confidence and for the growing public disillusionment with the political process.

It has also produced in some circles a reaction against the desirability of economic growth and an argument that our economic performance has failed to match international standards because we have deliberately turned our backs on growth. This is, however, no more than an *ex post facto* rationalisation of the fact that we have done badly what we have tried to do well, and it is totally contradicted by all the evidence of continuing demands from all quarters for improved standards of private and public consumption. All that is happening in Britain is that we are failing to keep up with the rising standards of other countries, not only in terms of personal living standards, but also in terms of our ability to secure social justice as between the privileged and less privileged and to maintain the fabric of our environment and civilisation. As long as economic growth can be secured through the more efficient utilisation of the resources available, it will be rejected only by those whom Anthony Crosland once described as 'pulling up the ladder behind them'.

In any case, the option of a stable-state economy is simply not open to us. Our rate of growth cannot be established in isolation; it depends crucially on the performance of other economies and the effect of this on our international competitiveness. We have to run in order to stand still. As long as we operate as part of the wider international economy, and as long as we need to trade in order to maintain our present living standards, we must either compete with and match levels of efficiency and productivity which continue to rise around the world, or else we must face the real prospect of economic decline and impoverishment.

It may be that, at some point in the future, economic growth will no longer be possible, but we are far from having reached that point yet. In the meantime, it is economic growth which permits us to improve our living standards – standards which are not measured simply in terms of personal material consumption, but are also determined by the level of public services. Growth is necessary not only so that the less privileged reach material standards already taken for granted by the better-off, but also in order to secure better education, housing and health services. The fruits of economic growth also provide the key to a safer and cleaner environment, since measures to reduce pollution and waste inevitably cost money. The margin of additional resources provides a lubricant, too, for necessary social and economic change and provides a guarantee of the social and political stability which we take for granted in a liberal democracy. Economic prosperity can help to make possible cultural and sporting achievements; it kindles a sense of national self-confidence and well-being which is reflected in the increased influence that a country with a successful economy enjoys in the world.

Given the importance of economic growth, it is surprising that so little attention has been paid to it by economic theorists and practitioners. There seems to be very little appreciation, in this country at least, of what economic growth is and how it can be brought about. British governments have become so immersed in the difficult problems assailing them from all sides that they have sometimes lost sight of the simple proposition that the central objective of economic policy-making is to produce more goods and services. In the absence of growth, great attention has been paid to other economic indicators – inflation, the balance of payments, the public sector borrowing requirement. These are, however, subordinate considerations, which, if important at all, are simply the means to the end of economic growth rather than ends in themselves. They would cease to dominate our thinking if the economy as a whole were performing well.

The British failure to secure growth at a rate comparable to that of other industrialised countries has provoked an increasingly frenetic search for explanations. As the extent of that failure has become more apparent over recent years, there has been a tendency to seek for causes arising from that more recent experience. In the 1950s, the less sophisticated complained that our industries were at a disadvantage because our factories had not been destroyed in the war and subsequently rebuilt. The more sophisticated emphasised the problem of lower labour productivity, and teams were sent to the United States to learn how we could lower our costs by more intelligent use of our existing manpower and machinery resources, thus perhaps unwittingly repeating an exercise carried out nearly a century earlier and illustrating the fact that our problems have been with us for a long time.[1] In the early 1960s, we tried to break out of the descending spiral by a 'dash for growth' and, when this failed, we were told that the right policy was to create through mergers huge firms able and willing to rationalise and re-equip to make use of new technologies. Throughout this period, we were assured that our problems would be solved by joining the EEC. Other explanations have become fashionable in the cold reality of the 1970s; we have identified in turn, as the reasons for our failures, overconsumption and underinvestment, low profitability, trade union power, the shift from manufacturing to public employment, excessive public expenditure and a failure to control the money supply, amongst many others.

Many of these explanations are no more than attempted rationalisations of political prejudice. Almost all of them overlook the fact that our decline has now been going on for a century or more[2] and is therefore not to be attributed to any relatively recent development, such as the increase in trade union power or the rise in public expenditure. A recognition of the long-term nature of our problems is indeed essential to accurate analysis. Otherwise, it becomes difficult to disentangle cause and effect. Long-term economic decline inevitably produces its own long-term consequences; these include defensive attitudes on both sides of industry – restrictive practices and overmanning on the part of labour and an unwillingness to innovate or risk investment capital on the part of management – which eventually become problems in their own right and are accordingly regarded as original causes rather than symptoms.

Among the consequences of our long-term comparative decline are what are now described as 'supply side' problems. These include apparent shortages of investment capital, skilled labour and components, and problems of industrial organisation and industrial relations. Much effort has been devoted to identifying these problems and, through national plans, industrial strategies and ministerial exhortations, to the means of resolving them. But to identify these difficulties is merely to restate the problems. The real questions still await answers. Why is investment capital lacking? Why is there a shortage of skilled labour? Why do bottlenecks arise through shortages of parts? Why are there defensive attitudes in industry? Most importantly, why do these problems inhibit the British economic performance when they are successfully overcome in other economies? The attempt to answer these questions simply leads us back to the starting point of our enquiry.

As far as investment capital is concerned, it is certainly true that much of what is needed to bring about improved productivity will cost money – up-to-date plant and equipment, training workers, buying in components. But in the absence of growth, industry is not profitable enough to generate sufficient capital for reinvestment; and such capital as is available goes to other things, because the conditions in which it makes sense to invest in manufacturing in Britain do not exist. Similarly, with labour shortages; productivity can be inhibited by bottlenecks in the labour market, but there is no shortage of labour, even of skilled labour. What is missing is the ability of manufacturing industry to pay a high enough price to divert labour from less productive jobs, to prevent the loss of skilled men to the non-manufacturing sector and to train the existing workforce to a higher level of skill. In the same way, shortages of materials and components could easily be made up if manufacturing industry were profitable enough to afford to buy them in; from abroad if necessary. Our industrial performance would benefit enormously from improved attitudes on both sides; but these attitudes, too, can only improve if the overriding preoccupation to defend jobs and status is replaced by the prospect of expansion, increased job opportunities and rising standards.

In other words, 'supply side' problems are the consequence

rather than the cause of a low rate of economic growth. They describe but cannot explain our failure. The shortages of capital, labour, components and goodwill are not absolute shortages. There is no reason intrinsic to the British economy which makes them any more difficult to overcome than, say, in the German economy. The real question for British economic management is why these problems are not resolved.

It is our thesis that all of these problems could be resolved if the right macroeconomic conditions could be established. There is no reason to suppose that the British economy would not respond to those conditions as other economies have done. Our failures have arisen because we have consistently pursued mistaken policies which have made it virtually impossible for our economy to keep pace with our more successful competitors.

The roots of those mistaken policies and of our comparative industrial decline lie somewhere in the latter part of the nineteenth century, when our pre-eminence as an industrial power was first seriously threatened by the rise of important rivals, and when our share of world trade first began to decline significantly. We began to develop an economy based on financial power rather than manufacturing. The income from our huge investments abroad meant that we did not need to pay for our import bill by selling exports. Indeed, our overseas earnings not only removed any incentive to remain competitive but made it increasingly difficult to do so. We demanded payment in gold and, because the Bank Act of 1844 meant that any increase in the gold supply was reflected in an increase in the supply of money, domestic costs and prices were bound sooner or later to rise to a level that would make our goods less competitive at home and overseas.

These developments could have been counteracted by determined policy measures, but the prevailing orthodoxies – many of them still with us a century later – made this almost impossible. London had inevitably become the financial centre of the world, and all the efforts of the City of London were directed towards protecting the value of our investments and the interests of those who held and dealt in financial assets. In the scale of values then established, the needs of manufacturing industry, of those who make and sell things, were given a relatively low priority. We fell into the habit, fatally, of attaching more importance to the money economy than to the real economy. While our more successful competitors erected tariff barriers, fixed their ex-change rates and decided their monetary policies in the interests of manufacturing industry, including in particular the new science-based industries, we were more concerned to preserve the stability and reputation of the City of London as a financial centre.

These attitudes led to a fundamental misapprehension as to the nature of economic growth. We watched with increasing be-wilderment as our own economic performance was outstripped by more successful countries, who entered a virtuous circle of increasing productivity and competitiveness which led in turn to growing financial strength. Our own preoccupation with financial rather than industrial power meant that we repeatedly sought to break into this virtuous circle at the wrong point. We tried to take a short cut to economic growth through policies of extreme financial orthodoxy which ignored the underlying health of the real economy and indeed inflicted considerable damage. We failed to recognise that the first and essential function of a successful economy is that it should produce real goods and services and that, in the end, no other measurement matters but the quantity of goods and services which are made, provided and sold. Financial strength is the concomitant rather than the progenitor of a successful economy; but in the absence of real economic strength, financial orthodoxy can be an obstacle to economic success and leads inevitably, in the longer term, to financial weakness as well.

This failure of analysis, engendered by mental habits estab-lished a century ago, continues to influence economic policy-making today. Although modern British governments, like their predecessors, continue to seek the elusive goal of economic growth and competitiveness, success is as far away as ever. This is because we have failed to break free from policy attitudes which began to store up trouble a century ago, even when our economy was one of enormous financial power, and which are even more harmful and inappropriate today when we have to earn our living in the world. We have failed to analyse the policy requirements of a successful industrial economy with sufficient rigour and, even when we have correctly identified what is needed, have failed to pursue the necessary policies with suf-ficient vigour.

It is our belief that these deficiences can be made good. In the following sections of this chapter, we explain what we believe is the key to economic growth, why growth is much faster in some countries than others, and, in particular, why the British record has been so poor.

PRODUCTIVITY AND GROWTH

Economic growth is about increasing the production of goods and services. A higher total output can be achieved in a number of ways. It can happen because labour inputs are increased either by more people working or by the same people working longer hours or more shifts, or by a combination of these two. Or it can happen because the output per hour of those in employment rises. Increasing the number of hours or shifts worked can be a significant factor, because it increases the productivity of capital, although this cannot be relied on too heavily at a time when there are pressures to reduce the working week. Increasing the labour force is only possible beyond a certain point, even if the population is expanding – and then of course the increased output is diluted because it has to be spread over more people. The key to long-term economic growth and raising living standards therefore lies in increasing the average output of each worker per unit of time he or she is actually at work, or in other words, increasing productivity.

Increased productivity can be brought about in several different ways. It can be achieved by increasing investment in plant and equipment which means that less labour is required for each unit of output. It can be attained by improved working methods, perhaps based on better training and education, but often arising from quite basic and common-sense changes in working practices, so that unnecessary steps and over-complicated procedures are eliminated. Higher productivity on average can also be obtained as resources of labour and capital move from low to high productivity areas in the economy and as the economy as a whole concentrates on those things it is best at doing.

The scope for productivity increases varies from one part of the economy to another. In some fields of economic activity, productivity has hardly altered at all over the last two centuries. On the other hand, some computer applications now involve outputs per employee which are literally thousands of times higher than was possible two or three decades ago. The areas in the economy where very rapid gains in productivity can be achieved are to be found where there is a combination of certain key characteristics.

First, some economic activities provide large-scale scope for labour-saving mechanisation. Almost everyone's job can be helped to some extent by machines, but in light industry in particular, and in some parts of the service sector such as in communications, the possibilities for increasing productivity are very great. The output per employee achievable from modern computer-controlled lathes, moulding machines, assembly operations and process equipment is now orders of magnitude greater than it was even a generation ago.

Secondly, because resources for investment are limited, it will be those machines which offer the greatest increases in productivity over existing equipment, and which take the shortest time to develop, build and install, which will provide the most rapid cumulative increases in output. It is a great mistake to believe that all or even a major part of this type of machinery is the product of fundamentally new research. In fact, most of it is the result of piecemeal improvement, often very sophisticated technically, but generally brought about by the practical, speedy and intelligent exploitation of technology which is readily available.

Thirdly, in those areas where the most rapid improvement is possible, it is essential that there is an institutional economic framework which allows for the maximum amount of experimentation and interchange of knowledge. Improvements in productivity are extremely difficult to ordain by administrative action, whether in the public or private sector. Governments can raise productivity by, for example, improving transport and communications systems, but most productivity improvements are discovered almost at random and depend on a series of small, detailed changes which are very difficult to identify and plan for at national or even industry level. Hence, we are sceptical about industrial strategies to improve economic performance, especially in light industry where the scope for productivity increases is very high but the means of achieving them is almost infinitely varied; for the same reasons, while large firms and undertakings might improve productivity to some extent through rationalisation, we would expect more important gains to be made in the smaller enterprises where the need to innovate and to respond flexibly are likely to be more evident.

Fourthly, there is the crucially important question of economies of scale. It is a key characteristic of many of the most effective ways of increasing productivity that they involve greater volumes of output and, as a consequence, falling unit costs of production. More intensive use of expensive capital equipment and longer production runs make it possible to achieve profitable production at lower and lower costs. Lower production costs allow the market to be enlarged, either by absorbing higher transport and other costs so that wider areas are covered or by reducing prices so that demand increases within existing markets. It is in those areas, therefore, where the techniques of mass production can be utilised and where marginal reductions in price lead to substantially enlarged markets, that the most important productivity gains can be made.

These factors are significant in identifying those areas of the economy where productivity is likely to increase fastest. But the overall economic climate is, in our view, the most important single determinant of trends in productivity for the economy as a whole. This is not to say that productivity cannot increase in the absence of economic growth. Nevertheless, an environment of growth is important, both as a stimulus to improved productivity, for the reasons we explain shortly, and because improved productivity in the absence of growth can be a mixed blessing. If the size of the economy is static and productivity rises, the consequence is increased unemployment rather than more output. Thus, it does not necessarily follow that the national income will increase, even if productivity in the economy is rising, unless a further vital condition is fulfilled. The total level of demand for the goods and services which the economy actually has on offer must increase sufficiently rapidly to ensure that productivity improvements lead to increased national output and not to increased unemployment. A deficiency in demand will not only mean static output, but also, by removing incentives to both capital and labour in the longer term, inhibit improvements in productivity.

Improvements in productivity therefore depend crucially on the existence of readily accessible markets for the goods which the economy produces. It is not just the absolute size of these markets which matters, however; productivity will be stimulated particularly if the demand for the economy's products is rising and if the available markets are expanding. The process of raising productivity is a dynamic one; the flexibility, co-operation and innovation on which a reduction in unit costs depends is much more easily achieved when the economy as a whole is working with it rather than against it. A high level of demand and a sizeable market are important in static terms, but it is the rate of growth that will really make the difference.

An industry which is expanding rapidly is much more likely to build completely new manufacturing plants and to place them in advantageous new locations which reduce its production costs to a minimum; and, because such an industry is almost certain to be very profitable, the wages, salaries and morale of its workforce are likely to be very high, so that good management and workers will be attracted from other industries and the industrial relations climate will be favourable. An industry which is on the defensive, on the other hand, is forever trying to make do and mend, putting such new machinery as it can afford piecemeal into unsuitable buildings, often scattered on one site, or, as in the case of British Leyland, a multiplicity of sites; and, because its market is not expanding, it can only increase its productivity by shedding staff and paying less than the going rate, with all that that entails for morale and the firm's ability to hold on to the more competent among its existing staff.

The classic example of the influence of growth on productivity is the motor car industry. The UK share of the world market for cars has declined for nearly thirty years, despite the government's efforts to force the industry to sell more of its production overseas by restricting demand at home. These efforts were quite literally counterproductive. They included severe hire-purchase restrictions and increases in purchase tax of up to as much as 60 per cent of the wholesale price in the case of home sales. The effect was to raise unit costs and to reduce the industry's profitability, the inevitable result being that investment in labour-saving plant was reduced to only a fraction of the amount made available to its continental competitors and, in particular, to the rapidly expanding Japanese industry. The British industry was therefore ill-equipped to meet unrestricted competition within the enlarged Common Market from contintental manufacturers enjoying much larger economies of scale. This was not, as some would have us believe, the result of exorbitant wage demands. In fact, real wages in the British motor vehicle industry fell by nearly 20 per cent between 1958 and 1978, by comparison with

industry generally, and since then have again fallen substantially
as a result of the low settlements agreed in 1979. In other
countries, real wages have risen steadily and car workers' wages
have risen even faster. Little wonder that low productivity and
industrial relations problems have become endemic and have
reinforced the damage that was originally inflicted by the restrictions which the monetary and exchange rate policies of successive governments imposed on the capacity of the industry to
expand its markets at home and overseas.

The relationship between productivity and growth was emphasised by the Department of Trade in an article on export
performance in *Trade and Industry* on September 1 1978. The
Department drew attention to the close correlation between falling labour productivity in the UK, the declining UK share of
all industrial countries' GDP, and our loss of share in non-
Commonwealth markets. It also pointed out that, in international comparisons, high rates of productivity growth are
generally associated with high rates of output, export growth and
employment in manufacturing. It did not, however, draw any
conclusions about the direction of causality.

A strong indication that productivity depends on growth,
rather than vice versa, is however provided by the experience of
the principal industrial countries since 1963, as shown in Table
1.1.

The differences between the period of high growth from 1963

TABLE 1.1   *Average annual percentage increase in GDP and output per person-hour
in manufacturing, 1963–79*

| | 1963–73 | | 1973–6 | | 1976–9 | |
	GDP	OPPH	GDP	OPPH	GDP	OPPH
Japan	10.2	11.2	2.5	2.0	5.8	7.7
France	5.5	6.7	2.8	3.9	3.2	3.9
Germany	4.7	5.7	1.3	4.5	3.4	3.7
Italy	4.7	7.0	2.1	2.3	2.8	3.0
USA	4.1	3.7	1.1	3.4	3.8	2.1
UK	3.3	4.5	0.4	1.3	1.3	1.2

SOURCE: UK figures are from *Economic Trends* and exclude oil and gas. Other
countries: cols 2, 4 – OECD, *Economic Outlook*, no. 26 (December 1979); cols
3, 5 – NIESR Review; cols 6, 7 – OECD, *Main Economic Indicators* (April
1980) p. 168 and country tables.

to 1973 and the period 1973 to 1976, which was dominated by the 1975 recession, are strikingly clear. Even in countries such as Japan, with enviable records of productivity growth, and where the docility of the labour unions is legendary, productivity fell quickly as the rate of growth fell; this was the clear experience of four of the six countries.

In the United States and Germany, on the other hand, a very severe fall in the rate of growth caused only a relatively small fall in output per person-hour, in part because the numbers employed had to be drastically reduced as a result of closures and in part because, in the case of Germany, foreign workers were being replaced by better-trained German workers who would otherwise have been unemployed. The recovery in output and employment in these two countries after the recession was likewise accompanied by a fall in output per person-hour as marginal labour was reabsorbed. The conclusion over the period as a whole, however, is nevertheless unavoidable: for Britain, and other countries too, productivity responds to a high rate of growth.

The relationship is even closer in the case of the UK, if we take the comparison back to 1955 and compare the average annual increase in total output in manufacturing with the corresponding figure for output per person-hour, as in Table 1.2.

TABLE 1.2 *Manufacturing output and output per person-hour in the UK, 1955–79*

	Manufacturing Output	Output per Person-Hour
1955–62	2.2	2.2
1963–73	3.6	4.5
1973–9	−0.75	1.4

SOURCE: OPPH for 1955–62 is from the NIESR Review. Other figures are derived from *Economic Trends*.

The barrenness of the Thorneycroft and Selwyn Lloyd years in terms of both output and productivity is well shown. The faster growth initiated by Reginald Maudling produced a substantial improvement in productivity. That growth was interrupted by Roy Jenkins's two budgets, but the much-maligned 'Barber boom' allowed output per head in manufacturing industry to increase by almost 18 per cent in the period from the first quarter of 1971 to the third quarter of 1973, compared to an increase of little more than 2 per cent for the rest of the economy. The recession which followed reduced output per head in manufacturing by nearly 7 per cent in the 21 months to the second quarter of 1975, even though productivity in the rest of the economy fell by not much more than 1 per cent.

It cannot be argued that those substantial variations in productivity increases caused the differing rates of growth which accompanied them, since the rate of growth was in each case strongly affected by factors which were quite independent of productivity levels –factors such as the deflationary or expansionary domestic policies pursued by successive governments, and the impact of world trading conditions. Nor are the variations explicable in terms of some of the explanations generally offered for our disappointing economic performance. The trade unions, for example – the factor identified by so many current commentators – can hardly be said to have looked particularly kindly on Mr Heath's government and then reimposed restrictive attitudes when Mr Wilson returned to office. The only rational conclusion to be drawn from these figures is that productivity in the UK, as in other countries, rises when the rate of growth increases.

The link between growth and productivity has not been entirely overlooked, even in official publications. In the Economic Progress Report of December 1977, for example, the Treasury provided an admirable description of the virtuous circle in which growth and productivity play such important and interlocking parts:

Productivity is a key element in what is often described as the 'virtuous circle' of high growth: increased productivity – briefly and in summary, a reduction in the labour cost of producing any given amount of goods – provides cheaper products; increased demand for these cheaper products increases employment and is an incentive for investment in expansion, at the same time providing the funds for this investment; expansion enables sustained higher levels of output and employment while additional investment also enables further improvements in productivity. And so the 'circle' begins again, at a higher level of output and employment: economic growth becomes self-sustaining.

'The major weakness of this analysis is that it suggests that the 'virtuous circle' can be broken into through increased productivity, in the absence of growth, and that growth will then follow on as a consequence of increased productivity. The deficiences of this approach are evidenced by the continuing failure of policies based on this premise to launch our economy into the 'virtuous circle'; and they are particularly well illustrated by the impact of current policies.

As the recession bites deeper and unemployment rises sharply, there may be an apparent short-term revival in productivity, arising from the closure of plants which are less efficient than the average, even while nothing else changes; but this would be an improvement which could not be sustained. In the longer term, the downward pressure on real wages, the increasing threat to jobs, and falling output and profit margins, with their disincentive effects on investment, must inhibit the flexibility and preparedness for change which are essential if productivity is to rise. With output falling sharply, any attempt to increase output in future will be fatally handicapped by the weaker industrial base, the more disaffected and less skilled workforce, and the out-of-date plant and equipment with which that attempt at expansion will be made. The lesson from all our past experience of trying to improve productivity through restriction and retrenchment is that these are the very reverse of the conditions in which long-term productivity improvements can be expected and sustained.

THE IMPORTANCE OF INTERNATIONAL TRADE

If improved productivity is a function of growth, this means that the traditional British insistence on deferring policies for growth until productivity is somehow persuaded to improve is almost entirely misconceived. But if growth is the necessary precondition of increased productivity, how is growth to be secured? Growth can, of course, be domestically generated by full employment policies or, in the case of an underindustrialised country, by rapid industrialisation so that labour moves from subsistence agriculture into profitable industry; but there is an international dimension to growth which has become increasingly important over recent years. This is partly because economic failure in terms of international competitiveness can inhibit domestic policies for growth and partly because international markets are an increasingly important element in the demand for domestically produced goods.

It has always been worthwhile for international trade to take place, even when transport was much more expensive and risky than it is now, because of the enormous differences in relative costs of producing goods and services. If, at a given rate of exchange, a country can make one product more cheaply than it can another, and the position is reversed somewhere else, then it must be in the interests of both countries to sell to each other the product each is best at making, whatever the difference in living standards between the two countries. Both of them gain.

In the days when trade between countries largely comprised goods which were not produced by mass-production methods, and when transport costs were high and numerous trade restrictions were in force, the volume of trade in proportion to the national income which was worth doing was fairly low. However, the last century and a half has seen a transformation in this situation. Transport costs in real terms have fallen enormously, many of the tariff barriers to trade, especially in manufactures, have been removed or reduced, and trade in mass-produced goods now dominates international exchange. As a result, growth in world trade has been far greater than that of world GNP, and this is reflected in a rise in the proportion of national incomes derived from international transactions. This huge growth in international trade in manufactured goods has had a number of extremely significant consequences.

In the first place, the really huge expansion in trade has taken place in those categories of goods which are either mass produced or cost a great deal to design and develop so that unit costs fall with greater volumes of output – motor vehicles, electronic and electrical goods and household appliances. The markets for such goods are extremely price-sensitive; an initial advantage in cost will lead to a cumulative increase in market share and the economies of scale thus made available lead to further reductions in costs. Furthermore, the extra sales thus generated will lead to a further accumulation of advantages; increased profitability will make possible increased investment, incorporating the latest technology, and labour is attracted from lower to higher productivity sectors of the economy. There is thus a strongly built-in tendency for any country with expanding export industries to do cumulatively better than its weaker rivals.

Secondly, there is a very important difference between the pattern of trade in manufactured goods and that of the more traditional internationally exchanged commodities, such as food and raw materials. There will always be overwhelming geographical and geological reasons for obtaining supplies of particular commodities, such as certain agricultural products or fossil fuels or minerals, from those countries which are best placed to provide them, but there are no reasons in principle why most manufactured goods should be made in one location rather than another. What is crucial in the case of most manufacturing operations is the political and economic climate – a reasonably stable financial and political background, free access to important markets, wage costs per unit of output which are internationally competitive – all of which are susceptible to manipulation by governmental authorities. As a result, there is a strong tendency for manufacturing capacity to be concentrated in those parts of the world economy where governments are able to provide these conditions; and since this is easier done where an initial advantage is already enjoyed, there is a reinforcement of the cumulative advantages which successful economies possess.

Thirdly, as foreign trade assumes a larger and larger role for each country, so any imbalance between imports and exports develops an increasingly larger and more significant ratio to the national income. No country can run a balance of payments deficit indefinitely, and the importance of balance of payments difficulties, and the severity of measures needed to deal with them, are likely to loom increasingly large for any deficit country. An initial deficiency in international competitiveness can therefore be exacerbated by the interruption to expansion which is usually, and in the British case invariably, the consequence of policies to contain the problem.

SHARES IN WORLD TRADE

If international comparisons are made, it will be found that those countries which have the most rapid rates of growth are also those which are increasing their share of world trade, whereas slow-growth countries have a falling share of world trade.

This is brought out very clearly in Table 1.3, showing the percentage increase in each country's Gross Domestic Product, the increase in the volume of manufactured exports, and the increase in the share of exports of manufactures by the main manufacturing countries in each of the decades ending in 1963 and 1973, in the six years 1973–9 and over the whole period 1953–79.

TABLE 1.3   *Percentage increase in GDP, volume of manufactured exports and share of world trade in manufactures, 1953–79*

		1953–79	1953–63	1963–73	1973–9
(a)	*Gross Domestic Product*				
	Japan	699	134	170	27
	France	254	73	71	20
	Germany	231	83	57	15
	Italy	222	77	58	16
	USA	130	32	49	16
	UK	94	31	38	7
(b)	*Volume of Manufactured Exports*				
	Japan	3547	436	339	55
	France	890	136	176	52
	Germany	1106	230	177	32
	Italy	2816	434	250	56
	USA	265	27	121	30
	UK	205	36	85	21
(c)	*Share of Trade in Manufactures*				
	Japan	260	97	69	8
	France	16	0	7	8
	Germany	56	49	12	−6
	Italy	246 est.	146 est.	13	22
	USA	−39	−17	−25	−1
	UK	−67	−28	−39	−11

SOURCES: (a) OECD National Accounts 1950–78 and IMF *Statistical Yearbook* (1979). (b) UK figure for 1973–9 based on Table E1 of MRETS. Rest on UN Yearbook of International Trade – base 1958 for col. 2, rest on base 1970. (c) NIESR for 1953–63 and MRETS for 1963–79. Italy estimated for 1953–8. The UK figure for 1973–9 is based on volume and not value.

The greatest contrast is between the enormous achievement of Japan at home and overseas, and the wretched performance of the United States and the even worse performance of the UK; this contrast shows very strikingly the correlation between the rate of growth and the share of world trade. Two interlocking

explanations very strongly indicate that it is international competitiveness which plays a crucial role in generating rapid growth
in national income rather than the other way round. First, competitive export industries, especially those with falling cost
curves, enable an increasing share of world trade to be obtained
in a fashion which is extremely beneficial to the exporting
countries. Not only does increasing output, through the process
we have described, make export industries progressively more
competitive; it also attracts resources into the most productive
parts of the economy as a whole and the division of labour at the
international level allows the economy to drop more and more
those things it is less good at doing. Secondly, rapidly rising
export revenues reduce the chances of the government being
pushed into deflationary policies to deal with balance of payments problems, something which governments are still prone to
do, even with floating exchange rates. The resulting 'virtuous
circle' of increasing productivity in export industries combined
with lack of restraint on domestic expansion means that the
prosperity achieved by export success is spread throughout the
whole economy.

It therefore follows that the crucial determinant of any
country's growth in industrial output, compared with the world
average, is what is happening to its ability to compete in international markets. This ability can be broadly measured by
trends in its share of world trade in manufactured goods. If it is
losing share, then, both as a cause and a consequence, its industrial growth rate will be below par, and vice versa. We believe
this to be a proposition of universal application, especially taking
a long view, although we accept that changes in tariffs or quotas
will alter the relationships involved in the short term.

What options are open to a country which is losing its share of
world trade in manufactures, and therefore has a slower rate of
growth in industrial output than the world average? There is
only one answer if it is to reverse this situation in the long term.
It must make its internationally traded manufactured goods
more competitive. In particular, unit costs must be reduced in
relation to costs in other parts of the economy and to costs in
competing economies. Whether the costs themselves are high or
low is not the key factor; it is costs adjusted for productivity
which are crucial. If, in this sector, unit costs are significantly
different from the world average, then the growth rate of industry

will diverge from the norm. Indeed, we would go further. We would define unit costs in the internationally traded sector as satisfactory only if manufacturing output is growing at the same rate as in the world as a whole. If output is growing more slowly than the world average, unit costs in the internationally traded sector must be too high. This is, of course, the British experience for the greater part of this century.

We believe that to be competitive in this sense is much more important than is generally realised. All the evidence suggests that any country will improve its economic performance by reducing its prices for internationally traded goods. Numerous studies have established that the elasticities of demand for exports and imports are reasonably large and negative – and these are the conditions which need to be fulfilled. However, the standard economic concept of elasticity of demand is essentially one involving comparative statics. We habitually ask whether, if we reduce our prices by 1 per cent, the demand for them will rise by more than 1 per cent in volume terms so that more foreign exchange will be earned. This is to overlook, however, the fact that the relationship is not a static one, but is highly dynamic. A change which makes exports more competitive will not have a once and for all effect on improving export performance, measurable by a single figure comparing two static positions. It will have a cumulative effect which will alter a trend – this trend being the country's GNP growth rate compared to that of the world as a whole. The mechanism which causes this to happen is the one we have already described. Higher growth springs from the cumulative increases in market share as export sectors become progressively more competitive and past successes provide the platform for the next round of market penetration. If export costs become less competitive, the reverse process takes place, and in Britain, the damage has always been aggravated by the measures which the government has taken in response to that loss of competitiveness.

The major consequence of a lack of competitiveness is, of course, a lower volume of exports than would otherwise have been achieved, combined with a greater volume of imports. The result is that a lower proportion of demand at home and abroad is met by British industry, and this leads to lower growth in manufacturing output. During the period up to the First World War, and to a lesser extent during the inter-war period, the resulting trade deficits were masked by the country's vast invest-ment income from abroad. More recently, oil and gas have per-formed a similar function. However, especially since the end of the Second World War, balance of payments difficulties have recurred every few years on an increasing scale. The remedy to which we always have recourse is deflation. The objective has been the immediate one of reducing imports by depressing demand in the domestic economy, while hoping – without much evidence in support – that this would free resources for export and encourage firms to go out and look for orders from abroad.

The disadvantages of this policy are enormous. Not only does deflation directly reduce the national income by causing an immediate and very substantial loss of output in the short term; its long-term effects are exactly the opposite of what is required. It is precisely those industries which are most significant in exporting which, because of the importance of economies of scale in the internationally traded goods sector, are hit hardest by declining home demand. With falling demand and output, their average costs rise in relation to other parts of the economy and to competing economies, so that they are in no position to win back orders on the highly competitive export market. The loss of competitiveness engenders a further fall in demand and loss of output and an intensification of the competitiveness problem because, unlike firms in the non-internationally traded goods sector, export firms have no option but to compete; they have no captive market to absorb their cost increases. The result is that the very firms and industries upon which the future of the econ-omy depends are forced by lack of sales prospects and volume production runs to cut back on research and development, in-vestment and expansion; and in a growing number of cases, they are forced out of business altogether. Our export sector loses ground to other parts of the domestic economy and to competing industries abroad.

The long-standing nature of this vicious circle of contraction and falling competitiveness is well described and illustrated in the following extract from the Minority Report of the Royal Commission on Depression of Trade and Industry in 1887; it is, they said,

inevitable that any industry which is engaged in a hopeless struggle against insuperable difficulties must sooner or later fall into a condition of languor, and of decreasing ability to meet competition. Those in it lose heart and hope; capital and talent are gradually withdrawn from it; and as it offers reduced remuneration and diminished prospect of advancement to skilled labour, the quality of labour employed in it tends continually to decline and its production deteriorates.

There can hardly be a better summary of the century-old decline of British manufacturing industry, a decline to which our perennial underrating of the importance of international competitiveness and our belief that productivity can be improved through contraction rather than growth have contributed so much.

CONCLUSION

For the better part of a century, British governments of all political persuasions have failed to appreciate the real causes of economic growth and, by confusing the symptoms with the cause of the British disease have prescribed remedies exactly the reverse of what is required. As a result, they have condemned this country to the worst economic performance of any developed country in the world. It is other countries which have benefited from the economies of scale which success in world markets makes possible. Mass production at a low rate of profitability per unit has resulted for them in a high level of profitability. This has created a renewed incentive and ability to invest in new technologies, to develop skilled workforces and new plant, and to make available sales and servicing facilities which in turn reinforce the ability to exploit growing world markets for mass-produced goods.

For these countries, free trade is an ideal climate in which to prosper. The favourable cost curve in the export sector, and the resultant high levels of productivity and profitability, have meant that they can combine rising living standards and increasing costs at home with increased competitiveness in the internationally traded goods sector. It is inevitable, therefore, that there is a close correlation between those countries with a rising share of world trade in manufactures and those with a high rate of economic growth. Such countries can avoid the balance of payments constraints and deflation to which less successful economies have

felt obliged to resort. The advantages secured for export industries benefit the rest of the economy through factors such as a
better educated workforce and better management skills, and
export-led growth inevitably attracts resources into the most
productive parts of the economy. Their success has been based
entirely on establishing the competitiveness of their manufactured goods in world markets; once this is done all else flows from
it.

Our own experience in Britain has been almost exactly the
reverse of this. We seem almost deliberately to have eschewed the
course successfully pursued by our competitors. In place of
international competitiveness achieved through expansion,
economies of scale, high profitability and growing markets, we
have preferred to tackle our long-standing problem of falling
competitiveness through deflation, restriction and retrenchment.
The consequences have been disastrous. Output has been held
back. Unit costs have risen. The brunt of these damaging policies
has been borne in the internationally traded goods sector with
the result that resources and talent have been drained away from
the most productive part of the economy on which we must
depend if we are to achieve a high rate of growth.

We have exacerbated our failure to tackle successfully the
problem of falling international competitiveness through the
consistent attachment of successive British Chancellors to an
overvalued exchange rate – yet another manifestation of an
excessive concern for the interests of those who hold money
above the needs of those who make and sell things. The diminish-
ing export markets, growing vulnerability to imports, and shrinking profitability which are all the inevitable consequences of an
overvalued currency have had such a marked disincentive effect
over such a long period of time that the British economy has
simply become accustomed to living without the expectation of
real growth. This has in turn produced a lack of new investment
and an entrenchment of defensive attitudes which have further
weakened the British industrial performance.

We have consistently denied to our manufacturing industry
the one essential precondition for success and growth. Instead of
ensuring, through a proper level of demand at home and a proper
level of competitiveness abroad, that there are profitable and
expanding markets for our goods, we have constantly held back
the level of demand and paid no more than lip service to the

need for international competitiveness. If we are right, and the existence of growing and profitable markets at home and abroad is the precondition for economic growth, then our economic policy has been entirely misguided.

The current monetarist fashion expresses these perennial errors in a more than usually damaging form. Monetarism is an updated version of our unfailingly unsuccessful attempts to deflate our way out of our problems and it is accompanied by our familiar attachment to an overvalued exchange rate. We explain in Chapter 2 the theoretical and practical deficiencies of monetarism, and of the policies currently pursued in its name; and in Chapter 3 we set out the errors underlying the view, usually described as international monetarism, that movements in the exchange rate affect the inflation rate but do not influence the real economy.

The errors of international monetarism are particularly damaging because they encourage policy-makers to overlook the importance, in establishing the conditions for growth, of giving overriding priority to our international competitiveness in the traded goods sector. Only if this is done will our manufacturers have both the incentive and the means to overcome the problems which have held us back for so long and which orthodox policies have so gravely exacerbated. All else should be subordinated to this requirement; it should be the major objective of macroeconomic policy. We explain in Chapter 4 that a correctly aligned exchange rate is the key to international competitiveness and we deal with the misapprehensions concerning devaluation which have inhibited us from establishing the rate for sterling at a competitive level. In Chapter 5, we look in detail at the errors that have been made in measuring our international competitiveness and which have led the British authorities to take a consistently overoptimistic view of our ability to compete.

In Chapter 6, we consider some of the elements of current orthodoxy which reinforce the damage being done by monetarist inflation and an overvalued exchange rate. We then compare the most widely favoured alternative strategy, that based on import controls, with the strategy we advocate of establishing through the exchange rate a level of competitiveness which will stimulate exports as well as import substitution.

We set out, in the final chapter, our reasons for believing that our present course is doomed to failure and that only an appreciation of the real nature of economic growth, and of the policies needed to secure it, will enable us to escape from the vicious circle of de-industrialisation and decline. The required policies – a competitive pound, low interest rates, a high level of demand, the full utilisation of resources, some measure of protection where necessary – are explained in detail. We believe that, provided these policies are implemented, there is nothing inherent in the British situation or in the British character which precludes us from emulating our more successful rivals. On the contrary, British skills and resources need only be allied to correct policies to transform our prospects and secure for us the fruits of economic growth.

Brit. gov⁵ mao concerned with deflation on policies than with intend export to achieve growth. to balance trade deficit

2 The Monetarist Cul-de-sac

The most significant development in economic policy since 1975 has been the conversion of those concerned with the management of the British economy to the doctrine of what has been rather misleadingly described as monetarism. Although this doctrine is presented as providing a fundamentally new analysis and technique for dealing with our problems, it is in fact no more than a revival of what has always been known to students of economics as the quantity theory of money. The deficiencies of this essentially primitive view of the way the economy works were well established in the nineteenth century. It has returned to the centre of the stage, partly because of the work by Professor Milton Friedman at the Federal Reserve Board of St Louis and subsequently at the University of Chicago, and partly because it provides a powerful reinforcement for both traditional financial orthodoxy and for prevailing political beliefs. The failings of current British economic management cannot be fully understood without considering both the importance and the defects of monetarism.

WHAT IS MONETARISM?

The basic monetarist claim is that prices are determined by the supply of money. All that a government has to do, in order to control the level of price increases, is to obey a fixed monetary rule which would permit the money supply to increase by no more than the anticipated growth in output. Any departure from this rule, or any attempt to use other means, such as fiscal measures, to influence economic developments, will be self-defeating.

The basis for these claims has been most fully advanced by Professor Milton Friedman in *A Monetary History of the United States, 1867–1960*, written in association with Anna Jacobson

Schwartz. According to Friedman, the United States' experience over this period shows that (1) changes in the behaviour of the money stock have been closely associated with changes in economic activity, money incomes and prices; (2) the inter-relation between monetary and economic change has been highly stable; and (3) monetary changes have often had an independent origin – they have not simply been a reflection of changes in economic activity.

These three propositions have become embodied in a body of doctrine which can be summarised[1] as follows:

(a) Past rates of growth in the stock of money are the major determinants – indeed, virtually the only systematic non-random determinants – of the growth of GNP in terms of current prices. It follows from this that fiscal policies do not significantly affect GNP in money terms, though they may alter its composition and also affect interest rates, and that the overall impact on GNP in money terms of monetary and financial policies is for practical purposes summed up in the movements of a single variable, the stock of money. Consequently, monetary policy should be exclusively guided by this variable, without regard to interest rates, credit flows, free reserves or other indicators.

(b) Nominal interest rates are geared to inflationary expecta-tions and thus, with a time lag, to actual inflation. Although the immediate market impact of expansionary monetary policy may be to lower interest rates, it is fairly soon reversed when premiums for the resulting inflation are added to in-terest rates.

(c) The central bank can and should make the money stock grow at a steady rate equal to the rate of growth of potential GNP plus a target rate of inflation.

(d) There is no enduring trade-off between unemployment and inflation. There is, rather, a unique natural rate of unemploy-ment for each economy which allows for structural change and job search but which cannot be departed from in the long term. Government policy will produce ever-accelerating in-flation if it persistently seeks a lower than natural rate of unemployment; if it seeks a higher rate, there will be an ever-accelerating deflation. The natural rate of unem-ployment cannot be identified except through practical experience; it is the rate which will emerge if the proper steady-growth monetary policy is pursued.

The attractive simplicity of this doctrine is easily recognised. The essence of the monetarist position is that increases in prices and wages can be held in check by nothing more complicated than the apparently simple device of controlling the amount of money in circulation. Ideally, a condition of nil inflation is achieved when the increase in the money supply equals the increase in the real output in the economy. Since both wage and price increases can only occur if extra money to finance them is made available, no increases will take place if no more money is provided. If attempts are made by firms or wage-earners to gain an advantage by putting up the cost of their goods and services on the one hand or labour rates on the other, a constant money supply will mean unsold goods and services for the firm and the loss of jobs for labour. Thus, as long as the government is prepared to control the money supply, everyone will see it as being in his interests to exercise restraint, and inflation will be reduced to whatever level is deemed to be acceptable.

WHAT IS MONEY?

It is immediately apparent that the efficacy of this apparently simple doctrine depends crucially on there being an accurate and measurable definition of money which has a close and stable relationship with the national income and which can be easily monitored and controlled by government. Monetarists believe that money is different from all other kinds of assets and that this quality of uniqueness means that it is possible to define and measure money with sufficient accuracy for the purposes of controlling the money supply.

In the real world, however, the position is rather more complex. The man in the street thinks of money primarily in terms of cash, but a moment's thought will persuade him to include in his concept of money the credit balances which he holds in his bank account. He might then be persuaded without too much difficulty to extend his definition to include credit balances held in building society accounts and in other similar forms of saving. He might then be induced to treat as money for certain purposes other kinds of savings, e.g. bonds and securities of various sorts, and also the purchasing power made available to him through credit facilities such as bank overdrafts or the use of credit cards.

It would be clear to him by now that money is not the simple concept with which he started. Money turns out to be anything which the community recognises as making valid claims on resources held by others. Money can take an almost infinite variety of forms; indeed, the whole history of money is of the continual invention of new kinds of money, for reasons of greater convenience or because of a shortage of officially-approved forms. The growth of bank credit, for example, was a response to both the short supply and inconvenience of gold. Credit cards are a further and relatively recent example of the introduction of a new form of money. An even more recent and striking example of the flexibility of the concept occurred during the 1978 Irish bank strike, when people created their own forms of money and proceeded quite satisfactorily without recourse to the banking system at all.

The truth is that the concept of money, in its various forms, represents a continuum of declining certainty and liquidity so that the point at which a particular range of assets ceases to be money is virtually impossible to ascertain. While there are some assets, e.g. coins and notes, which are indisputably money and nothing else, there are other assets, e.g. government bonds, which may be regarded as money for some purposes and at some times, but at other times and for other purposes are indistinguishable from assets such as property or jewellery.

There is no escape from this difficulty by trying to draw a distinction between 'active money' and 'idle money'. No asset is in action as a medium of exchange except in the very moment of being transferred from one owner to another. All money is idle between transactions; in the case of demand deposits, for example, many customers retain a minimum working balance in order to enjoy 'free' banking. If, on the other hand, activity is held to mean readiness against possible use in exchange, all monetary assets are active all the time. It is not merely that we cannot easily earmark for statistical assessment the quantity that is active; there is no such quantity, except in the all-embracing concept of what constitutes that money which influences total effective demand for goods and services, interpreted widely enough to include credit that can be brought into existence concurrently with the decision to exercise demand. This not only means bringing in the readily callable liabilities of financial inter-mediaries, but also 'trade credit' extended by manufacturers and traders to their customers, the swing in which was found by the Radcliffe Committee to dwarf, from one year to another, changes in bank balances and bank credit employed by companies engaged in manufacturing, building and distribution quoted on the Stock Exchange.[2]

The slipperiness of the concept of money inevitably makes monetarism a less certain instrument than its proponents claim. A policy which depends entirely on controlling the money supply cannot very well be implemented if money means only what people agree from time to time that it should mean, and if new or different forms can be invented or extended in use to circumvent control. That is however only the beginning of the difficulties.

WHICH DEFINITION OF MONEY?

One aspect of the problem of definining money is that it is possible to use for different purposes dozens of different definitions. It is said that the 24 members of the OECD have between them 23 different definitions of money for regulatory purposes. In this country alone, there are many different views as to how money should be defined. The following is a list of the definitions of money which are most commonly used for official purposes in the United Kingdom:

Notes and coins in circulation with the public.
Retail M_1 – Notes and coins plus sight (i.e. current account demand) deposits of the UK non-bank private sector in banks and the discount market, but excluding those on which in-terest is paid, generally known as Wholesale Deposits.
M_1 – Retail M_1 plus the interest-bearing sight deposits of the UK non-bank private sector excluded from Retail M_1.
M_2 – M_1 plus deposits of the UK public sector and time de-posits of the UK non-bank private sector in banks and the discount market, but excluding Certificates of Deposit (which are marketable claims to a fixed-term deposit) and Wholesale Deposits.
Sterling M_3 – M_1 plus time deposits in banks and the discount

market plus Certificates of Deposit of the UK non-bank private and public sectors plus sight deposits of the UK public sector.

M3 – Sterling M3 plus foreign currency deposits of UK residents in banks and the discount market.

M4 – Sterling M3 plus UK non-bank private sectors' holdings of Treasury bills, tax instruments (mainly certificates of tax deposit) and Acceptance Credits.

M5 – M4 plus Building Society deposits.

The Bank of England, which is responsible for the control of the money supply, uses M1, Sterling M3 and M3 for statistical purposes.[3] It is Sterling M3, however, which has become the touchstone of monetary performance. When monetary targets were first announced in the budget of 1976 (and they were then little more than a forecast), M3 was thought to reflect all the most important financial flows in the economy – the public sector borrowing requirement, bank lending, sales of debt and flows across the exchanges. But when the definition became a firm target a year later, the overseas sector was excluded because the figures were liable to alter following changes in the exchange rate and this was thought to be misleading.

The case for Sterling M3 is that it is relatively easy to forecast because so many of the variables are known or can be predicted with reasonable accuracy. There is little to be said, however, in favour of a measuring rod which, like Sterling M3, excludes sterling deposits held by non-residents and foreign currency deposits of residents, particularly now that, with the abolition of exchange controls, anyone can switch into and out of sterling at will. We can borrow abroad what we cannot borrow at home and a measure which cannot take account of changes in the foreign balance must be fatally flawed from an operational point of view because it can give the same reading when credit is restrained as it does when it is excessive.

This is not of course a criticism which ardent monetarists dare to make of the present system of control because of its implications for any system of control which is directed exclusively at the supply of money in conditions of free exchanges. They have concentrated instead on suggesting other measuring rods. Some have argued the merits of M1. The Governor of the Bank of England claimed in 1978 that the relationships between this measure and incomes and interest rates have over a period of fifteen years been closer than any other.[4] It has, however, ceased to be reliable because it includes the very volatile Wholesale Deposits, e.g. the cash balances of multinational companies, which can fluctuate according to whether overnight interest rates are higher or lower than other interest rates, such as those on seven-day deposits; and because it can also fluctuate with changes in the gilt-edged market, since funds raised by the sale of gilt-edged stock are often placed in the money market overnight pending re-investment. Others have therefore expressed a preference for Retail M1, but it too can be misleading because the banks can generally get their larger customers to increase their non-interest-bearing sight deposits by one means or another when they themselves come under pressure to reduce their interest-bearing liabilities. Samuel Brittan has also criticised Retail M1 on the grounds that it is demand-determined – those who want to hold more cash can draw on their current accounts and replenish them at will from their deposit accounts – and that it failed to predict the inflation of 1974–5.[5]

The problem is that Sterling M3, the Bank's chosen variable, is subject to even bigger distortions. Money can easily be switched, for purely commercial reasons or simply in order to evade control, from a short-term asset which falls within the definition of money supply to another which does not. Practices such as 'round tripping' (where large sums are borrowed from the banks at interest rates tied to base rate to invest in, for example, Certificates of Deposit, thus inflating both Sterling M3 and bank lending to the private sector) and 'soft arbitrage' (where a great deal of money is switched from banks deposits to Certificates of Deposit, thus reducing Sterling M3 but leaving M4 unchanged) distort the figures in unpredictable and virtually unquantifiable ways.[6] For these and other reasons, some have argued the case for M5, the widest of the accepted definitions.

The problem about relying on any single definition is that those whose interests might be adversely affected by a tightening of control are bound to do all in their power to avoid that control. That is what competition is all about. This has given rise to what is known in the City as Goodhart's Law – named after a Bank of England economist who is reputed to have said that 'any observed statistical regularity will tend to collapse once pressure is put on it for control purposes'.

The incentive to manipulate the figures would be reduced if there were more than one measuring rod. The Governor of the Bank of England, however, has rejected this idea as a 'recipe for confusion'.[7] The problem he had in mind was no doubt the awkward fact that different definitions tell a different story at different times and indeed sometimes move in opposite directions.

The real problem is that the authorities have been hoist on their own petard, so that, having preached the virtues of simple-minded monetarism, they must needs give the appearance of being in control of the situation. Sterling M3 is the only statistic which they can manipulate with any confidence because the kinds of money covered by this definition are under very close supervision by the Bank of England and can be more or less kept under control by the purchase and sale of government securities.

PROBLEMS OF CONTROL

Even with the advantage of a monetary measure chosen for its ease of manipulation, the government has had difficulty in bringing Sterling M3 within the target range at times when the demand for credit has been strong. In addition to the normal operations in the gilt-edged market, the authorities therefore resorted in times of stress to a more direct form of control on liquidity, by specifying a maximum rate of growth in interest-bearing deposits and other interest-bearing 'eligible' liabilities (IBELS). If this rate was exceeded, the offending bank was required to deposit with the Bank of England free of interest an amount equal to a proportion of the excess, calculated on a sharply rising scale. This method of control, known as supplementary special deposits or 'the corset', had to be abandoned because the abolition of exchange controls meant that borrowers could obtain overseas the money which they could not obtain at home.

The 'corset' was in any case less effective than was hoped. The banks were able to rearrange their business in such a way that they avoided the penalties but were able to carry on much as before. Gordon Pepper, of Greenwell and Co., showed in a brilliant piece of detective work how the banks inflated their IBELS when they had good reason to believe that the corset might be reintroduced, thus improving their reference base for further lending, and then relieved the pressure by subsequently deflating them artificially. In some cases, the banks persuaded their customers to switch from interest-bearing deposits (which were an eligible liability and part of Sterling M3) to non-interest-bearing deposits (which were neither), but the principal avenue of escape was the 'bill leak', through which bank-accepted commercial bills were sold for cash in the discount market.[8] To the holder, such bills are no less liquid than a certificate of deposit of comparable term, and to the borrower they are a very close substitute for direct bank credit. The effect of these forms of 'disintermediation' – the process under which the banks cease to be the financial intermediary – is to reduce Sterling M3 and bank advances below what they would otherwise have been, largely circumventing the attempt at control. The fact that Minimum Lending Rate (MLR) had to be raised to a record 17 per cent in November 1979 and retained at that level for many months, and the apparent sharp increase in Sterling M3 when the 'corset' was removed in July 1980, are ample testimony that the control was largely ineffective.

Money is created in three ways; by printing bank notes, by cheques drawn on the Bank of England and issued by the government in payment for goods and services, and by banks providing overdraft facilities which are drawn on to discharge debts. There is no means of controlling this process from the supply side because the Bank of England as the lender of the last resort is committed to supply the Discount Market with whatever funds it requires to meet the demands of the banking system, in return for which the Market undertakes to buy whatever amount of Treasury Bills the Bank decides to issue to finance government expenditure, take foreign exchange into the reserves and manage the money market. The supply of money is therefore essentially demand-determined: the banks will in principle go on lending money to their customers as long as they are willing to pay the price in terms of higher interest rates. This point is implicitly acknowledged in the Green Paper on Monetary Control where interest rates and fiscal policy – both public expenditure and tax policy – are identified as the principal means of controlling the money supply.[9] The aim of fiscal policy is to reduce the public sector borrowing requirement (PSBR) and the role of interest rates is of course simply to reduce the demand for credit. These are of course the traditional weapons of deflationary demand management, and they point up the essential similarity between what is now passed off as monetarism and old-fashioned deflaton.

This is anathema to those strict monetarists who believe that money should be controlled at the point of issue. They oppose the present system because it gives the authorities discretion in controlling monetary conditions and enables the government to go on borrowing from the banking system when it suits them. They have argued instead for a monetary base system of control under which the banks would keep at least a known proportion of their deposits with the Bank of England in the form of base money. The authorities would then either control the amount of base money in existence or use divergences of the base money figure from the desired trend as a trigger for a change in interest rates intended to correct the divergence. The first would limit the increase in the money supply – because the banks' balance sheets cannot exceed a multiple of the base – and the limit would then generate the interest rates necessary to bring the rate of growth of the money supply back towards the desired path. The second would either be discretionary or would be determined by a scale set in advance by the authorities.[10] The Bank would no longer be able to provide unlimited support to the banking system as a matter of routine and interest rates would be set automatically at market-clearing levels.

The definition of the monetary base favoured by Pepper, who has been one of the most active and most influential advocates of this form of control, would include only bankers' deposits at the Bank of England, but there are other definitions and almost as many proposals for operating the scheme as there are monetary economists. All have been condemned by the authorities on the grounds that, given the known costs and the uncertain benefits, the case for a monetary base system has not been made out. They argue that it would require a major change in the structure of the money markets, resulting in less flexibility; that it would give rise to practical operational difficulties because the authorities cannot accurately estimate on a day-to-day basis either the actual base that would be consistent with the seasonally adjusted target path for the money supply or the base that the banking system may obtain; that the evidence that it would produce less undesirable disintermediation is weak; that it would take several years to establish whether there was a predictable relationship between money and the chosen base; and at the end of the day there would be no assurance that monetary control would be any better than at present.[11] One might add that the seasonal adjustment is constantly changing and is itself affected by cyclical factors which could well vary from one cycle to another. There is also the wider question whether any system of control can be made effective in the absence of a constraint on overseas borrowing.

In any case, it is clear that, as Hawtrey noted as long ago as 1926, a contraction of credit may have very little effect on the amount of bank deposits and therefore on the size of the monetary base; when Bank Rate was raised to 7 per cent in 1920, and the most intense deflation was set in train, the total amount of deposits actually increased.[12] In modern conditions, over the period from 1972 to 1979, Lewis has shown that only 40 per cent of the liabilities of the four different categories of financial intermediaries can be explained by the movement of interest rates; and that, within the total, the response of the deposit banks was much slower than in the case of other banks, non-banks and the insurance and pension funds. Lewis concluded from this that any system of monetary base control must, in order to be effective and to avoid discrimination between deposit banks and other financial intermediaries, employ the dual weapons of imposing a quantity restraint upon the deposit banks' intermediation and a price constraint upon other institutions.[13]

The problem is that the demand for money rises not only in response to an increase in real economic activity but also in response to inflation. Borrowers may need extra credit to finance involuntary increase in stocks and increased interest charges. Demand for money is therefore not necessarily matched by the supply, and when it is not, the rate of interest ceases to function as a market-clearing mechanism. The demand for bank deposits in fact increased during each period of monetary restriction in the 1970s. The deposit banks in particular have relied more on rationing their customers than on trying to price some of them out of the market.[14]

We can be thankful for this small mercy at least. Industry, which used to raise most of its finance through the Stock Exchange, has had to rely more and more on the banks because the corporate bond market has collapsed and because the scope for raising money by a rights issue is limited when the economy is depressed. The result is that industry cannot reduce its borrowing from the banks without reducing its wealth-creating capacity. There is therefore no way under the present system of rapidly reducing bank advances short of deflating the whole economy.

The other objection to a monetary base system, and indeed to the existing commitment to a monetary target, is that it rules out intervention by the authorities in the foreign exchange market to control the exchange rate. A rise in interest rates, however determined, would thus lead to an increase in the exchange rate and the consequent debilitation of the real economy, regardless of the circumstances in which the increase occurred. It could happen simply because the oil producers wanted to keep their surplus funds in London or because the demand for credit had increased to finance asset speculation, as happened in 1972–3. The result is to put the monetary cart before the wealth-creating horse. As with so much of monetarist theory, the attempt to control the money supply in practice runs into virtually insoluble problems; but its lack of success does not prevent the attempt from inflicting substantial damage on the real economy.

DOMESTIC CREDIT EXPANSION

The best measure of the underlying rate of inflation is the rate of expansion of domestic credit (DCE), the one measure which monetarists totally ignore because it is determined by the flow of funds over a period rather than by the stock of money and because its control requires a dynamic rather than a static analysis of the kind on which monetarist theories are based.

To appreciate the significance of this point, we must first consider the difference between the official measure of liquidity and the measure of domestically created money. As we have seen, Sterling M3 comprises notes and coin in circulation with the non-bank private sector together with all sterling deposits (including certificates of deposit) held with UK banks by UK residents in both the public and private sectors. Domestic Credit Expansion (DCE) can be defined as the change in non-bank holdings of notes and coin, plus the change in total lending in sterling by UK banks to the non-bank private and public sectors, plus the change in overseas and bank lending to the public sector; but it can also be defined as comprising the public sector

borrowing requirement, plus the increase in sterling lending to
the non-bank private sector, plus the increase in bank lending to
overseas, less the net acquisition of public sector debt by the
non-bank private sector.[15]

The importance of DCE is that, unlike Sterling M3, it takes
into account changes in the balance of payments on both capital
and current account. It allows for the importance of external
finance as a source of credit when the non-bank sector is in
balance of payments deficit for whatever reason. This means that
DCE is larger than Sterling M3 when the balance of payments of
the non-bank private sector is in deficit and usually smaller when
it is in surplus. In banking terms the difference between the two
can be defined as the increase in the banks' (net) non-deposit
liabilities plus the external and foreign currency financing going
to (1) the public sector, mainly from changes in the official
reserves and in sales to non-residents of public sector debt, and
(2) the banking sector, comprising the changes in the banks'
foreign currency liabilities (net) and in sterling deposits held by
non-residents.

The failure of the politicians to understand this recondite
matter has led many people to believe that the monetarist
policies pursued since 1976 were enjoined upon the government
by the terms exacted from them by the IMF. The truth is in fact
very different; not only did the IMF not require the government
to pursue the monetary policy which it subsequently chose to
pursue, but the conditions imposed by the IMF would have
required a monetary policy very different and very much more
satisfactory in terms of the interests of the real economy.

The Letter of Intent which Healey signed on 15 December
1976 was a charter for export-led growth, built on two un-
ambiguous undertakings – that 'stability in the exchange
markets would be maintained consistently with the continued
maintenance of the competitive position of United Kingdom
manufactures at home and abroad' and that the expansion of
domestic credit (DCE) would be kept to £9 billion in the banking
year ending 20 April 1977, and to £7.7 billion and £6 billion in
the two subsequent banking years.[16] We shall deal with the
exchange rate in a later chapter; all that need be said at this point
is that the IMF undertaking was designed to maintain sterling at
its then unusually competitive level. For present purposes, the
significant point is that there is no mention in the second under-

taking of monetary targets, for the simple reason that such targets would not have allowed the unrestricted opportunities for import-saving and export-led growth which the competitive exchange rate then offered.

The significance of the IMF's preference for domestic credit expansion, as opposed to monetary targets expressed in terms of Sterling M3, lies in the fact that, as we have seen, DCE accommodates changes in the balance of payments on both capital and current accounts. It was deliberately chosen as a corollary of the export-led growth which the exchange rate policy they recommended would have produced. An improvement in our balance of payments, and particularly the earning of a surplus, would have added to the domestic money supply but would have left domestic credit expansion untouched. The IMF, in other words, recommended a monetary regime which would allow virtually unlimited monetary growth, provided that this was brought about by an improvement in our balance of trade. Their only requirement was that we should live within our means.

For reasons which have never been properly explained, the government adopted a course which was almost exactly the opposite of what was required in the national interest and which expressly contradicted the undertaking so recently given to the IMF. No sooner was the ink dry on the Chancellor's signature, than the exchange rate was allowed to rise by over 5 per cent despite our much higher inflation rate. More importantly, and more puzzlingly, the decision was taken early in 1977 to set a limit to the increase in the money supply in terms of Sterling M3. The Treasury maintained that these targets 'were set consistently with the agreed limits on DCE' but there was no way in which a restricted money supply could have been consistent with any figure for DCE, provided the balance of payments continued to improve. The Letter of Intent was indeed quite specific on this point. It said that 'the exact implications of the target set for DCE for the growth of the money supply would depend on the speed of progress in achieving our balance of payments objectives'; there is no hint in this that monetary targets would be set which would effectively prevent us from attaining those objectives.

What happened was that Sterling M3 exceeded the top of the target range as soon as our balance of payments began to improve – as it did by the second quarter of 1977 in response to the fall in the exchange rate in the fourth quarter of 1976. This gave the vested interests in the City, who had gambled on a rise in the exchange rate, the excuse to press for sterling to be 'uncapped' on the grounds that the authorities would otherwise lose control of the money supply. The huge increase in the reserves which appeared to the uninitiated to substantiate the monetarist case would not in any case have materialised if the Bank of England had not guaranteed every speculator a profit by intervening in the markets to slow down the fall in interest rates and by putting a floor under sterling. What no one was ever told was that, throughout this period, the expansion of domestic credit was running far below the ceiling laid down by the IMF; indeed, domestic credit actually fell by a seasonally adjusted £282m immediately before sterling was uncapped. Equally, no one seems to have realised that the increase in the money supply required to finance the improvement in the balance of payments was not and could not have been inflationary so long as there were abundant resources of labour and capital available to meet the increase in the demand for UK goods and services.

The distinction between liquidity and credit in an open economy like that of the UK is vital to an understanding of what has been happening in the UK in recent years, as shown in Table 2.1.

TABLE 2.1   *Expansion of the UK money supply and domestic credit: £m*

	£M3	DCE
1974	3255	6934
1975	2331	4529
1976	3565	7462
1977	4130	1085
1978	6772	8023
1979	6583	10340

SOURCE: CSO, *Economic Trends*, Annual Supplement (1980).

In 1974–5 and again in 1979 the economy was depressed by a savage reduction in the real money supply, i.e. the increase in the supply of money was far less than was required to accommodate the rate of inflation. We therefore borrowed abroad what we could not borrow at home, the enormous deficit on the balance of

visible trade in both cases being financed by an inflow of specu-
lative capital. The counterpart of this has been the destruction of
a large part of our industrial base. The great exception was 1977,
when we were still benefiting from the devaluation of late 1976.
DCE was then only a quarter of the increase in the money supply
and one tenth of DCE in 1979.

Why the Chancellor defaulted on the undertakings he had
given to the IMF is shrouded in mystery. He may have been
persuaded that an increase in the real exchange rate would raise
real wages by reducing the real cost of imports and thus encourage wage restraint. He may have been influenced by the
monetarist outcry that the influx of foreign exchange would be
reflected in an increase in the money supply and that this would
add another twist to the inflationary spiral. It needed only a
touch of common sense however to realise that much of the inflow often referred to as 'hot money' would remain highly liquid
and two Treasury economists, Lomax and Mowl, have shown
convincingly that the effect of external flows – in both directions
– on the monetary aggregates depends ultimately on the portfolio
behaviour of the banks, the private sector and overseas residents,
as well as on the way the monetary authorities themselves
react.[17] The seasonally adjusted increase in Sterling M3 in the
third quarter of 1977 was in fact a good deal lower than in any
subsequent quarter to date.

The Chancellor may also have been misled about our competitiveness (as we suggest in Chapter 5). In any event, the decision
to introduce firm monetary targets based on Sterling M3 is in-
explicable and in our view raises doubts about the quality, and
possibly the impartiality, of the advice which he was given. It
certainly meant a much more rigid monetary policy than even
the IMF thought appropriate.

THE VELOCITY OF CIRCULATION

Even if monetarist economists could agree on the meaning of the
concept of money, even if they could choose a definition or definitions which were appropriate in all circumstances, even if they
could devise measures for controlling the money supply which
were foolproof, they would still not have achieved very much.
They would have done nothing to establish the validity of their

basic premise: that over the period relevant to monetary policy
the demand for money is constant, without which there could be
no presumption that a fixed monetary rule would lead to stable
prices. This issue can best be illustrated by reference to what is
universally known as the Fisher Equation, written as $MV = PT$,
where M stands for the quantity of money, V for the velocity with
which money circulates, P for the level of prices and T for the
number of transactions or what would now be described as the
Gross Domestic Product. This equation, as an equation, cannot
be faulted, but there can be and indeed have been arguments
about what is comprised within each of its components. The
error is in regarding the equation as a theory and not as a mere
identity. We cannot assume that there is a stable relationship
between MV and PT such that an increase in M necessarily
results in an equivalent increase in P; we cannot in other words
assume that V and T are in fact constants.

This is particularly true of V, the velocity of circulation of
money. The mere adding up of the quantity of money in the
economy tells us very little of what we need to know, unless we
also know to what use the money is to be put, or in other words,
how much demand there is for it. This is not a new point. The
principal elements in this argument are all to be found in the
report of the Select Committee on the High Price of Bullion,
written as long ago as 1810. The Committee pointed out that the
'mere numerical return of the amount of bank notes in circulation
cannot be considered as at all deciding the question whether
such paper is or is not excessive . . . the quantity of currency
bears no fixed relation to the quantity of commodities . . . and
any inference proceeding on such a supposition would be entirely
erroneous'. They concluded that 'the effective currency of a
country depends on the quickness of circulation . . . as well as on
the numerical amount' and that 'all the circumstances which
have a tendency to quicken or retard the rate of circulation
render the same amount of currency more or less adequate to the
needs of trade'.

The significance of this can be grasped by looking at the
figures for the velocity of circulation of money during the 1970s in
this country. In the third quarter of 1971, the velocity of Sterling
M3 (i.e. the number of times this kind of money would have had
to circulate to produce the money national income in that
quarter expressed as an annual rate) was as high as 3.223. This

was at a time when money was in short supply owing to the deflationary policies which Roy Jenkins had adopted as Chancellor. His immediate successors pursued different policies and as a result, the velocity fell almost continuously in the second half of Heath's term of office to 2.370. Under the new Labour Government in 1974, the velocity of circulation increased again as the real money supply tightened, reaching a peak of 3.460 in the fourth quarter of 1977. The reduction in velocity of 26 per cent under the Conservatives was thus more than offset by an increase of 46 per cent under Labour. Thereafter, the velocity fell marginally but, under the present government, it rose to a new peak of 3.526 in the first quarter of 1980. Not since the third quarter of 1976 has it fallen below the deflationary peak reached in 1971.

It is clear that the stock of money was in much greater demand in the second half of the 1970s than it was during the Barber boom. In the last 30 months of the Heath administration, the money supply rose 77 per cent, but this was offset by a decline of 26 per cent in velocity and an increase of 9 per cent in GDP. The net impact on the price level could therefore be put at 29 per cent. In the next 45 months, under the orthodoxy of Healey, the money supply rose by 42 per cent, but the velocity increased by 45 per cent and GDP by only 3 per cent. The net impact on prices might therefore be put at 98 per cent.

The absence of any evidence to support the basic proposition of the monetarist case is, on these figures, quite remarkable. The velocity of circulation is of course only a statistical relationship – in this case the ratio of Sterling M3 to the National Income – and we must avoid falling into the same trap as the monetarists by assuming that either the money supply or its velocity tells us very much about credit; but the fact remains that the evidence in this and other countries does not support the claim that the level of prices is determined by the money supply in such a way that it would make economic sense to adopt a fixed monetary rule. David Smith of the National Westminster Bank has shown that between 1900 and 1977 the velocity of five different measures of money have each changed enormously and that, apart from the broader definitions during the Barber boom, there has been an almost continuous increase in velocity since the late 1940s.[18] The Radcliffe Committee assumed in 1959 that the increase in velocity would cease when the liquidity which had built up during the Second World War had been worked off, but they reckoned without the restrictive policies of successive British governments. Over a long period, the velocity of circulation in the UK has risen faster than in any other industrial country. The trend rate of increase in the UK between 1953 and 1976 has been put at 2 per cent per annum, compared to a reduction of no less than 4 per cent in the case of Germany, and in our view this largely explains the difference between the economic performance of the two countries.[19] Germany had a falling velocity of circulation because of an accommodating monetary policy which facilitated export-led growth. We had the reverse.

Monetarists generally argue as if the problem did not exist. When taxed with it, they tend to dismiss it by saying that the changes are temporary and not sufficiently predictable to be offset by official action. Some go further and argue that the monetary authorities would make the maximum feasible contribution to minimising velocity fluctuations if they kept the money supply growing at a well-publicised and non-inflationary stable rate.[20] The velocity of circulation, however, is a reflection of changes in the level of activity as well as of changes in the quantity of money, and one clear lesson of the Gold Standard is that changes in velocity are minimised when the supply of money is varied to conform to the needs of trade. The fact that the road ahead is not clearly visible is no excuse for letting go of the steering wheel. A constant rate of monetary growth might be appropriate if we were driving on an economic motorway, but the road we have to travel is full of twists and turns; if we want to arrive at our destination safely and with the minimum of delay there is no substitute for the monetary accelerator and the brake.

The conclusion is indisputable that, in addition to all its other uncertainties, controlling the money supply is an even blunter weapon than monetarists claim because variations in the velocity of circulation will normally offset to a large degree differences in the rate of increase in the supply of money. When money is plentiful, the velocity will slow down and, fortunately for the British economy, when money is tight, the velocity will increase.

This is not to say that a restrictive monetary policy, maintained over a long period, will not be effective in slowing the economy down; there is a limit to the extent to which the velocity of circulation can be increased to offset the shortage of money. But the responsiveness of the velocity of circulation to changes in the actual money supply adds considerably to the uncertainties with which monetarists already have to grapple.

THE TRANSMISSION MECHANISM

Assuming that monetarists could overcome all the problems so far considered, they have still to demonstrate that controlling the money supply would actually have the consequences which they postulate. In particular, they have to demonstrate that an increase in the money supply causes an increase in prices and not vice versa. A number of transmission mechanisms have been suggested by monetarist economists. One, the exchange rate, is that favoured by those normally described as international monetarists and this will be considered in the next chapter. Another leading contender is the notion that an increase in the money supply increases the real demand for goods which in turn pushes up prices. However, as Tarling and Wilkinson have demonstrated,[21] the connections between the money supply and real demand, and between real demand and prices, are far from well established and do not provide a sound base for monetarist theory.

Perhaps the most confidently advanced 'transmission mechanism' at present is the concept of 'rational expectations'. The essence of this view of how monetary control determines the inflation rate is that those who make wage claims and fix prices must be made aware of the government's determination to adhere to strict monetary targets. Once they are convinced that the government will not budge, even in the face of trade union power or rises in commodity prices, wages and prices will be fixed in accordance with 'rational expectations', i.e. in line with the degree of inflation permitted by monetary policy, and the inflation rate will fall accordingly.

The notion that monetarist policy depends in the end for its success on an uncertain forecast about behavioural patterns is somewhat surprising in a doctrine whose initial appeal rests on its supposed mechanistic simplicity, certainty and directness. It is not as though economists find it easy to identify and predict 'rational' responses to economic phenomena. This is well illustrated by what was thought to happen to the savings ratio in times of high inflation. For years, the orthodox view was that the rational response to high inflation was to increase spending and reduce savings; but this confident prediction has been confounded by recent experience which shows that savings tend to increase as the inflation rate rises. The 'rationality' of economists is clearly not always shared by the general public.

The difficulty of accurately forecasting a rational response is even greater in the case of monetary phenomena. Most of those who make wage claims or fix prices are blithely unaware of the latest monthly figures for Sterling M3; their opportunities for rational responses to these figures are therefore somewhat limited, and, as we have seen, they would in any case have been totally misled as to the true state of affairs. Furthermore, many of those who set the pace in determining wages and prices will not themselves pay any penalty for 'irrational' behaviour; indeed, in the preferred monetarist climate of the free play of market forces, the rational response to monetarist discipline of those workers with industrial muscle or those industrialists with a captive market will be to ignore money supply targets altogether. They will demand and obtain what the market will provide; and in the case of wage-earners, a rising exchange rate means that it is 'rational' to take advantage, through higher wages, of the increased consumption which the appreciating rate suggests the economy can afford. Those who will pay the penalty – school-leavers, for example – will do so involuntarily without ever having the chance to make a choice, whether rational or otherwise.

Stripped of the quasi-psychological element of 'rational expectations', monetarism must rely for its counter-inflationary effect on nothing more than the deliberate use of unemployment as a means of restraining wage claims. Its real impact comes not from the rational connection which workers and businessmen might make in advance between money supply targets and wage or price levels, but from the reality of rising unemployment and bankruptcy. The elegant monetarist theory becomes in practice nothing more than the familiar deflationary squeeze; the theory's only importance is that it encourages the policy-makers to push deflation to even more extreme lengths than are usually tolerated.

There is therefore a gaping hole in the theoretical basis of monetarism. Because no monetarist economist has yet succeeded in proving the elusive transmission mechanism, monetarists are therefore forced back to purely empirical conclusions, derived from their interpretation of the evidence provided by the monetary experience of various countries. Even here, there is little to back their claims.

THE BRITISH MONETARY EXPERIENCE

In this country, the crude version of the monetary theory was first given popular expression by an article in *The Times* of 13 July 1976, in which the editor argued that an average annual increase of 9.4 per cent in what he termed the 'excess money supply' in the nine years 1965–73 had resulted in an average annual increase of exactly 9.4 per cent in retail prices after a time lag of two years, i.e. in the nine years 1967–75. This remarkable correlation seemed to him amply to confirm the Friedman conclusion that there is roughly a two-year interval between an increase in the money supply and an increase in prices, after taking account of the increase in output and the money required to finance it. So confident was Mr Rees-Mogg of the validity of his findings that he even went on to proclaim that the excess money supply was like water flowing from a tap attached to a hosepipe about two years in length. Once the tap had been turned on, nothing could stop the water coming out of the other end in the form of price increases.

No doubt this earthy explanation appealed to many *Times* readers, but it could not have taken more than a moment's pause to realise that Rees-Mogg's figures bore all the hallmarks of a statistical fluke. What was true of the whole nine-year period was by no means true of every or any pair of years within that period, or of any other period. The average increase in prices over the whole nine years may have been exactly equal to the average 'excess money supply' but the variation in any one year was as much as 8.1 per cent above in 1969 to 7.3 per cent below in 1972.

A simple explanation for this statistical fluke is that the demand for money varies in the course of the trade cycle, increasing in the upswing and falling in the downswing, and this means that, provided the calculation embraces the whole of one or more cyclical periods, or begins and ends at the same point on the cycle, the excess money supply will be roughly equal to the increase in prices. This is so because we know, *ex post facto*, how much has been produced and, by definition, the amount of excess money. We have ended up, as Rees-Mogg did, by describing an identity, but we have discovered nothing about causal relationships. What is merely a tautology, in relation to a long period, cannot be relied on for policy prescriptions.

If we look at a different period from that selected by Rees-Mogg, a quite different picture emerges. Let us take instead the nine years from 1969–77.

Table 2.2 shows that what Rees-Mogg called the excess money supply – the increase in Sterling M3 less the increase in GDP – was very small in the two years after the devaluation of 1967, rose very rapidly after the Conservatives returned to office in 1970 and fell to a low of 5.8 per cent in 1976 as a result of the deflationary policies introduced by Healey, which raised the level of unemployment from 512 000 in the fourth quarter of 1973 to 1 456 000 in the third quarter of 1976. However, the relationship between the excess in col. 4 and lagged retail prices in col. 5 is very different from that which Rees-Mogg would have had us expect. His monetary hosepipe may have been working in 1970 and 1971, when the rise in prices was much the same as the corresponding increase in the excess money supply, but in 1972 it had obviously sprung a leak, because prices rose much less than the increase in the excess money supply two years earlier. Since 1972 water appears to have got into the pipe from somewhere else because prices have risen a good deal faster than the excess

TABLE 2.2   *Relationship between the money supply and prices, 1968–77/79*

	DCE	Sterling M3	GDP	Excess Money	Prices After 2-year Lag	Col 5 less Col 4
1968		7.7	4.3	3.4	6.3	2.9
1969	0	2.1	2.4	−0.3	9.4	9.7
1970	6.6	9.4	2.0	7.4	7.3	−0.1
1971	6.6	12.9	1.5	11.4	9.1	−2.3
1972	34.1	24.0	2.5	21.5	16.0	−5.5
1973	32.6	26.7	7.0	19.7	24.2	4.5
1974	22.0	10.2	−1.7	11.9	16.5	4.6
1975	13.1	6.7	−0.9	7.6	15.9	8.3
1976	20.2	8.9	3.1	5.8	8.3	2.5
1977	2.7	10.1	1.9	8.2	13.4	5.2
1978	18.1	15.2	2.7	12.5	19.0 est.	6.5 est.
1979	20.2	13.4	0.5	12.9	?	

SOURCE: CSO, *Economic Trends*, Annual Supplement, 1980 edn.

money supply. In the four years ending in 1980, prices have risen on average 60 per cent more than excess money and it is abundantly clear that these years of monetary contraction did not have the effect on prices which monetarists predicted.

There are two reasons for this. The first and most important is the increase in the velocity of circulation. The second is the deterioration in the overseas balance. The two of course overlap to the extent that activity is financed by, for example, sterling deposits of overseas residents. It should be noted in this connection that Rees-Mogg's calculations were based on M3 (in 1976 Sterling M3 was still a backroom concept). M3 includes the foreign currency deposits of UK residents and the effect is slightly to reduce the figures, with the exception of 1977, when the foreign balance was rapidly improving. The significance of M3 is that it is actually demand-determined and in the absence of exchange controls it is bound to increase in times of monetary stringency. The second column of Table 2.2 shows how DCE has increased for the same reason, the mechanism in this case being the adverse balance of trade inevitably created by an overvalued exchange rate.

The reason why monetarists have been so successful in convincing so many intelligent people of the validity of their case is that the money supply does in general terms increase at a time of rapidly rising prices, and while this tells us nothing about causality, it is only too easy to convince a bewildered public that the cure for inflation is simply to 'turn off the tap'. But if we take a period when there was greater stability, we can see that there is very little evidence of a stable and causal relationship between the money supply and prices, as Table 2.3 shows.

There is an astonishing identity between the growth of the broader definition of the money supply (col. 3) and the growth of the gross domestic product (col. 5) but this, according to Rees-Mogg, should have led to stable prices.[22] In fact, there was an increase, with a time lag of two years, of 46 per cent.

What happened in the early part of the period is even more revealing. From 1947–51, the money supply increased by no more than 8 per cent, less than the increase in the gross domestic product. Prices nevertheless rose in the period 1949–53 by no less than 27 per cent. This was not primarily due to the increase in wages, though there was undoubtedly a secondary wage effect. The real reason, as can be inferred from Table 2.3, was the

TABLE 2.3 *Relationship between the money supply and prices, 1949–62*

Year	Money IMF	Money LCES	Retail Prices	GDP	Bank Advances
1949		93	79	90	86
1950		94	81	92	96
1951	97	96	89	96	110
1952	97	96	97	96	107
1953	100	100	100	100	100
1954	104	104	102	104	104
1955	103	105	107	108	107
1956	103	105	112	109	109
1957	102	108	115	111	112
1958	104	111	119	112	116
1959	113	116	120	116	152
1960	113	121	121	121	183
1961	116	125	125	126	202
1962	109	128	130	127	205

SOURCE: Cols 2 and 5, from IFS *Yearbook* (1939), cols 3, 4 and 6 from London and Cambridge *Economic Service Bulletin* (1964).

increase in prices as a result of the Korean War, coming on top of the unexpectedly small price rises as a result of the 1949 devaluation. This was a clear case of cost-push inflation operating despite a negligible expansion of the money supply.

Recent experience shows much the same story. In the spring of 1980, we should have enjoyed an inflation rate of only 7.5 per cent if the monetarists are right about the two-year time lag and about 11 per cent if there is only a one-year time lag, but the actual rate of inflation was about 20 per cent. What use is a theory with so little relevance to reality?

Even in those cases where a 'statistical relationship' can be discerned between increases in the money supply and increases in price levels, the monetarist difficulty in showing how the transmission mechanism works suggests that the connection may not be the causal one which they assert. When other factors in the real economy cause prices to rise, e.g. when raw material import prices rise, the money supply may rise in order to accommodate those factors. The relationship would then, however, no longer be one in which increases in the money supply caused inflation, but rather the other way round; it would simply be, as the Select Committee put it in 1810, a response to the needs of trade. The difficulties which monetarists have in this regard are well

summed up by a recent announcement from Professor Milton
Friedman to the effect that the connection which he postulates
between money supply and inflation rates is subject to time lags
which are both variable and unpredictable. If this is the best that
a monetarist theoretician can do, there is nothing left to support
monetarist theory but empirical observation and that, as we have
seen, is almost entirely destructive of monetarist pretensions.

COMPARATIVE MONETARY POLICIES

We have examined the record for a number of other countries for
the years 1960–70 and 1970–8 for evidence to support the
monetarist case that there is a stable link between money and
prices. In Table 2.4 we give for each period the percentage
increase in the money supply compared to the percentage increases in output and prices. We also give in columns 8 and 9 the
increase in the money supply in each period divided by the
product of the increase in the GDP and the increase in prices, but
without allowing for a time lag, in view of the length of each
period.

TABLE 2.4   *Increase in money supply, output and prices, and the ratio of money to
output and prices, 1960–70 and 1970–8*

Country	Money	Output	Prices	Money	Output	Prices	Money ÷ Output × Price	
	1960–70	1960–70	1960–70	1970–8	1970–8	1970–8	1960–70	1970–8
France	144	76	49	144	35	99	89	85
Italy	314	73	47	299	24	167	204	128
Holland	129	67	54	132	29	84	82	96
Belgium	90	64	35	102	31	81	74	74
Ireland	102	56	59	199	37	171	69	73
Germany	112	61	32	120	23	51	100	140
UK	45	31	49	170	18	170	47	78
USA	54	42	31	62	30	68	63	52
Japan	415	187	75	223	52	111	103	101

SOURCE: USA and Japan – *International Financial Statistics Yearbook.* Rest – Eurostat, *Basic Statistics.*[23]

The results are obviously rather crude, but it is significant that
few of the figures in the last two columns approach unity (100),
i.e. where the increase in the money supply over the whole period
is equal to the increase in output multiplied by the increase in
prices. The country which goes closest is Japan, the most successful country in the world from a purely economic point of view.

Japan had the highest rate of inflation in the 1960s and a significantly higher rate than most countries in the 1970s, but, as we
shall see later, this was not reflected in export prices. The high
wages earned in the traded goods sector as a result of high investment forced up costs and prices in the rest of the economy and it
seems that the demand for money went up *pro rata*. The Germans
also came close in the 1960s, when they had a high rate of
growth, but they allowed the money supply to increase rapidly in
the 1970s, when they had one of the lowest rates of growth.

The contrast is very striking between the UK and the USA on
the one hand and the successful economies on the other. The UK
had the lowest rate of monetary growth in the 1960s and a high
rate of inflation. Italy, whose rate of monetary growth was seven
times faster, had a slightly lower rate of inflation. The French
had the same rate of inflation as we did, but more than three
times the rate of monetary growth. In the 1970s, the Italians
again had a very much higher rate of monetary growth and a
marginally lower rate of inflation than we did. The UK rate of
inflation was over three times higher than that of the Germans,
but the rate of increase in the UK money supply was only 42 per
cent higher. Over the whole period 1960 to 1978, the United
States had the lowest rate of monetary growth and the second
lowest rate of inflation, but the penalty for this seems to have
been a rate of growth which lagged far behind all but the UK. In
each of the three years 1976–8, the rate of inflation was much
higher in the United States than in Germany and the rate of
increase in monetary growth was much smaller. In 1978 the rate
of increase in the money supply in Germany was twice that of the
United States, but two years later the rate of inflation was not
much more than one-third of the United States figure.

It seems that the countries which have been most successful
are those which have had a relatively high rate of growth of the
money supply. The question arises whether their success was
despite or because of what monetarists would describe as their
excessive monetary growth. Monetarists have circumvented this
problem through the simple expedient of attaching a label to the
phenomenon which contradicts their theory. They say that
countries such as Germany have a natural propensity to require
a higher money supply increase for a given rate of inflation than
countries such as the United Kingdom. They therefore postulate
for each country a 'warranted rate of monetary growth'.

This is no more than an admission that, in order to finance growth and productivity on the German scale, a higher degree of monetary expansion is required than is currently permitted by monetarist doctrines in this country, and that it does not necessarily lead to a higher rate of inflation. This seems to be an excellent reason for abandoning a doctrine which is so deficient in theory and so lacking in practical evidence to support it. The notion of 'warranted' growth is not so much a theory as a description of an awkward fact (awkward that is for monetarists) that in some countries a high rate of increase in money supply means not a fall in the exchange rate and a rise in inflation, but the reverse. Monetarists are forced to explain this away by treating trends in productivity as though they were entirely independent of economic growth, a view which, as we have seen, is contradicted by all the available evidence.

OLD-FASHIONED DEFLATION

Although the politicians who have recently embraced monetarism appear to believe that the doctrine offers them a new instrument for tackling our problems, most monetarist economists would concede that the practical effect of their policies is indistinguishable from the deflationary policies pursued by almost every Chancellor since the end of the war. For these economists, the only difference between, let us say, Roy Jenkins and Sir Geoffrey Howe, is that the former was applying monetarist policies but did not know it, whereas the latter consciously framed his deflationary policies on the basis of monetarist theory.

While the arguments used to justify the action may vary, the practical measures chosen to implement the policy differ very little from earlier deflationary policies. Cuts in public expenditure, restrictions on credit, high interest rates, are precisely the measures which have been tried repeatedly by successive Chancellors in an attempt to reduce comparative costs and improve competitiveness. Monetarist jargon will not make these policies any more successful, or any less damaging, than their predecessors have been.

No one doubts that severe deflationary policies will, until they are again relaxed, squeeze profits and that this will slow down the rate of wage and price increases. It will do so, however, only at the cost of overwhelmingly damaging consequences for growth in the real economy. The debilitating effect of such policies means that growth will be brought entirely to a halt long before inflation has been eliminated, and that as soon as the attempt is made to resume growth, inflation will rise rapidly in an economy whose real base has been seriously eroded.

The point has been well illustrated by Professor Sir John Hicks in Figure 2.1, produced in the course of an exchange with the late Professor Harry Johnson.[24] The horizonal and vertical axes represent zero inflation and zero growth respectively. Maximum output is represented by the vertical line *FF*. The position of the economy at point *A* reflects a given rate of monetary expansion. Professor Hicks accepted that the curve described by *A* must in the end become nearly vertical as it moves upwards against limited capacity and as the growth in the money supply increases. He argued however that it was unlikely to go vertically downwards as growth in the money supply contracted. The prospect he saw was that the curve would move horizontally to the left and that the end result would be inflation and negative growth (*AC*) rather than nil inflation and positive growth (*AJ*).

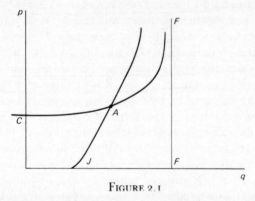

FIGURE 2.1

In the end, a tight monetary policy suffers from exactly the same logical defect as destroys every attempt to deflate our way out of our problems. If it is a necessary precondition for the success of deflationary policy that a certain proportion of resources should be kept out of use, growth can never be achieved, because as soon as the underutilised resources are drawn into use the necessary precondition for success has been destroyed. Those managing the economy will be compelled by the logic of their own theory to intervene to restrict growth. Deflation, whether based on monetarist doctrines or otherwise, can offer no solution to our problems.

THE BATTLE AGAINST INFLATION

We are constantly told, amidst the mounting evidence of industrial decline and destruction, that this horrifying damage is the price which has to be paid in order to conquer inflation. Whatever its other demerits may be, monetarism, it is claimed, at least guarantees that inflation can be brought under control. But even in these terms, the claims of the monetarists fall far short of their ability to deliver and are in fact contradicted by the practical effect of the policies which monetarism dictates.

The strict application of monetary targets compels the policy-makers to introduce measures which run directly counter to attempts to reduce inflation. The attempt to squeeze the money supply may mean that both tax rates and the rate of interest have to be raised, both of which have unavoidable consequences for the inflation rate. Increased tax rates, particularly in indirect taxes, and record interest rates directly increase inflation and indirectly stimulate inflationary wage claims and settlements. Forced increases in public sector rents, in the cost of public services and in the prices of nationalised industries, intended to reduce the public sector deficit, also push up the cost of living.

The conventional monetarist explanation for these measures is that they would not be necessary if public expenditure were reduced to an appropriate level. We shall consider the merits of public expenditure cuts in a later chapter, but what is incontrovertible, for the purposes of the battle against inflation, is that a reduction in public expenditure, at a time when the private sector is in serious recession, can only lead to a substantial fall in the level of demand and a further twist of the contractionary screw. This also has inflationary implications; as demand falls, and output falls in response to that falling demand, the inevitable consequence of any small increase in costs must be inflationary.

This becomes an even more serious factor if one accepts, as monetarists are not inclined to do, that in the real world, inflationary pressures may arise for other than monetary reasons – through a rise in the cost of imported raw materials or in wage costs in the absence of an incomes policy. It is this impact on unit costs which is the most serious inflationary defect of monetarist and other deflationary policies. At the very time that tax rates, interest rates and other factors are ensuring that fixed costs remain high and that overheads continue to rise, the only possible impact of a monetarist squeeze on output is to increase the cost of each unit of production.

According to monetarist theory, when costs rise in response to external pressures, controlling the money supply will force other costs correspondingly to fall, and will therefore prevent the overall level of costs from rising. Even if the theory should work like this in practice (and for all the reasons given this seems most unlikely), the problem is that those parts of the economy in which monetarist discipline tries to force a reduction in costs, in order to make room for unavoidable increases elsewhere, would be unlikely to survive the monetarist squeeze. They will simply go to the wall, caught between inflationary cost pressures on the one hand and a government-imposed deflationary squeeze on the other. As they go out of business in increasing numbers, the supposed counter-inflationary effects of the squeeze go with them. The only parts of the economy which survive are those in which the inflationary pressures can be tolerated – in practice, those firms operating in the non-internationally traded goods sector – who have an escape from this dilemma since they can pass on the cost increases to their customers. In the internationally traded goods sector, however, there is no such escape route available; the customer is unwilling to pay higher prices when the international market provides him with alternatives at lower prices.

The outcome is a depressing one on two counts. First, in terms of inflation, controlling the money supply does nothing to restrict cost increases in those parts of the economy which are able to pass them on to the consumer and the supposed levelling-out effect of costs in the economy as a whole is diminished by the fact that those parts of the economy which are supposed to reduce their costs are simply driven out of existence. Secondly, the dynamic effect of this process is particularly damaging, since it is the internationally traded goods sector, with its high productivity potential and crucial role in maintaining our competitiveness and growth possibilities, which is forced to bear the brunt and which is squeezed out of existence. It is hard to imagine an anti-inflationary policy which is less effective in reducing costs and more damaging to the real economy. The consequences of this misguided policy, both in terms of inflation rates and growth rates, are not only predictable but have already manifested themselves; our manufacturing capacity is shrinking rapidly while those parts of the economy which survive are inflamed by inflation.

THE APPEAL OF MONETARISM

If monetarism is as defective in principle and practice as we argue, how is it that it has achieved such pre-eminence in government policy-making? The first explanation of its popularity is that it revives and reinvigorates a continuing theme of British economic management for the past 100 years. We have consistently run our economy in the interests of those who hold assets, and particularly financial assets, as opposed to the interests of those who make and sell things. Financial orthodoxy has always been the prime concern of British economic managers; we have repeatedly given priority to purely financial objectives. The current preoccupation with the public sector borrowing requirement is the latest manifestation of this viewpoint, which led also to the earlier obsessions with the Gold Standard and with maintaining the parity of sterling.

The significance of monetarism can indeed best be appreciated by considering the parallels between our present situation and the crisis which brought down the Labour Government of 1931. Then, as now, the government insisted on a set of deflationary measures as a supposed cure for the ravages of its own deflationary policies. Then, the irrationality of what was proposed was obscured by the supposed importance of adhering to the Gold Standard; now a similar irrationality is overlooked or ignored because of the supposed importance of reducing the public sector borrowing requirement. In both cases, the measures imposed were not only extremely damaging in real terms, but were also self-defeating even in terms of securing the identified objective.

Monetarism's appeal is reinforced by the support which it lends to prevailing political prejudices. As disillusion with the effectiveness and desirability of government intervention has grown, there has been a swing of political opinion and fashion in favour of non-interventionist policies. Monetarism fulfils a useful role in appearing to provide an objective theoretical under-pinning, in terms of economic theory, to this set of political beliefs.

The doctrine is particularly useful in rationalising a concern which has long dominated the thinking of many of those who are most influential in economic policy-making. A strong and grow-ing body of opinion, exemplified by the editor of *The Times*, has reached the conclusion that our problems are entirely due to the monopoly power of the trade unions. On this premise, the over-riding objective of economic policy must be to reduce the power of the unions, both through legislative restriction and more importantly, through the use of a high level of unemployment to reduce their industrial bargaining power. The use of unemploy-ment for this purpose has often tempted governments of a right-wing persuasion, but the post-war consensus, and the availability of Keynesian techniques for maintaining full employment, have prevented the full rigours of this policy from being put into operation. Now that the post-war consensus has broken down and Keynesianism is virtually forgotten, monetarism has a valu-able role to play, for those who wish to implement this policy, since it provides a theoretical explanation for high unemploy-ment and further, explains that the responsibility for high unemployment rests on trade unions rather than on the govern-ment. A monetarist government, after all, is merely holding the ring; it is neutrally controlling the money supply and leaving it up to trade unions to decide whether to take the available money in terms of jobs for the many or increased real living standards for a few.

Monetarism is particularly popular in the City for all these political reasons and for financial reasons as well. It is no accident that the application of monetarist policies has meant a damaging squeeze on industrial profits but a bonanza for bank profits. Monetarism, whatever the theory may say, has meant in practice record interest rates and a corresponding boost to the profits of the banks. The Bank of England, perhaps the principal proponent of monetarism in this country, is in the last resort a bank itself – the bankers' bank; its primary loyalties are to the banking system rather than to the national economy and it is hardly surprising that it should urge priority for a doctrine which so well suits the financial interests which it represents.

There is a further sense in which monetarism is particularly congenial to the City. If the only criterion of the success of economic management is the control of the money supply, and if the money supply is in the end determined by the actions of financial institutions, it is only to be expected that the financial institutions will welcome a doctrine which gives them such influence and power over the management of the economy.

A good example of the power which monetarist doctrine places in the hands of the City can be seen in the period following the 1978 Budget. The Chancellor had introduced a mildly reflationary set of measures but found himself hoist on the petard of his own earlier emphasis on the importance of controlling the money supply. The money markets, calculating the effect of his Budget on the money supply, decided that it would rise beyond the desired level and that an increase in interest rates would be necessary to encourage an increased sale of gilt-edged securities. Because no investment manager worth his salt will buy gilts while interest rates are rising and the price of gilts is falling, the sale of gilt-edged came to a halt and the prophecy of a rise in the money supply, at least in terms of Sterling M3, became self-fulfilling. The Chancellor was thus forced to increase interest rates (thereby reversing the reflationary effect of his Budget) in order to bring the money supply under apparent control again.

The whole episode was regarded as a vindication of the importance of monetary targets, but all that had happened was that the money markets had expressed a judgement unfavourable to the Budget and were given the power, by virtue of the importance quite wrongly attached to monetary targets, for forcing a reversal of the Budget strategy.

A further and not entirely frivolous explanation of the popularity of monetarism in the City and elsewhere is that it is apparently so simple. If controlling the money supply is all there really is to economic policy, and if the success or failure of that policy can by measured month by month in terms of the monthly Sterling M3 figure, then everyone can, with complete confidence, be his own Chancellor. The mysteries of running the economy suddenly become accessible to even the lowliest of City functionaries. For those who have been irritated and bewildered by the uncertainties and complexities of economic management for so many years, the attraction of a doctrine which reduces the whole problem to one simple equation should not be underestimated.

CONCLUSION

The appeal of monetarism lies in its simplicity. It provides a panacea for all our economic ills, based on the simple proposition that inflation can be stopped, without in any way retarding the maximum sustainable rate of growth, merely by reducing the rate of increase in the money supply according to a precise and well-publicised timetable to a level which does not exceed the long-term rate of growth. Monetarists admit that hardship will be caused to some on the way, but argue that this is the inevitable consequence of the previous neglect of monetarist principles and indeed that the longer we delay in recognising their eternal verities, the greater these hardships will be. There is more than a hint of Marxism in their philosophy – with accelerating inflation replacing the inevitability of capitalist crisis – and like Marxism, it is nicely tailored to appeal to political prejudice, but with the trade unions rather than monopoly capitalists as the bogey men responsible for creating the reserve army of unemployed! Our problems are attributed to political interference with the free play of market forces and those who doubt the advisability of cutting government expenditure are assured that failure to do so will make it impossible to keep within the monetary targets on which all else depends. Only one path is provided to salvation.

There are signs, during the course of 1980, that the quasi-religious certainties of monetarism are beginning to crumble, even in the minds of its most fervent adherents. Reference has already been made to Professor Friedman's statement about the variability and unpredictability of the time lags; John Biffen, the Chief Secretary to the Treasury, has also recently confessed that there is no 'mechanistic connection' between the money supply and price levels, a clear admission that the transmission mechanism so essential to monetarist theory does not exist. An equally damaging admission has been made implicitly by all those ministers, including the Prime Minister and the Chancellor, who are urging a fall in real wages as a means of reducing inflation and who attribute rising inflation to the increase in world commodity prices; once it is conceded that these factors are important elements in determining the level of prices, there is nothing left of the monetarist claim that inflation is caused entirely by, and can be controlled only by, changes in the money supply.

3 International Monetarism

As we have seen, monetarist theory has never succeeded in showing exactly how changes in the money supply determine the level of prices. One school of monetarist economists, usually described as the international monetarists, have however advanced their own view as to how this transmission mechanism works. Their argument is that, under a regime of floating exchange rates, changes in the domestic money supply will cause the exchange rate to rise and fall and that it is this movement of the exchange rate which governs the level of prices. This argument warrants special attention for two reasons; first, it has been, until recently at least, very influential in UK policy-making; and secondly, it leads to policy prescriptions which are almost diametrically opposed to those which we believe are desirable in the interests of the UK economy.

The non-monetarist approach to the balance of payments concentrates on the relative price and income effects of a change in the exchange rate. The success or failure of a devaluation depends, according to this view, on the price elasticities of demand for imports and exports, the duration of the price advantage and the capacity of the economy to supply additional goods and services for import substitution and for export. The general view has been that the elasticity conditions are likely to be fulfilled because the volume effects (higher exports, lower imports) outweigh the adverse effect on the terms of trade (cheaper exports, dearer imports) and that the price advantage gained in the traded goods sector will be eroded only slowly, if at all, by price rises in the domestic economy; hence, all that is necessary is to ensure that there is sufficient spare capacity to meet the increase in export demand. This is clearly not a problem when the economy's resources are not being fully utilised; but, in conditions of full or near-full employment such as existed in the 1950s and 1960s, expenditure-reducing and expenditure-switching measures would also be required to shift resources from consumption and investment into the foreign balance. The only problem which then remains is the so-called J-curve – an initial deterioration of the balance of payments immediately after a devaluation because the improvement in the volume of trade takes time to offset the deterioration in the terms of trade –but the volume improvement will quickly assert itself and produce an improved balance of payments at a higher level of output.[1]

Exchange rate policy, combined with the appropriate fiscal policies, is thus seen as an instrument to reconcile full employment and a satisfactory balance of payments, either using fiscal policy to determine the employment level while the exchange rate is varied to secure balance of payments equilibrium, or, following Meade, using financial policy to maintain the external balance while the exchange rate is varied to secure internal equilibrium. Surpluses and deficits in the balance of payments are then simply treated as flow equilibria, assuming, explicitly or implicitly, that the monetary consequences of a continuing balance of payments surplus or deficit can be offset or sterilised by the monetary authorities.[2]

By comparison with this orthodox view, the distinctive feature of the monetarist approach to the balance of payments is that it stresses the implications for the money stock of the continuing flow of financial assets required to finance a balance of payments surplus or deficit. These surpluses and deficits are represented as substantial phases of stock adjustment in the money market and are not treated simply as equilibrium phenomena.[3] It is argued that these monetary inflows or outflows cannot be effectively sterilised within a period relevant to policy analysis, and must therefore influence the domestic money supply and consequently the level of prices, given a stable demand function for money.[4]

The belief that balance of payments surpluses and deficits must be considered in terms of changes in the money stock leads international monetarists to the conclusion that the exchange rate can affect only money phenomena, such as the general price level, and not the underlying real phenomena such as the trade balance or the terms of trade.[5] At the centre of the analysis is the assumption that the private sector has some desired long-run relationship between wealth and income so that additions to net wealth, as a result, for example, of a balance of payments surplus, will spill over into higher private sector expenditure.[6] This means that an improvement to the balance of payments as a result of devaluation can only be transitory because the balance of payments surplus feeds into the money supply and sets in motion an inflationary process which restores the price level of the devaluing country, measured in foreign currency terms, to its pre-devaluation level. At this point the external surplus disappears and the country is back to its original position, but with a once-for-all increase in its reserves, accumulated while the price adjustment was occurring.[7]

It follows from this that, in a world of fixed exchange rates, the authorities of a small open economy cannot control the money supply or the domestic price level. They can control the level of domestic credit, but any attempt to control the money supply will be defeated because money can be obtained from abroad through the mechanism of the balance of payments. Control over the money stock, therefore, can only be secured by letting the exchange rate float. The exchange rate can then be used to control the inflow and outflow of the foreign reserves, enabling the authorities to regain control over the money stock and thus over the price level. The floating rate is therefore seen as a means of determining the rate of inflation rather than of achieving balance of payments equilibrium and full employment. International monetarists nevertheless claim that full employment – or what they describe as the minimum sustainable rate of unemployment – is still a natural (and, in the long term, unavoidable) characteristic of their policy, with the added advantage that the overseas payments problem ceases to exist.[8]

The London Business School, and in particular the Centre for Economic Forecasting, have been the principal exponents of the international monetary approach in this country and have achieved a great deal of publicity through their periodic forecasts in the *Sunday Times* and through the writings of Samuel Brittan in the *Financial Times*. Their views have to be taken seriously because they are said to be shared by the present Prime Minister and several members of the Cabinet, and because Terry Burns, the former Director of the Centre, has been put in charge of the Government Economic Service to ensure that economic policy is based on the monetarist approach. We should therefore sum up this exposition of international monetarist principles by repeating the substance of the first three paragraphs of an article on exchange rate policy by Terry Burns in *The Times* on 11 July 1977.

Burns argued that exchange rate behaviour is the crucial link between inflation and monetary policy. The target movement of the exchange rate must therefore be judged primarily in terms of the desired relationship between United Kingdom and world inflation rates. If the UK is content to experience a similar inflation rate to the rest of the world, it is necessary to design a fiscal and monetary policy that is appropriate to exchange rate stability. If the UK target is price stability (nil inflation), then exchange rate appreciation will be necessary in an inflationary world and fiscal and monetary policy needs to be tighter than the world average. Burns admits that this apparently simple choice is complicated by what he describes as the short-run trade-off between exchange rate movements and industrial price competitiveness; depreciating countries will experience a temporary improvement in price competitiveness as long as the depreciation is unanticipated, while a country with an appreciating currency will normally suffer some loss of competitiveness in the short term. The decision as to which policy to pursue must therefore be judged in terms of the perceived advantages of price stability compared with the initial loss of price advantage. The decision is, however, made simpler, once it is realised that exchange rate movements cannot improve price competitiveness in the long term and that both export and domestic prices are really determined by world prices, irrespective of what happens to the exchange rate.

The view that a country's price level is pegged to the world price level and must move rigidly in line with it derives from the purchasing power parity theory of exchange rate determination. This theory, described by international monetarists as the 'Law of One Price', states that traded goods must have the same price in each of the markets in which they are traded and that, because of the domino effect of any change in the price of traded goods on wages and other prices, what is true of traded goods must also be true of those which are not traded. A given basket of goods will therefore cost the same in all markets, whatever currency is used to denote the price. This may not happen at once, because the proportion of traded goods may be relatively small or because of imperfect knowledge, including money illusion; but it must happen eventually. Because, on this view, an open economy is in the long term a price-taker on world markets, devaluation cannot permanently affect the foreign currency price of exports, and the benefits to be gained from a devaluation are necessarily short-lived.[9]

THE FLAWS IN THE MONETARY ANALYSIS

The validity of the monetary approach to the balance of payments very much depends, like so much else in economic theory, on the simplifying assumptions used in constructing theoretical and econometric models. Model-building has become a great industry; but, as Alfred Marshall – the father of modern economics – wrote in 1901, every economic fact, whether or not it is of such a nature as to be expressed in numbers, stands in relation as cause and effect to many other facts, and since it never happens that all of them can be expressed in numbers, the application of exact mathematical models to those which can is nearly always a waste of time and in the large majority of cases is positively misleading.[10]

This is a judgement with which we heartily concur. Our case against the monetary approach to the balance of payments is precisely that it is almost wholly based on theoretical concepts for which the empirical evidence is at best ambiguous, and that opinion formers have been 'taught to believe what their common sense, if they had relied on it, would have told them was absurd'.[11] We shall examine the Theory of One Price in the next section of this chapter, but the fact that the cost of living is not and never has been the same in all countries should be reason enough to cast doubt on the view that 'each country's price level is pegged to the world price level and must move rigidly in line with it'.[12] In this section, our main concern is with the effect of international flows on the domestic stock of money, but here again, the evidence of what has happened in the case of Germany should cast doubt on the proposition that monetary inflows and outflows cannot be sterilised within a period relevant to policy analysis. The German mark has been undervalued over long periods since 1950[13] but, as Professor Ottmar Issing has pointed out, the German monetary authorities have been very successful in sterilising the inflow of foreign reserves to make sure that their goods were not priced out of home and overseas markets.[14]

The monetarist case is nevertheless based entirely on the assumption that the monetary flows which stem from a change in the exchange rate cannot be sterilised by open-market intervention. The disturbance to stock equilibrium in the private sector brought about by exchange rate movements will set in motion changes in expenditure to restore the balance between wealth and income, a balance which international monetarists believe is invariable in the long run and which in their view must restore the level of costs and prices to what it was before the movement in the exchange rate took place.

This highly abstract view of the working of the monetary system not only tells us very little about the real world, in which there is little or no evidence of a stable relationship between income and wealth, but is also defective because it takes no account of changes in the public sector. It is true that a balance of payments deficit/surplus cannot be offset in the long run by open-market operations if we assume that the public sector is in balance, because in that case a continuing balance of payments surplus would result in a continuing private sector surplus and it is unlikely that this would remain unspent indefinitely. But, as Professor Currie has pointed out, this excludes the possibility that sterilisation can be effected by running a government (budget) surplus/deficit corresponding to the balance of payments surplus/deficit, in which case there need be no continuing disturbance to private stock equilibrium and no unavoidable change in the money supply. General equilibrium necessarily includes balance of payments equilibrium, but it does not preclude a private sector surplus matched by a public sector deficit in conditions of full employment.[15]

Professor Currie concluded from this analysis that international monetarists had overemphasised the importance of monetary factors in the balance of payments and had underestimated the importance of expenditure-switching and expenditure-reducing policies as a means of sterilising monetary movements. The analysis of the balance of payments in the longer run should therefore concentrate on changes in fiscal policy and other real factors, rather than on the accounting identity between the money stock, and reserves and domestic credit, on which the monetary analysis focuses.

Professor Harry Johnson argued, however, that the monetary authorities will not be able to sterilise the effects of balance of payments disequilibria on the money supply, not because of any supposed theoretical problem, but for the practical reason that they will sooner or later exhaust either their international reserves or the stock of domestic assets.[16] In the case of a deficit, it is certainly true that the reserves could eventually be exhausted, though a short-term deficit on current account can generally be financed by foreign investment and/or assistance from foreign banks and, in the case of a larger country, huge deficits and surpluses breed countervailing flows which leave the money stock in the private sector relatively untouched. The Americans, for example, have been able to finance their current account deficit for years on end.

There is no reason in the case of a surplus, however, why a country should not go on accumulating reserves, provided the authorities are prepared to use fiscal measures to offset the inflationary impact and provided other countries are prepared to countenance a corresponding reduction in their reserves and increase in their budgetary deficits. As we have seen, the Germans were able to sterilise their balance of payments surplus between 1950 and 1970, despite the undervaluation of the Deutschmark over a long period.

The concept of equilibrium used by international monetarists is in any case extremely dubious. We are told that the surplus on the balance of payments must disappear because the devaluing country's prices are forced up by the inevitable inflation to the international level, and that devaluation will therefore lead only to a once-for-all increase in the foreign reserves in conditions of equilibrium. But what would happen if the process were to continue indefinitely, as the German example suggests it could? The consequences postulated by international monetarists in terms of domestic inflation and international competitiveness simply did not materialise. What happened instead was a continuing increase in the German share of world trade in manufactures, a factor which international monetarists completely overlook.

This last point is important because the studies which have been carried out by monetarists – referred to in a later section – completely ignore the crucial issue, so far as policy is concerned, that some countries have been able to increase their share of world trade substantially over a long period at the expense of others. Equally, there is nothing in international monetarist theory which would allow a country with a consistently overvalued currency, as evidenced by a persistent balance of payments deficit and a falling share of world trade in manufactures, to escape from that predicament. The starting point to which, according to international monetarists, any attempt to vary the exchange rate must eventually return may be equilibrium in terms of the theoreticians' model, but in the real world it is all too likely to be a state of long-term decline. Monetarists who argue that changes in the exchange rate cannot permanently change the underlying real phenomena thus appear to have no monetary explanation for the very real shift in resources and economic activity which has taken place between debtor and creditor countries.

THE THEORY OF ONE PRICE

The international monetarist view that changes in the exchange rate can only affect monetary phenomena, such as the general price level, is based on the purchasing power parity theory of exchange rate determination. This theory, as we have seen, assumes that a basket of goods and services will cost the same in each market at an equilibrium rate of exchange, so that in the long run any change in the rate of exchange will be offset by price movements which will restore the real or barter rate of exchange between each country.

The purchasing power parity theory – now usually referred to as the Law of One Price – has gained almost universal acceptance, although a moment's thought would suggest that it has no foundation in reality. A world in which costs and prices in each country are determined by world costs and prices would be a world of economic convergence. The world in which we live is actually one of increasing economic divergence. The theory has nevertheless been accepted by economists of such widely different outlook as Professor Kaldor on the one hand – it is the basis of the so-called Kaldor paradox – and Professor Terry Burns of the London Business School on the other. The Treasury accepts its validity and a massive survey of the literature undertaken by Professor L. Officer[17] for the IMF concluded that the theory was sound. What is the basis for this?

The purchasing power parity theory was first expounded by Gustav Cassel in 1916 and elaborated in a memorandum submitted to the International Financial Conference at Brussels in 1920. He argued that the substantial movements which had taken place in the rates of exchange before and after the First World War reflected changes in the purchasing power of the respective currencies. He admitted, though, that purchasing power parity would not prevail where there were tariffs or other restrictions on trade; and since a tariff is a form of exchange depreciation, this should have warned him and others that the relationship between prices and exchange rates was by no means as straightforward as he believed.

In any case, the figures told a much less clear story than he suggested. As Jacob Viner pointed out as long ago as 1937, the divergences between actual exchange rates and those postulated by the purchasing power parity formula are in fact frequently substantial; the 'disturbances' from which such divergences result need not by any means be temporary and may in fact increase progressively.[18] Viner showed that, even under the Gold Standard, it was easy to conceive of changes in costs or demand conditions, or both, which would so change the relative demand of two or more countries for each other's products in terms of their own as to bring about an enduring and substantial relative change in their levels of prices, including the prices of domestic commodites and services.

Viner appreciated that under a paper standard there would be a mutual influence of prices on the exchange rate and of the exchange rate on prices, with no satisfactory way of apportioning to each set of influences its share of responsibility for the actually resultant situation. It is doubtful, though, whether he realised that a change in the exchange rate could be destabilising in the sense that it can lead to a change in unit costs in the traded goods sector which is bigger than the change in the exchange rate. It is this essential, but little appreciated, point which undermines the purchasing power parity theory and explains its deficiencies.

International trade, as we have seen, consists in large part of goods which are produced continuously or in large batches and which are therefore subject to economies of scale. The larger the market for such goods, the longer the production runs; and the longer the production runs, the further unit costs can be reduced. Because the markets for internationally traded goods are extremely price sensitive, a relatively small reduction in costs can have a disproportionate effect on sales, and a further and cumulative benefit to unit costs. In such cases, improved competitiveness, whether brought about by devaluation or otherwise, enables the producer to reap a double advantage; he can increase his revenue by putting up prices in terms of his own currency and, provided the increase in prices is less than the margin of improved competitiveness, he can reduce his costs by expanding sales. Indeed, where his plant is working at far less than capacity it may pay him not to increase his prices at all and rely on increased output and sales to provide a bigger return for workers and shareholders alike. This could well be the case in the UK at the present time, where many industries are working at far below capacity and where marginal costs must be a great deal less than average costs.

The significance of this is that those firms engaged in international trade, which are by definition the most efficient firms in the most efficient industries within a given economy, will have cost curves which describe a different and more favourable path over time than does the cost curve of industry generally. It follows from this that economic growth is subject to a Law of Continuous Causation which undermines the Law of One Price and which also explains the so-called Kaldor paradox – the fact that some countries are able to combine rising exchange rates and industrial costs generally with increasing international competitiveness. For such countries, export-led growth, often generated by a competitive exchange rate, feeds on itself as the market expands at home and abroad; unit costs in the internationally traded goods sector then fall faster than in other parts of the economy, enabling competitiveness to be maintained or improved even when industrial costs generally are rising as a result of higher living standards, or currency appreciation, or both. The opposite process is at work in the case of a country with falling competitiveness in the traded goods sector; the virtuous circle of export-led growth is then replaced by the vicious circle of import-led contraction.

This very simple explanation of the relationship between internal growth and external equilibrium does not appear to have been grasped earlier. The IMF survey previously referred to noted that changes in relative prices within a country are indicators of real changes in the economy in question and concluded that this could lead to a divergence between purchasing power parity and the exchange rate, but the significance of this in terms of the price of traded compared to non-traded goods and services does not appear to have been grasped. Bela Balassa also noted that, although a high-income country is more productive technologically than a low-income country, the comparative advantage is not uniform.[19] He too failed to grasp the significance of the point. The problem is that economists almost everywhere look at competitiveness in terms of unit labour costs generally and not in terms of export costs and prices. It is true that in most cases they look at costs in manufacturing industry, but this fails to take account of the fact that most firms engaged in manufacturing are not significantly affected by foreign competition at home and abroad because they are not making the kinds of goods which can easily be marketed over a wide area.

The issue has been further confused by the IMF, who have constructed an index showing relative normal unit labour costs in manufacturing based on full capacity working; this index is now widely used as a measurement of competitiveness. We shall be considering the problem of measuring competitiveness in Chapter 5, but it is extraordinary that the Treasury should rely on this index, which is relevant to manufacturing industry generally rather than to the internationally traded goods sector, in preference to an indicator which shows more accurately what is actually happening to Britain's international competitiveness.

Our scepticism concerning the Law of One Price is supported by the work of Peter Isard of the Division of International Finance of the US Federal Reserve System, who has shown conclusively that, in the case of the USA and Germany, the Law of One Price is in practice flagrantly and systematically violated by empirical data and that exchange rate movements substantially alter the relative dollar-equivalent prices of the most narrowly defined domestic and foreign manufactured goods for which prices can readily be matched.[20] This is largely confirmed by the results of our own researches into the validity of the conclusions reached by the NEDC in a paper on price competitiveness, to which we refer in the next chapter.

The importance of the relationship between export and domestic prices can be seen from Table 3.1, showing for the period 1952–78 the increase in (a) the consumer price index and (b) the unit value index for exports of manufactures, in each case as a percentage of the increase in the wholesale price index and for each of the principal manufacturing countries; together with the increase in export prices in each case, as a percentage of the UK increase in 1978 and the first quarter of 1980.

Table 3.1 shows only the movement of relative prices within each country. It does not tell us whether the country was gaining or losing competitiveness either at the beginning or at the end of the period, but the first three lines do show how far export prices diverged from domestic prices;[22] and the rest of the table brings out very clearly how the competitive position of the UK, and to a lesser extent the USA, had weakened by 1978 and even more so by the first quarter of 1980, when the effective exchange rate was 72.2 of the Smithsonian (1971) parity compared to 63.0 in 1978. The effective exchange rate by the end of October 1980 was 79.9 and this understates the movement in the real exchange rate brought about by our higher rate of inflation.

TABLE 3.1   *Increase in consumer and export prices as a percentage of wholesale prices, 1952–78*

	UK	USA	Germany	Japan	France	Italy	Belgium	Holland
A. Consumer	119	103	130	242	121	116	158	173
B. Wholesale	100	100	100	100	100	100	100	100
C. Man. exports	115	116	78	62	97	67	73	66
Increase in (C)								
1978	100	82	89	62	76	58	66	72
1980 1st qtr	100	73	68	45	67	52	58	61

SOURCE: Chain-linked to 1978 based on 1958, 1963 and 1970 UN series. OECD, *Economic Outlook*, no. 27, for the last line.[21]

These comparisons are necessarily broad brush. The coverage of the price indices varies from one country to another and over time, the export price index takes no account of goods which are priced into and out of the market, the varying rates of inflation in the different countries may have had differing effects on home and export prices, and the cut-off date in each case may be unrepresentative for a particular country, e.g. just before or just after a change in the exchange rate. The figures are nevertheless very striking. Export prices in the less successful economies – the UK and the USA – have risen a good deal faster than wholesale prices. The opposite is true of the successful countries.

The conclusion must be that even if the Law of One Price is accepted as having some broad validity (in the sense that there is a limit to which prices can diverge without a change in market shares), it tells us very little of what we need to know. It obscures the crucial fact that countries with a successful and expanding export sector are able to hold down costs in that sector in relation to other parts of the economy, and are thereby able to move resources into the export sector with a consequent increase in their share of world trade. The reverse is true of economies that are failing to compete.

EMPIRICAL EVIDENCE

What evidence, apart from assertion, have international monetarists advanced to support their case? The first attempt in the UK seems to have been made by Messrs Ball, Burns and Laury of the London Business School, using a large-scale quarterly econometric forecasting model to examine the effect of a change in the exchange rate upon the balance of payments, financial flows, price level and expenditure components of the UK economy.[23] They constructed four elegant wage–price models and concluded to their own satisfaction that, with free collective bargaining and no fiscal or monetary measures other than the indexing of government grants and tax rates, the impact of an exchange rate change is likely to be temporary. They were nevertheless forced to admit that none of the models could explain why the UK economy had had a persistent tendency over a long period of years to run at a higher rate of inflation than that of our principal competitors, such as the United States and Germany. They did not, however, conclude that the models were deficient, which would have been the reaction of the non-economist. They decided instead, because only this was consistent with their model, that the devaluation of 1949 must have been excessive, that as a result sterling was essentially undervalued until the mid-1960s, and that because of this wages and prices had to rise (in accordance with monetarist theory) until our competitive advantage had been eliminated. They advanced this remarkable theory, even though this process led us back to a position of disequilibrium rather than the equilibrium postulated by their model and was accompanied by an immense fall in our share of world trade in manufactures. They were so convinced of the validity of their theories, however, that they insisted on the corollary: that because of the undervaluation of sterling, the level of output was higher, unemployment was lower, and the balance of payments better than it would otherwise have been. If the basic premise of undervaluation were really correct, what better case for a competitive exchange rate could one have than that?

Messrs Ball, Burns and Laury did not advance a shred of evidence to support their view that sterling had been undervalued, but, as we shall see in the next chapter, the evidence is conclusive that both sterling and the dollar were overvalued from 1950 onwards. It is in any case absurd to describe a currency as being undervalued when the country in question is losing its share of world trade and of its home market at a rate which is without parallel in recorded history.

This brings us back to the fatal flaw in the monetarist approach; they ignore changes in market share and consider everything in terms of money and prices, forgetting that a balance of payments equilibrium could be restored despite a loss of market share. They tacitly assume that every devaluation starts from a point of equilibrium and are quite unable to explain how their theory works if the devaluation is no more than sufficient to correct a previous overvaluation. Their problem is an intellectual one; their theory does not really admit that a currency *can* become overvalued.

What is needed in the real world is a monetary theory which explains changes in both output and prices in terms of an equilibrium rate of exchange which enables each country to maximise its rate of economic growth with external equilibrium in conditions of full employment. A reduction in a country's share of world trade in conditions of less than full employment would then be evidence of a disequilibrium which needs to be corrected by appropriate monetary measures, including a reduction in the exchange rate.

A different approach was adopted by Messrs Robinson, Webb and Townsend in a very detailed study made by the Directorate General for Economic and Financial Affairs of the EEC in 1978 of the effect of exchange rate changes on prices in eighteen industrial countries between 1954 and 1976.[24] The study is important because it shows how misleading this kind of exercise can be. The purpose was to test the conclusion of the so-called Scandinavian Theory – which is the basis of the Law of One Price – that relative prices are stable under fixed exchange rates and cannot be changed in anything but the short run by a change in the exchange rate.

The authors realised at the outset that prices were likely to be more responsive in an open than in a closed economy and that differences in productivity between the manufacturing sector and the rest of the economy in different countries could lead to a change in relative prices, but they do not appear to have asked themselves why these differences should occur, nor do they appear to have grasped their significance for the theory itself.

We are in any case very critical of their statistical methods. We appreciate that their task was almost impossibly complex, but this was a good reason for not attempting it. The period 1954–76 was characterised by very great changes in trading relationships which must have had an effect on prices. Quantitative restrictions on trade were removed on most trade between industrialised countries in the late 1950s and there was a steady reduction in tariff levels over the whole period. Commonwealth preferences were eroded, but substantial new preferences were created in the EEC and EFTA. These changes could have been as significant for some countries as changes in the exchange rate. The comparison on the other hand includes foodstuffs, where the link between world prices and domestic prices is to say the least tenuous in seventeen out of the eighteen countries, as it has been even in the UK since it joined the EEC. The inclusion of exports of services in the calculations is a further complication. We would have much preferred a straightforward comparison of export prices of manufactures, the wholesale price of manufactures less foodstuffs, and consumer prices.

A much more fundamental criticism is that this study also takes no account of changes in market share. The authors claim that the figures show that export prices do indeed follow the world price, but this seems to us economically meaningless unless it can be shown that market shares remain the same. It is obvious that an exporter cannot charge a great deal more than his competitor for an identical product sold in the same market and expect to stay in that market for any length of time. Indeed, there is a sense in which everything exported is competitive, since otherwise the buyer would have looked elsewhere. What really matters is the price of goods that could not be sold because they were not competitive and on this vital issue the method adopted by Messrs Robinson *et al.* tells us nothing.

We are equally unimpressed by the conclusion that domestic prices were found to be stable under a system of fixed exchange rates. The changes they found of up to 2 per cent in a given year and up to 5 per cent in five years are not insignificant, particularly in view of the fact that the average rate of return on sales in manufacturing industry in the UK is only of the order of 8 per cent before interest and tax, on an historic cost basis.

It is nevertheless of interest that the figures did not show a strong link between wholesale prices and changes in the exchange rate. In about half the cases, the coefficients reflecting the quarterly response of wholesale prices to changes in the exchange rate were insignificant and erratic in sign. A number of countries had in fact succeeded in bringing about what the authors described as a permanent increase in either wages or in profits in the exporting industries as a result of devaluation. In those countries, changes in parity had in fact resulted in a change in relative export prices.

International monetarists have become increasingly conscious of the fact that relative prices have been changing. This has been particularly obvious in the case of Japan, where, despite the rapid rise in the cost of living, the Japanese have enjoyed an increasing price advantage in world markets. In October 1977, Professor Burns published an article in the *Sunday Times* which in effect substantially modified the conclusions reached in the article published earlier that year in the *Economic Journal*. He was now suggesting that attention should be fastened on the 'real exchange rate' – which he defined as the actual rate in terms of dollars multiplied by the ratio of retail prices – adjusted to take account of changes in productivity growth in manufacturing and/or changes in the price of a major product which the country is buying or selling, including the gain from the discovery of a natural resource such as North Sea oil. Acknowledging as it did that the divergence of relative export prices has to be explained somehow, this was a major step towards our own Theory of Continuous Causation, which we had first outlined in a Fabian pamphlet published at the end of September 1977, but it was still quite unnecessarily complicated and failed to take account of the important dynamic differences between the behaviour of costs in the internationally traded goods sector and elsewhere in the economy.

Professor Burns's emphasis on retail prices reflects the continuing preoccupation with the 'shopping basket' approach of the purchasing power parity theory, without which the international monetarist case of course falls to the ground; and, while he was certainly right to take account of changes in productivity, these

are of importance in the context of the exchange rate if and only if
they have an effect on the relative cost of producing internationally tradeable goods and services. Nethertheless, the invention of
the concept of a 'productivity-adjusted real exchange rate' does
show that international monetarists are now aware that the Law
of One Price does not provide an adequate or accurate explanation of what happens to relative export policies and international competitiveness.

CONCLUSION

International monetarists maintain that the exchange rate will
rise if money is too tight and/or if unemployment is above what
they describe as the minimum sustainable rate and it will fall if
money is too plentiful and/or unemployment is too low. If the
exchange rate rises too high, the apparent loss of competitiveness
will be offset by a rate of inflation lower than that of other
countries, and if it falls too low, the gain to competitiveness will
be wiped out by a higher rate of inflation.

It follows that we are powerless to determine our economic
fate. Any attempt on our part to influence events can do no more
than postpone the inevitable and indeed will cause undue suffer-
ing by making matters worse than they would otherwise have
been. The greatest good is thus achieved by leaving everything to
the hidden hand of market forces.

The difficulty we face in analysing this deterministic view of
the way the economy works is that its values are entirely subjec-
tive. We cannot judge whether the exchange rate is too high by
reference to the rate of unemployment because international
monetarists are not prepared to say whether the minimum sustainable rate is 1 per cent, 5 per cent or 10 per cent. They talk
constantly of equilibrium, but they do not tell us how equilibrium is to be defined, where it is to be found and how we are to
recognise it when we get there. One thing seems clear from all
their writing; equilibrium is concerned only with changes in price
to the total exclusion of changes in market share. As we shall see
in Chapter 5, this raises the question of how changes in price are
measured, but still leaves us with no economic benchmarks
against which to test the validity of their theories. This of course
gives them an enormous advantage in public debate. Whatever

the level of unemployment, they can still argue that inflation is
the fault of the unions and/or that the government is spending
too much of the taxpayers' money. They give no hostages to
fortune which might strip them of their academic pretensions
and lay bare their political prejudices.

Nevertheless, the theoretical deficiencies of international
monetarism, its tenuous connection with what happens in the
real world, and its inability to explain what has happened to the
UK and other economies over recent years, means that the exchange rate cannot be the elusive transmission mechanism so
long sought by monetarists. Even more conclusive and damning
is the sheer weight of the practical experience of the UK over the
past three years. During that period, the exchange rate for
sterling has appreciated continuously; this, according to international monetarist theory, should have meant a British inflation
rate substantially lower than the international average. Instead,
the UK has experienced an inflation rate which, at and following
the time of sharpest currency appreciation, has itself risen
sharply to a level well above the world average. Even the London
Business School seem to have acknowledged the frailty of their
theories; in their forecast of April 1980, they predicted a UK
inflation rate at the end of 1980 of 19 per cent, still well above the
world average. The hey-day of international monetarism seems
to be over, though its influence seems likely to persist in Whitehall for some time to come.

4 The Exchange Rate

As we have seen, international monetarists argue that the exchange rate is irrelevant in determining the direction of the real economy and affects only monetary phenomena, such as the level of prices. This view was put to a practical test from 1977 to the time of writing (October 1980), when sterling was permitted, if not encouraged, to appreciate almost continuously as a result of the saving to the balance of payments from North Sea oil and of the massive inflow of foreign capital in 1977 and again in 1979–80 to take advantage of high interest rates.

The supposed benefit to the inflation rate clearly failed to materialise; the appreciation of sterling was accompanied and followed by a sharp acceleration in the inflation rate which rose from a low point of 7.8 per cent in 1978 to 22 per cent in the second quarter of 1980. On the other hand, the predictable damage to competitiveness and profitability, with the inevitable consequences for investment, employment and output, were all too apparent. There are now very few academic commentators or financial journalists, and even fewer practical businessmen, who do not believe that the exchange rate for sterling was grossly overvalued in late 1980. Even an international monetarist might be tempted to concede that a 40 per cent appreciation in the nominal value of the pound against the Japanese yen in the space of little over a year, from January 1979 to February 1980, might produce consequences in terms of price competitiveness which the UK's foreign customers are unlikely to ignore.

THE EFFECTS OF OVERVALUATION

This experience enables us to go further than the usual academic assertions about the influence of the exchange rate and to draw upon a practical example which is still fresh in most memories. It demonstrates that two types of damage are inflicted in such circumstances. First, there is a straightforward loss of competitiveness. The price of exported manufactures rises by comparison with those of foreign manufactures and exports therefore become more difficult to sell. At the same time, the price of imported manufactures falls and imports therefore become more difficult to resist. The demand for British goods falls, both at home and abroad, output falls as a result, and there is a debilitating effect on employment and investment.

The second type of damage occurs even in respect of those goods which the UK still manages to sell in the internationally traded goods sector. An overvalued exchange rate means that these sales are much less profitable than they would otherwise be. Again, the squeeze applies to all goods in the internationally traded goods sector, whether sold on the home market or abroad. The consequence is that there is less money to pay the wages needed to compete with other industries, less money to hold stocks or to invest in new plant and equipment, and less incentive to make the necessary investment.

The peculiarly damaging thing about both of these sets of consequences is that they are felt exclusively in the internationally traded goods sector, the very sector of the economy to which we should be looking for growth and innovation. An overvalued exchange rate inevitably deals a double blow, both to competitiveness and profitability, in the very sector on which, as the experience of the UK and of other countries shows, the future of the economy depends.

If an overvalued exchange rate is maintained over a considerable period, these two types of damage are compounded. As the earnings of both capital and labour are depressed, because the needless exposure to severe competition from foreign firms destroys both markets and profitability, resources, both human and material, are moved wherever possible out of manufacturing industry into areas offering a better or more secure return. More and more employees at every level leave the wealth-creating industries in which pay and prospects are deteriorating, and less and less money is spent on new equipment, new product development and sales promotion. More and more skilled employees emigrate and more and more production is transferred from the UK to subsidiaries or associated firms overseas. Unit costs rise faster than those of UK competitors, in part because of a loss of talent at every level, but more particularly because production falls in absolute or in relative terms. This process is accelerated by the efforts of successive governments to grapple with the consequent balance of payments problem. Governments squeeze domestic demand in a vain attempt to get costs down and to compel firms to export at little or no profit, a policy which can only be made to produce its essentially short-term effects by repeated and ever stiffer doses of the same medicine.

The car industry is a very good example of the debilitating effects of such policies. British Leyland, for example, has been able to invest only one-twelfth as much per worker as Toyota, whose labour productivity is, not surprisingly, five times as great. The public have been taught to blame the trade unions for the problems which face the industry, but the unrest among car workers, both skilled and unskilled, can be sufficiently explained by the drop of 20 per cent in their earnings relative to those of other industries between 1958 and 1978. Little wonder that, in these circumstances, which are inimical to the interests of both capital and labour, there are defensive attitudes on both sides of industry which, in turn, become obstacles to efficiency and innovation.

Such circumstances are the very reverse of those which are required for growth. They are, in fact, so damaging to the real economy that they are also the best recipe for a continuing long-term depreciation of the currency, which must over a long period move in conjunction with the fortunes of the real economy. An overvalued exchange rate guarantees that the rate must fall in the longer term, not just by enough to eliminate the initial overvaluation, but by an additional margin reflecting the weakened state of the real economy which the overvaluation has brought about. In the longer term therefore, even the financial interests, who are usually the strongest supporters of the highest possible exchange rate, suffer from overvaluation of the currency.

A HISTORY OF OVERVALUATION

It is our belief that the British economy has been saddled with an overvalued currency, not just over the past three years, but as a constant element of economic policy, for most of the past century. Much of the economic history of the UK over that period can be

explained in terms of the burden which an overvalued pound has
constantly imposed on British industry.

Certainly, the problems which an overvalued exchange rate
are currently imposing on British industry are closely parallelled
by the impact of the return to the Gold Standard at an overvalued parity in 1925. Britain had left the Gold Standard in 1914
and soon after the end of the war the value of the pound fell
rapidly, reaching a low of $3.44 in October 1920 compared to the
pre-war figure of $4.85. The American economy had been greatly
strengthened by the war and there is no reason to believe that the
reduction in the rate for sterling had been overdone, but the
authorities nevertheless decided on the advice of the Cunliffe
Committee to return to the Gold Standard at the pre-war parity,
thus repeating the mistake that had been made after the
Napoleonic Wars. Other countries returned to gold, but did so at
a competitive rate. The result was that, despite massive unemployment, the exchange rate was gradually forced up by
methods which are now familiar until the pre-war level was
reached. At that point, the currency with much acclaim was once
again tied to gold. The pound could now 'look the dollar in the
face'.

National honour was presumed satisfied, but the effect on the
UK economy of the measures needed to restore the parity was
disastrous. Wages fell by 37 per cent between December 1920
and September 1925, and although export prices fell by nearly
half over the same period, they were still 85 per cent higher in
1925 than in 1913, compared to a 53 per cent increase in the case
of imports and 70 per cent and 75 per cent respectively, for wages
and retail prices. Prices fell after the return to the Gold Standard
on 28 April 1925, but they were falling in other countries too and
by the end of that year UK prices in terms of gold were still 25
per cent higher than those of France and Germany relative to
1913. For this, the appreciation of 40 per cent in the nominal
value of the pound between 1920 and 1925 must take full responsibility. The effect on UK trade was disastrous. Imports by
volume were 8 per cent higher than in 1913, but exports were 24
per cent lower. Unemployment in the principal export industries
– cotton, wool, coal, steel and engineering, including shipbuilding – accounted for 19 per cent of the insured population
compared to 9 per cent in other occupations. Production was
only just above the 1913 level, a far worse performance than any

other industrial country apart from Germany. There was some improvement after the General Strike but in the second half of the decade the UK rate of growth was far slower than that of most other industrial countries. Unemployment never fell below 9.7 per cent after the post-war boom and was far higher than anywhere else except Germany.[1]

The situation was inherently unstable. Sterling was over-valued by an estimated 15 per cent in 1929, despite a fall of more than 10 per cent in export prices after the collapse of the General Strike.[2] The huge deficit on visible trade was little more than offset by earnings on invisibles and the continuing substantial outflow of long-term capital could only be financed by Bank of England intervention in the money market to attract and hold short-term funds in London. The UK was thus driven to borrowing short and lending long, the bankers' recipe for financial disaster.

When the eventual crash came, and the policies which the Labour Government had pursued at the expense of its own supporters were abandoned within a few days of its leaving office, the combination of a devaluation of 30 per cent, a tariff of 10 per cent on imports from foreign countries and increased tariff preferences on exports to Commonwealth countries proved the right mix in an imperfect world. Imports of manufactures from foreign countries fell 48 per cent between 1931 and 1933 to only 41 per cent of the 1929 level in terms of sterling, but exports to foreign countries fell by only 7 per cent to 48 per cent of the earlier figure. The deficit of £78 millions in 1931 had turned into a surplus of £23 millions. This improvement enabled Bank Rate to be reduced to 2 per cent from June 1932 onwards and, under the stimulus of protection and a cheap money policy, industrial production rose much faster in the UK between 1930 and 1937 than in any other industrial country.

The fall of 36 per cent in the value of the dollar when the United States went off gold weakened the competitive position of the UK, and when France and the other Gold Bloc countries followed suit in 1936, the UK very foolishly entered into the Tripartite Agreement under which it agreed with the United States and France to manage the Exchange Equalisation Account to stabilise the rates of exchange at the new level. The UK surplus on trade in manufactures had turned into a deficit by 1936 and it would have been a good deal worse in the late 1930s if tariffs on steel, consumer goods and other sensitive items had not been substantially increased.

After the Second World War, the pre-war rate for sterling against the dollar was maintained for far longer than was justified. In the longer term, the UK had to face the fact that a much higher proportion of its imports had to be financed by exports than had been the case before the war, but the UK was extremely reluctant to concede that its exports could not compete with those of the United States, whose economy had again been greatly strengthened by the war. It took a great deal of pressure from the Americans and a huge run on sterling to persuade Sir Stafford Cripps to agree to devaluation.

What the 1949 devaluation could not do was settle the right relationship between sterling and other currencies. The war had turned the rest of the world upside down and it would have been pure chance if the sterling rate and the associated cross rates had proved viable in the long term. For example, German output per head was bound to rise fast; in the third quarter of 1949 it was only 72 per cent of the 1936 figure and exports were less than half the pre-war total. The UK was nevertheless chained to the new parity by successive governments for a period of 18 years, long after it should have been apparent to everyone that UK goods were becoming steadily less competitive at home and abroad. The UK share of world trade in manufactures fell from 25.5 per cent in 1950 to 16.5 per cent in 1960 and 12.2 per cent in 1967, while the share of the Germans, the Japanese and the Italians rose dramatically.

The devaluation of 1967 thus came only after the UK had inflicted enormous damage on itself by sacrificing internal growth to external equilibrium in defence of an overvalued exchange rate. This is clearly brought out in Figure 4.1, showing (1) the increase in the real exchange rate from 1955, the earliest date for which official figures are available, to 24 October 1980; (2) the movement in the nominal/effective exchange rate, measured after 1971 on the IMF (MERM) basis; and (3) the unlagged fall in the UK share of world trade in manufactures measured in terms of value, which respectively understates or overstates the UK share of the volume of world trade according to whether sterling is falling or rising.

UK prices had risen faster in almost every year from 1950 onwards than those of our competitors, with the exception of the

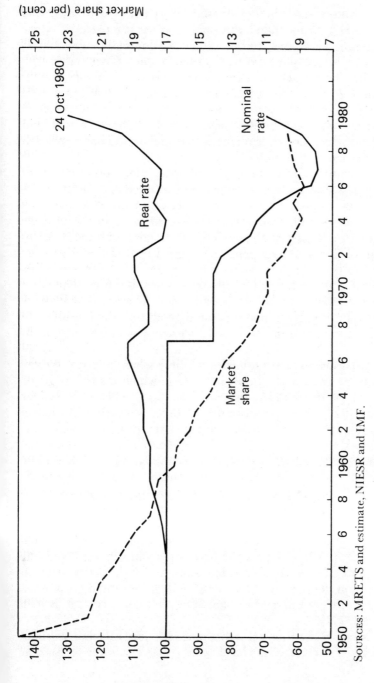

Market share (per cent)

FIGURE 4.1   *Changes in real and nominal exchange rates compared with changes in UK*
share of world trade in manufactures, 1950–24 Oct. 1980

SOURCES: MRETS and estimate, NIESR and IMF.

United States, and the devaluation of 14 per cent in 1967 was
even less significant than it appeared because it replaced a 15 per
cent import surcharge and a system of admittedly small export
rebates. UK relative export prices fell by only 6 per cent to the
level they had reached before 1962. This was not sufficient to
stimulate growth. The current account surplus which we enjoyed
in the years 1969–71 was secured only as a result of the massive
deflation engineered by Roy Jenkins in the Budgets of 1969 and
1970 and which no government at that time would have regarded
as permanently acceptable.

In December 1971, the United States obliged other countries
to accept a devaluation of 10 per cent in the dollar in return for
lifting their import surcharge. The UK very foolishly agreed to a
new parity of $2.55 and compounded the error in the next six
months by allowing, if not actively encouraging, sterling to rise to
a peak of $2.66, thus wiping out a good deal of the advantage
conferred by the 1967 devaluation at a time when UK unit costs
were rising much faster than those of other countries. The effect
was as disastrous as it was predictable. There was a massive
increase in imports of manufactured goods and the UK share of
world trade in manufactures fell to a new low of 8.8 per cent in
1974.

The damage was contained for a time when, in 1973, the exchange rate was pushed down to a level which made UK goods
more competitive than at any time since 1957. This accounted for
our relatively good performance in the worldwide recession of
1975. Unfortunately, the incoming Labour Government was
persuaded to use the massive inflow of Arab oil money to stop the
exchange rate falling fast enough to compensate for our rapidly
rising rate of inflation. It was this rate of inflation which made
inevitable the steep decline of sterling in 1976, when the Arab
money was withdrawn, but the government of the day virtually
exhausted the country's reserves in its attempts to shore up
sterling, and when stability had been restored to the foreign
exchange markets, it took the first opportunity to push the rate
up again. The sterling rate has since been allowed to rise 32
per cent on the strength of North Sea oil and record interest rates,
with all the familiar and damaging consequences for British
industry.

It is our contention that this long-standing attachment to an
overvalued exchange rate has been the major factor in the secular

decline of British industry and of its share of world trade in manufactures and is also, paradoxically, the main reason for the long-term depreciation of sterling. World trade has expanded much faster than world production and the success or failure of economies has therefore come to depend more and more crucially on their international competitiveness. The price exacted for having the wrong exchange rate has thus become increasingly severe. The current and extreme manifestation of this policy, made possible in this instance by the accident of North Sea oil, is the most damaging instalment in a long saga. It has had the advantage, however, of focusing attention on the exchange rate and on the huge disadvantages of an overvalued rate. There can be no doubt now that between 1976 and 1980 the pound was increasingly overvalued. Once this is conceded, the only remaining questions concern the optimum rate for sterling and how it is to be achieved. But if these questions are to be intelligently addressed and the exchange rate brought to a competitive level, the intellectual habits of a century will have to be abandoned, and the role of the exchange rate must be fundamentally reassessed.

THE ROLE OF THE EXCHANGE RATE

The first essential is to understand properly the role which the exchange rate plays in international trade. The scope for international trade arises not because certain things are produced more efficiently by one economy than by another but because each economy is better at producing some things than it is at producing others. The exchange rate allows each economy to specialise and to trade in those goods which it is relatively good at producing. It is thereby enabled to balance its trade, even where everything it produces could be produced more efficiently somewhere else. As a result, India is able to sell manufactured goods to the UK and the UK in turn is able to sell to the United States. Exchange rate equilibrium ensures that each country can remain competitive in respect of the things it produces most efficiently and that there is no general shift of economic activity to the most efficient economies. If the exchange rate is not correctly positioned, however, there will be a substantial shift, such as has occurred in the case of the UK, in favour of the Germans, Japanese, French and Italians.

Since it is the correct alignment of exchange rates, rather than the convergence of productivity levels, which makes international trade and the balancing of trade accounts possible, it follows that any imbalance in trading performance, as evidenced by a persistent deficit or a declining share of world trade, is due to a misalignment of exchange rates. When ministers stress the need to improve productivity, or to restrain wages, so that we can balance our trade and allow the economy to grow, and at the same time preach the virtues of a high value for the pound, they simply demonstrate their ignorance of the basic principles of international trade. If, at a given exchange rate, improvements in productivity or a fall in real wages are needed to allow us to grow or to balance our trade, this is conclusive evidence that the exchange rate is too high. A lower exchange rate would eliminate the problem and would also ensure, in the longer term, that, through the stimulus provided by growth, productivity would improve and permit a rise in the value of the currency.

This is not to say that productivity is unimportant – an improvement in productivity is necessary if we are to raise living standards – but to look for improvements in productivity as the primary means of eliminating an imbalance in our trade is to attack the problem with an inappropriate and unnecessarily difficult solution. It is extraordinary that after decades of futile pleas and exhortations, ministers still pin so many hopes on improving productivity, particularly when their macroeconomic policies make this virtually impossible to achieve. It is the exchange rate which is the key to international competitiveness; it is the exchange rate at too high a level which causes an imbalance in our trade; it is the overvalued exchange rate which makes it impossible for us to provide the growth conditions in which we can tackle our problems of poor productivity; it is the exchange rate which, unlike productivity levels, is directly susceptible to government policies.

The failure of ministers and others to understand these points leads policy-makers into some extraordinary errors which are well illustrated by the 1980 steel strike. The total cost of employment in the steel industry, including benefits, amounts to only 29 per cent of the cost of making steel; the cost of meeting the difference between the union claim and the Corporation's offer would therefore have added something like 2 per cent to total costs. The air was thick with governmental warnings, however, that workers who insisted on paying themselves this additional margin without increases in productivity would price their products out of the market and themselves out of jobs. It does not seem to have occurred to the Prime Minister, Sir Keith Joseph and the other ministers concerned that the increase in wage costs was minuscule compared to the 35 per cent increase in comparative costs brought about by the rise of 35 per cent in the real exchange rate since the fourth quarter of 1976, and the even larger appreciation against the dollar and the yen. No conceivable improvement in productivity could compensate for this blow to our competitive position. The resulting fall in sales must inevitably reduce productivity. Indeed, it is difficult to imagine a stronger example of the way in which a misplaced emphasis on productivity and wage levels can mean that the real determinant of our competitive position – the exchange rate – is totally ignored. The loss of business caused by the strike and by the further appreciation in the exchange rate has not surprisingly forced the government to lift its cash limits to enable the industry to stay in business, and the overall cost to the Exchequer of this episode will exceed the cost of the orignal wage claim by at least a factor of ten.

We have argued in Chapter 1 that international competitiveness is the key to economic growth; and, since the exchange rate is in turn the key to international competitiveness, it follows that the answer to the economic problems which have afflicted the UK for so long is to bring the exchange rate to a level which would guarantee the competitiveness and profitability of our internationally traded goods at home and abroad. Unlike so many of those who build theoretical models of the economy, we do not assume that our starting point is a position of equilibrium; indeed, one of the difficulties in analysing the problems of the UK is that our economy has been in fundamental disequilibrium for so long that we have lost sight of our potential. Our starting point is that the exchange rate has been substantially overvalued for most of the past century and that the regeneration of British industry cannot be achieved unless our exports are made more competitive (i.e. cheaper) and imports less so (i.e. dearer). The great merit of a competitive exchange rate is that it can do precisely that. If our prices are competitive, there will be sufficient demand for our goods at home and abroad to stimulate increased output. If our prices are not only competitive, but also provide a sufficient margin of profitability on exports as well as on home production, manufacturers will no longer have an incentive to turn back to what used to be thought of as the easier home market as soon as home demand rises. There could then be no excuse for putting a deflationary brake on expansion in the interests of balancing our trade. The profitability of exports will thus lead to a shift of resources to the internationally traded goods sector where the mainspring of growth lies.

It is not enough that this conjunction of competitiveness and profitability should be short-lived. What is needed is a long-term assurance that exporting will be set on a course of expansion and profitability so that investment in new capacity for export production will be encouraged. British industry has for too long been forced by an unrealistically high exchange rate to look upon exporting as a marginal activity and to be satisfied with levels of profitability based on the marginal cost of producing goods for export. What has been so noticeably absent is any suggestion that the exchange rate could be used as a positive instrument of policy, rather than something which is simply to be defended. Virtually no attempt has been made to decide an exchange rate policy which could launch British industry into a virtuous circle of sustainable rates of growth, investment, employment and trading performance. What would distinguish the strategy that we are suggesting from previous nominal devaluations is that it would be a deliberate attempt to establish competitiveness and to do so on a permanent basis by continuing to adjust the rate for as long as necessary to hold the ground regained. The ultimate objective would be a situation in which depreciation of the currency would no longer be necessary to offset the loss of competitiveness engendered by slow growth; competitiveness would be maintained and improved by the continuing growth which devaluation had made possible.

A competitive exchange rate would stimulate structural changes in the British economy and the speed with which these could be achieved would depend on two factors. The first is the need to move resources into the export- and import-competing industries. It has been fashionable among economic commentators in recent years to point to shortages of skilled labour as a ground for arguing that unemployment is more apparent than real and that measures to stimulate the economy would simply be inflationary; but this is to confuse cause and effect. The skilled labour has gone into more secure and better paid occupations in which their skills are frequently irrelevant. What is required is an exchange rate which will enable manufacturers to offer terms which will attract such people back and which would encourage young people to undertake the training required to acquire such skills. There can be no doubt that there is at present a huge reservoir of unemployed labour and capital which could be tapped if the burdens which the government have imposed on manufacturing industry were to be lifted. If shortages of components were to appear because some firms had gone out of business, the greater profitability of sales would enable them to be bought in from abroad, at least until such time as requirements could be met from home production. The existence of such shortages would indeed be the mark of success of government policy. Growth is about the overcoming of bottlenecks; they are successfully tackled when the prospect of higher profits and higher wages attracts labour and capital from the less to the more productive industries. An economy in which there are no bottlenecks is an economy in which there is no growth.

There can be little doubt that the second condition for a successful devaluation also obtains. This condition concerns the price elasticities of demand for British exports and imports. Provided that the sum of the elasticities is of a value greater than one and negative in sign, i.e. that a reduction in price will induce an increase in the volume of sales so that their value exceeds what it was before the fall in price, devaluation must succeed. A series of studies of these price elasticities has been summarised in a recent publication from the Trade Policy Research Centre.[3] Their 'best estimate' for the price elasticity of demand for UK exports was -2, i.e. twice as great as the minimum required and greater over the period 1960–76 than the corresponding figure for our five principal competitors. The Treasury have indeed never contested the view that the price elasticities are at least as great as would be required to allow for a successful devaluation. They admitted in 1976 that they would expect a 10 per cent devaluation to result in an increase in the volume of manufactured exports of no less than 15 per cent and a reduction in the volume of manufactured imports of 5–10 per cent.[4] The growth in imports since then suggests that this last figure is very much an underestimate.

One important point to grasp is that devaluation produces a

range of different effects, depending on the initial degree of overvaluation and the size of devaluation. In a profoundly un-competitive economy, such as ours is at the present time, an initial and relatively small devaluation would almost certainly be offset by changes in price. Importers who had made substantial profits as a result of the huge increase in imports in recent years would cut their margins and exporters would take advantage of the relief offered by a lower exchange rate to escape from the pressures which are currently driving them out of business by raising prices. There would of course be a different response from different firms; those which were stronger and who were export-ing profitably would be inclined to use devaluation as a means of improving their competitiveness and market share, whereas others in a weaker position would use the advantage to restore their financial health and profitability without necessarily reducing their foreign currency prices to any degree. It is because a small and belated devaluation often produces this response that many commentators have tended to underestimate the possible advantages of devaluation for competitiveness.

A more substantial devaluation would, however, have a dis-proportionately strong effect on competitiveness. The response would again be mixed, but more and more firms would be able, having restored their margins, to reduce their prices and to become a more competitive force in world markets. More and more importers would be forced to trade at a loss. It is in these circumstances that one could expect the demand for British-made goods to pick up dramatically, both in export markets and in the home market. Since this would be a demand for goods which could be sold at a higher profitability than hitherto, there would be every incentive for manufacturers to draw unused re-sources into use so as to provide new export capacity. A 40 per cent devaluation would therefore be much more than twice as effective as one of only 20 per cent.

FOREIGN EXPERIENCE

The experience of other countries shows without doubt that de-valuation can be made to work successfully, even when the economy is apparently fully employed. The French share of world trade in manufactures fell from 10 per cent in 1951 to 8 per cent in 1957, but the French responded to this by devaluing the franc in 1957/58 by no less than 29 per cent and their share of world trade then recovered to 9.2 per cent in 1959 and 9.6 per cent in 1960. There was a decline in the mid-1960s, to 8.2 per cent in 1968, but the reduction of 11 per cent in the value of the franc in the following year and an increase in the value of the German mark combined to push the French share to a new peak of 10.2 per cent in 1975. They ran into difficulties in 1976 only because they had made the mistake of tying themselves to the mark in the currency 'snake', but they soon recognised the danger, cut loose from the snake and let the franc fall by 17 per cent. Their share of world trade, which had dropped back to about 9.5 per cent, recovered to around 10 per cent and enabled French industry to grow as rapidly as that of most other EEC countries. French agreement to the setting up of the European Monetary System appears to have come from President Giscard d'Estaing, who has long been a convinced monetarist, and the check which this has imposed on three decades of French expansion seems a high price to pay for the supposed benefits. The franc is now becoming overvalued.

American experience tells a similar story of the influence of exchange rate movements on trading performance, illustrated in Figure 4.2, showing on an annual basis (1) the movement in the real exchange rate from 1963, the earliest date for which official figures are available, to 1979/80; (2) the unlagged movement in the nominal/effective exchange rate, measured after 1971 on the IMF (MERM) basis; and (3) the fall in the US share of world trade in manufactures, rebased in 1962 and measured in terms of value.

The decline of US exports and the increase in US imports after 1949 can be confidently attributed to the realignment of currencies when the pound was devalued in September of that year. The American share of world trade fell amost continuously from 27.3 per cent in 1950 to 16.1 per cent in 1972, but, following the devaluation of 10 per cent in December 1971, their share recovered to 18.7 per cent in the third quarter of 1975 before falling to a new low of 14.4 per cent in the first quarter of 1978. Other countries had pushed down their exchange rates, after the recession of 1975, to secure a larger share of world trade and the impact of this on the balance of payments forced the Americans to take action to remedy the position. The Germans and

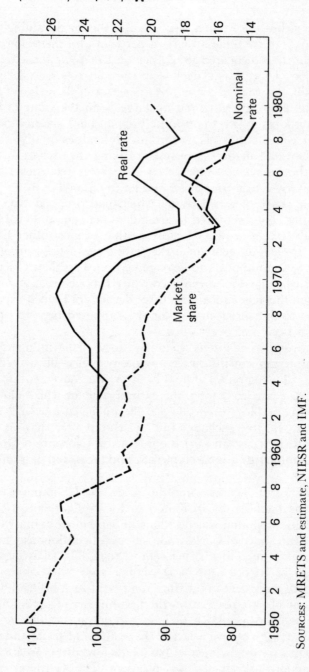

Market share (per cent)

SOURCES: MRETS and estimate, NIESR and IMF.   FIGURE 4.2   USA share of trade in manufactures compared with real and nominal
exchange rates 1950–80

Japanese were forced to let their currencies appreciate as the dollar fell against all other currencies except sterling. Unfortunately, the rise in oil prices in 1979/80 has added greatly to the cost of Japanese imports and as a result, the value of the yen fell by some 15 per cent between the fourth quarter of 1978 and June 1980, despite the much lower rate of inflation in Japan. The depreciation of 33 per cent in the value of the dollar against the yen between the first quarter of 1977 and the fourth quarter of 1978, and of 15 per cent in the effective exchange rate of the dollar, as calculated by the IMF, nevertheless had a very marked effect while it lasted. The US share of world trade in manufactures recovered to 16.4 per cent in the third quarter of 1979 and the Japanese share fell from the peak of 16.8 per cent in the first quarter of 1978 to 13.3 per cent. Industrial production in the USA between 1975 and the first half of 1979 increased as fast as in Japan and nearly twice as fast as in the EEC. The comparison in favour of the USA, moreover, loses nothing by reference to 1973 or 1974 instead of 1975.

BRITISH EXPERIENCE

Our own experience emphasises the overriding importance of price competitiveness. The devaluation of 1931 had a dramatic effect on our trade and when other countries followed suit we had to raise our tariffs to protect our home market. The 1949 devaluation served its purpose in eliminating the so-called Dollar Gap. It was not intended to protect us against competition from Germany and Japan and in such a fluid situation could not have done so. It has been frequently argued that the devaluation of 1967 did not work, but a detailed study by the IMF came to the opposite conclusion,[5] even though the margin of spare capacity was low at the time and wages had been rising very fast before the devaluation. The fall in the exchange rate in 1973/74 undoubtedly accounted for our relatively good performance in 1975 at home and overseas, and the fall in late 1976 was reflected in the sharp improvement in the visible balance in the third quarter of 1977.

This is brought out very clearly in Figure 4.3, comparing the relative export price for manufactures with the unlagged change

in the relative volume of imports and exports of finished manufactures.

Imports have fallen faster than exports during 1980 as a result
of the fall in economic activity, but no amount of ministerial
obfuscation can disguise the fact that our goods are being priced
out of home and overseas markets on a massive scale and that
there is nothing the firms in question can do to match the competition. It is true that our share of world trade in manufactures
rose from 8.3 per cent in the fourth quarter of 1976 to 10.2 per
cent in the third quarter of 1979, but apart from the fact that
there is a lag of about a year between a change in the exchange
rate and its effect on the balance of trade, the rise in the dollar
price of our exports overstates our share of the total because this
is measured in terms of value and not volume. An estimate based
on 1975 prices in fact reduces the figure for the third quarter of
1979 to only 8.8 per cent. In other words, we have temporarily
benefited from an inverted J-curve. The volume of world trade
has been increasing at about 4 per cent per annum and since the
volume of UK exports in the first half of 1980 was less than 3 per
cent higher than in 1977, our share of world trade must have
fallen in terms of volume since 1977, despite the advantage of
tariff-free entry into the Common Market.

If the theoretical basis for devaluation is so sound and if the
experience of ourselves and of other countries has been generally
so favourable, why, it may be asked, is there such resistance to
devaluation as a policy option in this country? The answer is a
complex one.

OBJECTIONS TO DEVALUATION

First, devaluation in the UK has been partially discredited by
the failure of most commentators to distinguish between a purely
nominal devaluation, which is simply the inevitable consequence
of a pre-existing loss of competitiveness, and a devaluation which
enables British manufacturers to charge significantly lower
prices and to provide a return to capital and labour on the scale
required to take up the slack in the economy. It is not surprising
that the man in the street, having watched the fall in the nominal
rate of sterling over a long period, and having been taught by the
media that the fall is inimical to his interests, is suspicious of
devaluation; he cannot be expected to understand that a sequence

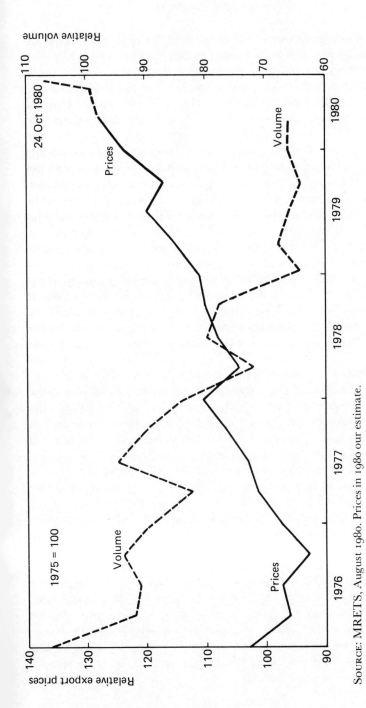

SOURCE: MRETS, August 1980. Prices in 1980 our estimate.

FIGURE 4.3   *Manufactures – relative export prices and relative volume, UK,* *1976–24 Oct. 1980*

of forced depreciations is a consequence of the failure of policies designed to prevent devaluation, rather than the deliberate implementation of a policy for devaluation itself.

The man in the street is not alone, however, in failing to grasp this fundamental point. Professor Terry Burns, of the London Business School, and now the Government's Chief Economic Adviser at the Treasury, said in an article in *The Times* in 1977 that the policy of depreciation was the pursuit of a price advantage at any cost.[6] What he did not seem to realise was that the long-term fall in the value of sterling was not a deliberate policy designed to secure a price advantage (in which it would notably have failed, since all the indices showed that our prices became less rather than more competitive by reason of our much higher inflation rate), but was rather a depreciation forced on a reluctant government by a decline in our competitive position.

A further factor which has always inhibited a competitive exchange rate strategy is the historical preference which financial institutions in the City have always had for a 'strong pound'. The very terminology militates against a realistic approach to the subject. When the pound is overvalued it is 'strong'; the news of the pound's appreciation has until recently been presented by the media as a beneficial development even if it meant an impoverishment of the manufacturing sector of the economy; when our export prices rise and import prices fall, we say that the terms of trade become more 'favourable'. All of this reflects well over a century's preference by the City of London, the Bank of England and the financial press for 'sound money', irrespective of the damage that it may do to manufacturing industry.

The basis of this preference is not hard to find. The Bank of England, which is primarily responsible for the implementation of exchange rate policy, is itself a bank and is officially responsible for and owes its primary loyalty to the banking system rather than to manufacturing industry. It is concerned to maintain stability and confidence in the City of London as an international financial centre and this is thought to require an unremitting resistance to currency depreciation. The Bank is also mindful of the commercial interests of the banks and of their major customers. Many of these are investment trusts, large firms and nationalised industries which borrowed abroad when sterling was high and would have to repay much larger sums if the pound were to be devalued.

There are also powerful political factors underlying the preference for an overvalued exchange rate. In the short term at least, an overvalued pound enables a government to sustain a higher standard of living than would otherwise be possible. Each overvalued pound does buy, after all, more imported goods than it would otherwise do. A government faced with an election within a year or two will be very loath to sacrifice this short-term gain for the sake of the longer-term health of British industry. Ricardo in fact saw the danger over a century ago when he pointed out that 'if we sell our goods at a high money price and buy foreign ones at a low money price . . . it may well be doubted whether this advantage will not be purchased at many times its value, for to obtain it we must be content with the diminished production of home commodities; with a high price of labour, and a low rate of profit.'[7]

In the last year or two, this political factor has been reinforced by an element of political doctrine. The Conservative Government which was elected in 1979 launched itself on a strategy in which a high exchange rate was to operate as a disciplinary element, which it was hoped would compel firms not to give in to excessive wage claims. While the level of wage increases has fallen, the discipline is less effective in the non-internationally traded goods sector, which already accounts for nearly three-quarters of the labour force and which inevitably becomes proportionately bigger in a shrinking economy as the traded goods sector, which does feel the impact of the strong pound, is squeezed into bankruptcy.

THE IMPORTANCE OF PRICE COMPETITIVENESS

One of the major reasons for scepticism about devaluation has been the view that price competitiveness is less important in the modern world than it used to be, and that non-price factors are now the major determinants of international competitiveness. In view of the manifest British failure to compete on price grounds, this smacks of wish-fulfilment, and is an argument which can only be supported by a resolute refusal to look at the facts.

It rests mainly on a misunderstanding of the effects of earlier depreciations. Those who are aware of the pound's fall in value, but who have failed to notice that, because depreciation has been nominal only, it has not made our goods any more competitive in price, may well conclude that exchange rate depreciation, with its presumed favourable impact on price competitiveness, has been relatively ineffective. The most sophisticated version of this view is that put forward by Lord Kaldor and described as the Kaldor Paradox. The paradox, as we explain in more detail in Chapter 5, arises because mistaken conclusions are drawn from unreliable indicators of competitiveness, without looking at what is actually happening to export prices. If the actual movement of export prices is given full weight, it will be seen that there is a close correlation between price competitiveness and trading performances. There is, therefore, no ground for concluding that price is not the major determinant of international competitiveness. Industries faced by Japanese and American competition have no illusions on this score.

It is one of the minor mysteries of recent economic policy that a government which is so dedicated to the principles of the free market and to the price mechanism as a means of making economic choices should be so ignorant of and oblivious to the importance of price in the internationally traded goods sector. This is a particularly damaging blind spot when it is precisely in the field of mass-produced and mass-market goods, which are so important in world trade, that marginal price advantages are so significant. Indeed, price competition has almost certainly become more, rather than less, intense over recent years in international as well as in national markets. We can hardly expect to improve our competitiveness if we blithely assume that price no longer matters and allow our prices to rise in relation to those of our major competitors.

There is in any case a paradox in official attitudes towards price competitiveness. Ministers and officials seem acutely aware of the importance of price so far as it is affected by wage and productivity levels, as witness their constant exhortations on these topics, but they have a blind spot in respect of the importance of price as a function of the exchange rate. What they do not seem to grasp is that the customer does not care whether a price rise is caused by wage levels, other costs, or the exchange rate; competitiveness is affected as much by one as by another.

In any case, there is no such thing as non-price competition in a market economy. Money is the medium of exchange and price is what determines the value of what is demanded and what is supplied. This is not simply a textbook proposition. The buyer in the real world is shopping around and has to decide what he can afford to pay for. The seller is looking for customers and has to decide what value he can provide for a given price. Both will measure what they can afford to buy and supply in terms of the money price. Value for money will increase, all other things being equal, if the price falls and decline if the price rises.

When Governors of the Bank of England and Chancellors of the Exchequer make speeches urging British industry to improve the quality, design and reliability of their products, and to back them up with better salesmanship, delivery dates and servicing arrangements, they should be asked how the money is to be provided to enable all these things to be done. All these desirable things cost money, and expenditure on them must affect profit margins and, sooner or later, price. Quality controllers cost money, more reliable components mean more research, improved production methods or better testing facilities, which all cost money; better delivery dates cost more money because of the high cost of holding stocks, interrupting production schedules to get more of a particular model or just building extra capacity; and better supply and servicing arrangements in export markets are particularly expensive to set up and maintain.

Professor A. J. Brown made the point in his Presidential Address to the Royal Economic Society in 1978 when he argued that low profitability inhibits investment in stocks and new productive capacity, and that this explains why British producers of mass-produced consumer goods, which require both great selling effort and ready availability of product, are so frequently unable to take advantage of opportunities when they arise.[8]

There are of course businessmen who assert that quality is what matters and that the rate of exchange is of no consequence because price is a minor consideration. One can only suppose that such people are incompetent. The businessman who is doing his job properly cannot but be hurt by a rise in the exchange rate. If he has made the right decisions as to price, market share and profitability at a given exchange rate, then a rise in the exchange rate must mean a fall either in profit margin or in market share, or both.

Of course, it would be desirable to improve quality, design and delivery dates and to secure higher levels of productivity generally. But simply wishing for them, or exhorting others to achieve them, is hardly likely to bring about the desired results, as over a century of futile hand-wringing demonstrates. The overvalued exchange rate so persistently pursued by successive governments in fact ensures that these desirable improvements will never be achieved since there is no way that an industry which is neither expanding nor profitable can possibly find the money to improve its performance in these respects. The pursuit of non-price competitiveness, to the exclusion of price competitiveness, is therefore an illusion; both are aspects of the same underlying lack of competitiveness which has so handicapped British industry and which is in the last resort a function of the exchange rate.

A variant on the argument that it is non-price factors which matter received a good deal of publicity in the spring of 1977, as a result of a paper which NEDC staff circulated entitled 'International Price Competitiveness, Non-price Factors and Export Performance'. This argued that the UK now produced goods which were less attractive to foreign competitors because successive devaluations had forced us to 'trade down' by selling on price alone rather than on quality. There was much talk about having become a 'bargain basement' economy and that we needed instead to emulate the German example by producing highly sophisticated products which could be sold in world markets, almost regardless of price. This argument naturally attracted a great deal of support from those who were at that time concerned to see sterling reverse its steep fall of 1976.

What the authors failed to notice was that we had not in fact 'traded down' because our prices for exported manufactures had actually risen faster than those of most of our competitors. They also failed to appreciate that much of the success of economies like the German and Japanese had been built on the sophisticated mass production of relatively low-cost products and that price competitiveness was originally, and still is to a large extent, a major factor in their success.

The NEDC had based its case on the fact that, in the case of most German and French exports, there was a much higher value per ton than for UK exports, and that in both cases the ratio of import to export values was also much lower than in this country. Much of this depended on a 'broad brush' approach to the statistical evidence; but a more detailed examination of the relevant categories shows that each category comprises a wide range of very different products, that average values per ton can accordingly be very misleading and that changes in price are in fact reflected in changes in relative volume. But in any case, it is hard to see why the NEDC thought that this factor was particularly significant; it is not a new development and has in fact not varied very much, if at all, over the last few decades. Like so many other long-term indicators of our economic decline, it is the inevitable outcome of slow growth and falling competitiveness. The British combination of a liberal trade policy with a restrictive monetary policy, designed to support an overvalued exchange rate, has allowed other countries to develop the more sophisticated products, forcing us to concentrate on relatively simple products which command a ready sale in non-industrial countries. There is nothing in the NEDC paper to suggest that we would not benefit, as other countries have done, from increased price competitiveness.

Loose thinking has also given rise to the belief, encouraged by the NEDC and others, that the United Kingom has a 'high propensity to import'; this phrase is less an explanation than a re-formulation of our problem. There are of course products, like French wine, which are bought because they are French, but no evidence has ever been produced to suggest that there is a natural tendency for the public to prefer foreign to British goods. In any case, the public does not know in most instances whether the goods they are buying are imported or home-produced. This is particularly true of clothing, but it is equally true of many other products – from refrigerators to motor cars – which may be purchased from a British supplier but which are in fact imported.

The propensity of the public is to seek value for money and anyone who doubts that should consider the enormous growth of cut-price retailing in the last ten years. It is the price advantage offered by importers which is so often decisive, a price advantage which manifests itself not only directly in cash terms, but also through factors such as easier credit, better service guarantees and more attractive special offers. There would be no propensity to import if British goods were cheaper and offered better value for money than imports.

DEVALUATION AND INFLATION

Over recent years, perhaps the major factor which has militated against devaluation as a policy option is the belief that devaluation carries with it an unacceptable inflationary cost. Again, this view seems to be supported by fashion rather than by facts. Many people seem to have a general recollection that the sharp fall of sterling in 1976 occurred at about the time of a very high inflation rate; what they do not seem to appreciate is that the inflation rate peaked before the sharp fall in the value of sterling and that the inflation rate then declined steeply, admittedly under the influence of a successful incomes policy. Equally, if there were any substantial connection between the movement of the exchange rate and movements in the level of prices, the rapid rise in the inflation rate during 1979–80, at a time when the pound was appreciating substantially, would not have occurred.

This is brought out very clearly in Figure 4.4, comparing the reciprocal of the percentage change in the effective exchange rate over a twelve-month period with the percentage change in the rate of increase in retail prices. There is therefore little, if anything, in the recent experience of the UK to suggest that devaluation is such a major inflationary factor as is generally supposed.

The cost of living objection was almost certainly, however, the main reason for the Cabinet's decision in 1976 that a further drop in the exchange rate had to be avoided at all costs and was also probably the major factor in the decision to allow sterling to float upwards in October 1977. It is of course futile to pretend that devaluation does not lead to an increase in import prices – that indeed is the intention in the case of competing imports – but we believe that the inflationary impact has been greatly exaggerated.

The exaggeration is based on a misapprehension as to what makes up the UK's current import bill. The myth dies hard that Britain is a country that imports foods and raw materials and exports manufactures. The truth is very different. In 1977, manufactures accounted for no less than 58 per cent of total imports and by 1979 the proportion had gone up to 65 per cent. These figures demonstrate that a policy of keeping the pound high, as a means of reducing the costs of imported materials for industry, means in reality that we are subsidising the very imports of manufactures which are closing down British factories and throwing British workers out of jobs.

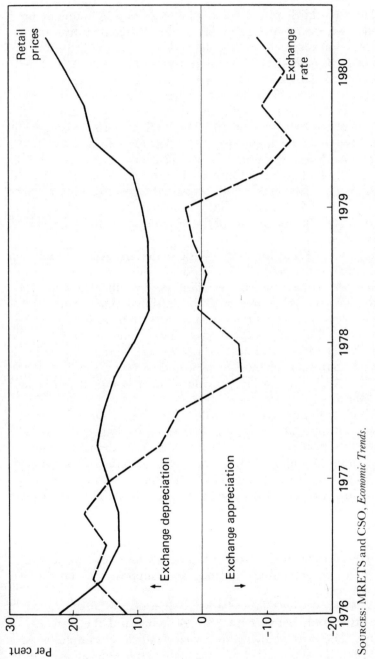

SOURCES: MRETS and CSO, *Economic Trends.*

FIGURE 4·4   *Percentage change in the effective exchange rate and in the rate of inflation: annual rates*

The two-thirds of our import bill made up by manufactured goods, whose price has to be made less competitive in any strategy for survival, are not the end of the story. Two-thirds of our imports of foodstuffs are subject to the Common Agricultural Policy and, so long as we remain in the EEC, their price is unaffected by a change in the exchange rate, unless the Green Pound is devalued as well, something which is within the discretion of our own government. Thus, a further 10 per cent of our imports would be unaffected by a devaluation, at least in the short run. Fuels accounted for 10 per cent of our import bill in the first half of 1980, but imports in the case of oil are balanced by higher-priced exports and, because the government now takes 87 per cent of the value of what is exported, the proceeds could be used to cushion the impact of the devaluation with no net cost to the economy.

This means that imports of basic materials, accounting for no more than 8 per cent of total imports, would be the only area in which we would immediately lose as a result of a fall in the exchange rate. While this would be detrimental to the interests of some firms and industries, such as newspapers, which are not subject to foreign competition at home and abroad but are heavily dependent on imported raw materials, the increased cost of such materials for most firms would be far outweighed by the boost devaluation would provide to their competitiveness and profitability.

There is in any case very little evidence that the lower import prices brought about by an overvalued exchange rate have a powerful effect on the rate of inflation in a stagnant economy. The price of imported fuel and basic materials in the fourth quarter of 1976 was 31 per cent higher than a year earlier. In the following two years the price fell by 4 per cent. The earlier peak was not exceeded until March 1979, by which time the rate of inflation – as measured by the retail price index – was already turning up sharply after reaching a low point in the second quarter of 1978. It then rose continuously for two years, at a time when an appreciating currency was supposed to hold down import costs.

What successive Chancellors have in any case failed to grasp is the distinction between the cost of living and the standard of living. The cost of living in Switzerland, for example, is very high, but the standard of living is higher still. A devaluation of 40 per cent might well raise prices by an average of 7–8 per cent but it would also lead to massive import substitution and to a flood of export orders. Firms would soon be paying out more in overtime and taking on more workers, and the increase in work in progress would feed back quickly into the service industries, including transport and fuels, which have a large margin of spare capacity. A high proportion of working people would thus be earning more, by the time the rise in import prices had worked through to the shops, so enabling them to maintain and in most cases increase their standard of living. The elderly and other disadvantaged groups could be given help from the Exchequer as a result of the huge increases in revenue from income, expenditure and petroleum revenue taxes, and of the reduction in unemployment and welfare benefits which would result from the increase in economic activity.

Not only is there no evidence from our own experience to suggest that devaluation would lead to an unacceptable inflationary burden; it is also difficult to see why the monetarists who now dominate policy-making can possibly argue that devaluation is inflationary. Indeed, some monetarists have taken this point and have argued that in monetarist terms a devaluation must be either deflationary or at worst neutral. Professor Harry Johnson, for example, has argued that since a devaluation reduces the value of the money stock, its effect must be deflationary.[9] Tim Congdon has also made the point that according to monetarist theory, a strict control of the domestic money supply must mean that while a devaluation may put up the prices of imported goods, this should be compensated for by a corresponding decrease in the price of home-produced goods.

In trying to assess the inflationary impact of devaluation, regard must of course also be had to its potential for reducing the inflation rate. For example, it would be an essential element in a devaluation strategy that interest rates should be brought down – to reduce the external value of the currency as well as to stimulate growth – and this relief from record high interest rates would certainly have a beneficial effect on mortgage rates and other components of the inflation rate. More importantly, devaluation would stimulate an immediate increase in output, without a corresponding increase in fixed and capital costs. Particularly in an economy such as ours, with very considerable spare capacity in manufacturing and back-up services, unit costs would fall substantially. Devaluation would therefore not only produce additional wealth to compensate for the higher cost of imports, but would also produce some valuable disinflationary effects which would help to bring the inflation rate down.

REAL WAGES

Resistance to devaluation, other than from the political Right, has been heavily influenced by the proposition that a devaluation necessarily means a squeeze on real wages. Wynne Godley, of the Cambridge Economic Policy Group, has argued that a large-scale devaluation would mean a severe squeeze on wages, lasting about four years, because he believes that the change in relative prices would make very little difference to output and employment in the short run, even though he concedes that it would eventually lead to higher real wages in the long term.[10]

We accept that devaluation would initially lead to a dispro-portionate increase in the profits of manufacturing industry as a whole, as the rate of economic activity increased, but this would be rapidly reflected in the higher wages which industry could then afford to pay. The return to both capital and labour must in any case be improved if British industry, both public and private, is to be regenerated and if management and labour of the kind that have left industry for lusher pastures are to be attracted back. The strategy propounded by the CEPG would have a simi-lar effect in this respect to devaluation, since the essence of their claims is that import restrictions would lead to a higher rate of growth. The criticism, if it is indeed a criticism, would be relevant to any strategy that would lead to higher growth. The CEPG do in fact make provision for a higher rate of profit in their policy for import restraint and we see no reason why – all other things being equal – the margin of profit should be significantly higher in the case of a strategy which relies entirely on a change in the exchange rate, rather than on a smaller change in the rate plus a tariff on imports. The effect on the cost of living of devalu-ation alone would be less than that of a devaluation plus a tariff for any given level of output, and this advantage would be re-inforced by the reduction in the cost of producing internationally traded goods and services under a strategy that gave weight to exports as well as to import-saving. The unit margin of profit could well be lower in the case of devaluation alone, if we are right in believing that the rate of growth would be higher.

In any case, an increase in the profitability of manufacturing industry, which is the desired objective of both a devaluation and an import control strategy, does not require and should not entail a fall in real wages in conditions of surplus capacity. While there would certainly be some time lag between a devaluation and the consequential rise in the level of economic activity, there would equally be a time lag between a devaluation and its impact on both imported, and even more, on domestic prices. Our own view is that a very substantial part of the benefit of a devaluation appears within a year and that the increase in domestic production would more than offset the increase in the real cost of imported goods. There would be a larger cake to share out. Again, what commentators seem to be doing is mistaking an increase in the cost of living for a fall in the standard of living. Our view is that while a devaluation, or any other strategy designed to reduce the price competitiveness of imports, might well produce a short-term and marginal increase in the cost of living, the advantages of increases in real output would mean that the standard of living would rise substantially. Any short-term pressure on real wages has to be considered in any case against the background of the long-term constraints imposed by the deflationary alternative.

RETALIATION

A further objection to devaluation, again advanced by the CEPG, has been that the large-scale devaluation required to promote export-led growth could not be achieved because other countries would retaliate. This is an odd argument from those whose own strategy is much more likely to provoke retaliatory reaction. Whereas increased tariffs and other restrictions on imports which were maintained for any length of time would certainly involve contraventions of both the GATT and of the EEC Treaty, a devaluation of the currency would not. In purely formal terms, therefore, a devaluation is much less likely to attract retaliation.

In any case, the retaliation argument can be stood on its head. Our deficit on trade and manufactures with the EEC Six in 1979 was no less than £4092 millions, compared to a surplus of £103 millions in 1970. Why should we put up with that? It is in effect we who should be doing the retaliating after years of self-destructive forbearance.

The fact is, too, that no one threatened retaliation in 1973 and in the fourth quarter of 1976 when the real exchange rate had indeed fallen to a level which promised to make our goods competitive at home and abroad. It was the Bank of England and not foreign pressure that killed our prospects. Our share of world trade is in any case now so small that the pressure on other countries to follow sterling downwards would not be very great.

THE MULTINATIONALS

Some people on the political Left are sceptical of devaluation, or of any other market-based strategy, because they argue that the domination of our international trade by multinational companies means that it is no longer the price mechanism which is the key to success. According to their view, multinational companies now organise production and trade to suit their own interests, which are often defined in terms of tax avoidance, and are able to override the normal determinants of competitiveness. There is, therefore, no point in paying much attention to, and bearing the inevitable costs of, establishing international competitiveness when those efforts can be undone by the pricing policies of the multinationals. Much better, it is argued, to grapple directly with the multinationals, and to bring them under national control through planning agreements and other forms of government intervention.

It is certainly true that a very high proportion of our international trade is conducted by a small group of very large firms, many of which are either UK-based or foreign multinationals. It is also true that their decisions as to pricing and production policies can and do have a large impact on the UK trading performance, as witness the large volume of foreign manufactured cars now imported into Britain and sold here by companies like Ford of Britain.

This may well mean that there is a strong case for attempting to limit the freedom of action of the multinationals, but it does not necessarily follow that such action and the establishment of international price competitiveness are mutually exclusive or that the one renders the other nugatory.

The fact that action of a specifically political nature may be required or desired to control the multinationals, as both exporters and importers, does not mean that it would not make sense to ensure that the market was working with, rather than against, such action. While the multinationals, with their greater size and autonomy, may not be as sensitive to market pressures in the short term as are smaller companies, they are possibly more rational in their response to the market in the long term. If a competitive exchange rate in the UK meant that, in the long term, it made sense for multinationals to manufacture and invest here, and to export British goods to their other markets just as they currently import foreign products to the UK, then they would do so. The chances of compelling the multinationals to act in the British national interest are greatly increased if the market is, at the same time, leading them to the same conclusion.

In any case, to argue that control is all that matters is to take an essentially static view of what we desperately need to become a dynamic process. A planning agreement is concluded with a multinational, but what then? Where are the prospects for growth and expansion, if an overvalued exchange rate means that no investor, public or private, can see any sense in making further investment in British industry? What of those companies, foreign or UK based, which are not at present investing in new export capacity but which must do so if we are to secure the expanding markets and economies of scale which have so benefited other countries? No political intervention, however successful and desirable, directed exclusively at those companies already established here as manufacturers and exporters, can generate the dynamic improvement in our trading performance which an overvalued exchange rate has frustrated for so long.

THE GERMAN EXAMPLE

A further factor which has produced opposition to devaluation is the fact that many people are impressed by the economic success of countries whose currencies have steadily appreciated. Such people point to the example of Germany to argue that economic growth does not depend on a depreciating exchange rate, but can rather accommodate and perhaps benefit from an appreciating rate.

This is a naive view. It is rather as though an athletics coach noticed that successful milers end their races with a high pulse rate and, identifying this as the key to success, tried to persuade less successful runners to begin their races in that condition – and then wondered why they collapsed with exhaustion half way around!

The truth is that the Germans did not begin their march to prosperity with an overvalued currency. Their prices were competitive at the time of the devaluation in 1949, even though output per man-hour was only 82 per cent of the 1936 figure. The improvement in supplies as a result of Marshall Aid and an increase in imports financed out of credits provided by the European Payments Union enabled productivity to be substantially increased. The beneficial effect of this on German competitiveness was compounded by the huge increase in the demand for German goods after the outbreak of the Korean War, which left them with a much freer hand in export markets as production in the USA and the UK was switched from exports to rearmament. Output per head exceeded the 1936 level for the first time only in the fourth quarter of 1950, having increased by 50 per cent since the third quarter of 1949. German exports were very competitive and this enabled them to reduce their prices by no less than 10 per cent between 1952 and 1955, despite the fact that wages had risen much faster and continued to rise faster than in the UK.[11]

With an undervalued currency and rapidly rising production, the German economy had no difficulty in launching itself on the virtuous circle of increasing productivity and competitiveness. Once the investment had been made, the plant and machinery were in place, the skilled workforce built up, export markets developed and the reserves built up through massive trade surpluses, of course the Germans could afford successive but marginal revaluations of their currency. Such revaluations will do little to reduce competitiveness in such circumstances and may indeed reinforce the strength of the economy through reducing inflationary pressures. It is also worth noting that for the Germans, entry into the EEC was itself a form of devaluation since it enabled them to put up tariffs against outside countries and to obtain free access to their principal markets within the

EEC; our own experience of EEC membership has been entirely the reverse since it has meant a loss of tariff preferences in our own traditional markets and the opening up of our own home market to competitors who already enjoy much larger economies of scale.

To argue therefore that currency appreciation would launch us on the same virtuous circle as the Germans have enjoyed is to defy logic. An appreciating currency may well be beneficial or at least not harmful to an economy which is growing in both size and competitiveness, but it is a fatal prescription for an economy whose competitiveness is declining. When our industrial decline has been arrested and reversed (and this in turn depends on the establishment of a competitive exchange rate), we can then look to the Germans as our model.

NORTH SEA OIL

Another, and superficially more credible view which has come to the fore over recent months, is that the immense benefit to our balance of payments arising from North Sea gas and oil makes it impossible to move the exchange rate down; and further, that it makes an appreciation of the rate inevitable. There are those who argue that an appreciating exchange rate, with its inevitably adverse impact on manufacturing industry, should be accepted, and indeed welcomed, since it is the price which is necessarily to be paid for the benefits which the North Sea confers.

This view, which is true to the traditional concern of our policy-makers for the interests of those who manipulate rather than create wealth, has been most notably advanced by the Institute of Fiscal Studies. They predict, on the basis of the 1976 pattern of production and overseas trade, that manufacturing output will fall by no less than 8.9 per cent as a result of North Sea oil and that this would raise the level of unemployment by 700 000. They argue that while these effects are produced by the impact of the oil on the exchange rate, it is not the exchange rate which is to blame. The real problem, they say, is that the pattern of domestic output must be restructured to accommodate the increased oil production and the rise in the exchange rate is simply the market's mechanism for bringing this about. According-ing to them, if we are to take the full benefit of North Sea oil, we must be prepared to accept a corresponding fall in manufacturing output.[12]

North Sea oil does present problems – indeed we raised them ourselves as long ago as the autumn of 1976, when few people had given any thought to the matter[13] – but the particular problem raised by the Institute is a false one. All that they are really doing is describing an identity – that the balance of payments must balance and that a change in one element must be offset by a corresponding change in another. There is nothing in this simple proposition, however, which tells us anything about the size of any of these elements or which imposes any limit on their growth.

The first warning that the Institute's view is not necessarily conclusive comes from the experience of other countries. There is nothing to suggest that anything but our own incompetence and wrong-headedness need prevent us from utilising the whole of our potential production, despite the supposed problems raised by North Sea oil. Australia and Canada are richly blessed with primary resources, but are not noted for having let their industry fall into decay. Australian imports of manufactures account for a smaller proportion of GDP than in our own case. Canadian imports are rather higher, but given the facts of geography this is hardly surprising and it is, in any case, significant that their imports are heavily concentrated in the engineering sector (SITC 7), which includes capital equipment required for investment in Canadian industry.

The experience of the Netherlands is particularly instructive because, or so it is argued, the discovery and exploitation of natural gas at Groningen has had much the same effect on the Dutch economy as North Sea oil and gas must have on the British economy. The increase in production of natural gas from 11 million tons of oil equivalent (mtoe) in 1968 to 55 mtoe in 1973 and a government-imposed peak of 75 mtoe in 1976 is said to have caused an appreciation of the guilder which in turn depressed manufacturing industry by pricing Dutch goods out of home and overseas markets. Thanks mainly to the writings of Sam Brittan, we soon became familiar with the symptoms of the 'Dutch disease' – the term coined to describe the adverse effect which it was thought that the rapid development of a valuable non-renewable natural resource would have on the economy if the addition to gross domestic product was largely spent on consumption of imported products at the expense of home production.[14]

As it happens, there could hardly be a better example of the way in which an argument largely based on myth has passed into the conventional wisdom. The balance of payments impact on current account of the production of natural gas was indeed very considerable – the Dutch Central Plan Bureau put it at the equivalent of 5½ per cent of GDP – and it is equally true that the share of GDP devoted to both public and private consumption increased over the decade 1968–78. We cannot legitimately conclude from this, however, that the increase in the production of natural gas caused a decline in manufacturing industry. This would have been a natural conclusion to draw if the prices of Dutch manufactures had risen relative to those of other countries and/or if competition from foreign manufactures at home and abroad had led to a reduction in profitability in the Netherlands compared to other countries. In fact, the price of Dutch exports of manufactures relative to those of other industrial countries has remained virtually unchanged since 1970,[15] and, although up-to-date figures are not available, the net operating surplus as a percentage of net value added in manufacturing in the years 1974–6 was actually higher on average than in any of the years 1965–73 and higher than that of any other industrial country except Japan; the figure of 33.6 per cent for the Netherlands was more than twice that of Germany and more than four times that of the UK.[16] There is certainly nothing here to suggest that Dutch exports had been priced out of home and export markets by the increase in production of natural gas.

The explanation for the stability of the Dutch currency and of Dutch prices is that both are heavily affected by the very close dependence of the Dutch economy on that of Germany, the bonds having been made even more secure by Dutch participation in the currency snake and, subsequently, in the European Monetary System. This means that, unless Dutch natural gas is thought to have influenced the German economy as well, the Netherlands cannot be used to support either the existence or the supposed inevitability of the 'Dutch Disease'.

The close involvement of the Dutch with the German economy also explains the slow-down in Dutch industry, such as it was. The profitability of German industry fell by one-third in the 1970s and this almost certainly had a disproportionate effect on the rate of growth in the Netherlands. Even so, between 1970 and 1977 manufacturing output grew faster in the Netherlands than in both Germany and the UK – 18 per cent compared to 15 per cent and 5 per cent respectively. In the seven years 1967–73 Dutch manufactures had increased their share of world trade by 20 per cent; the loss between 1974 and 1977 was only 9 per cent, from this very high point,[17] since when their share has remained constant. In 1979 it was still higher than in any year before 1972.

There has been, it is true, a decline in the share of GDP taken by gross fixed capital formation, as shown in Table 4.1. This gives for both the Netherlands and Germany the change in the percentage share taken by private final consumption expenditure, government final consumption expenditure and gross fixed capital formation as a percentage of GDP in 1973 and 1978, in each case since 1968.

TABLE 4.1 *Changes in private consumption, government consumption and gross investment as a percentage of GDP in 1973 and 1978 compared to 1968*

		Personal Consumption	Government Consumption	Gross Investment	Net Exports
Netherlands	1973	−1.3	0.4	−3.8	3.3
	1978	2.3	2.4	−5.6	0.0
Germany	1973	−2.7	2.5	· 2.0	−0.6
	1978	−1.0	4.4	−1.0	−1.0

SOURCE: Derived from tables in *National Accounts of OECD Countries*.

Table 4.1 shows that in 1973 the decline in the share of investment was not devoted to consumption; part was accounted for by a change in stocks, but the bulk was swallowed up by an increase in net exports. The increase in the production of natural gas was by then very substantial, but manufacturing industry was doing very well, with home and export markets booming. The situation had changed by 1978, but it must be remembered that the comparison made in Table 4.1 is with a particularly favourable year. In 1978, the external account was in balance and both private and government final consumption had increased their share by more than two percentage points. Apart from Denmark, however, the share of private consumption was still the lowest in the EEC and the share of investment was still higher than in the case of Germany, Italy and the UK. The increase in government consumption is moreover broadly in line with the experience of most other EEC countries, as we shall show in Chapter 6, though the huge increase in revenue from the natural gas no doubt encouraged the government to spend more than it would have done if it had had to raise new taxation.

We do not say that the discovery of natural gas has had no effect on the Dutch economy. What it seems to have done is to encourage investment in capital-intensive industries. This has raised real wages in those industries and generally, and reduced the competitiveness of such industries as textiles, clothing, foot-wear, vehicles and mechanical engineering, all of which are labour-intensive. The labour force in manufacturing has there-fore contracted more rapidly than in most other industrial countries, though unemployment in recent years has been con-siderably lower than in the UK. The Dutch chemical, steel and metal industries have been at or near the top of the EEC league table. Ours have been a long way behind. The Dutch have been using their resources. We are exporting ours for others to use.

The Norwegian example is equally instructive. Oil is much more important to the Norwegian economy than it is to us, but there are no signs that this has had the consequences predicted here. In 1977, imports of manufactures rose sharply and exports fell, but in 1978 the position was reversed and exports were 18 per cent up on 1975 compared to only 7 per cent for imports. The export figure may have been inflated by a drilling rig, but in 1979 production for export was 39 per cent up on the 1975 figure and although there had been no increase in output in manufacturing generally, unemployment had fallen to only 1.1 per cent of the labour force in the second half of 1979. It comes as no surprise that the real exchange rate – measured in terms of relative export prices – has actually fallen by 18 per cent since 1975.[18]

This suggests that there is nothing inevitable about the decline in British manufacturing which the Institute predicts and wel-comes. We are equally sceptical of their implicit assumption that the share of manufacturing industry in the productive process was satisfactory and offered no room for improvement in their base year of 1976. In fact, 1976 was a year in which we had a deficit in our visible trade of no less than £3911 million, com-pared to only £32 million in 1970 and a surplus of £190 million in 1971. Manufacturing output was 6 per cent less than it was in

1973, largely under the influence, as we argued at the time, of an exchange rate which was overvalued by between 10 per cent and 15 per cent.[19] The further deterioration which the Institute says is now in prospect and which we are urged to accept with equanimity represents therefore a worsening of an already unacceptable position.

The essence of the Institute's view is that the return on capital in manufacturing is already so low that it would not make sense to spend any of our new-found wealth on investment in this area. It follows, they say, that North Sea oil revenues will either have to be invested overseas – preferably by those who now purchase gilt-edged stocks – or spent on imports of goods and services to the detriment of British suppliers.

We see no justification whatsoever for the assumption that we could not, given the right policies, increase investment in manufacturing. Indeed, it should be increased by something of the order of £5 billion to take the total to £12 billion, if we are to match the levels achieved by our foreign competitors. In 1976, gross fixed capital formation in German manufacturing industry was twice as high as in the UK, and the French and American figures were three times as high. The real object lesson, however, is that of Japan. Ministers frequently refer to the Japanese success in increasing their productivity, but as Jorgenson and Nishimizu have shown,[20] this is substantially due to an increase in capital inputs relative to labour. They showed that the dramatic reduction in the difference between US and Japanese total output between 1960 and 1974 was due to the substantial increase in Japanese capital input relative to US capital input. Over the whole period, the average annual increase in capital was nearly three times the US rate and productivity grew at nearly four times the US rate. This confirmed the findings of previous studies that the relative rates of growth of output per unit of labour input in industrialised countries can be explained by the relative growth of capital intensity.

The Institute of Fiscal Studies is certainly right to argue that it is the low rate of return in British industry which acts as a disincentive to investment, and makes it difficult to use the oil revenues to regenerate British industry, but it is wrong to assume that this cannot be changed. The low rate of return is, in our view, the consequence of the monetary and exchange rate policies pursued by successive governments; that rate of return could be immediately raised if different policies, including a competitive exchange rate, were consciously pursued. If that were done, oil revenues could then be sensibly invested in British manufacturing industry. If we want to increase our rate of growth even to equal that of other countries, and if we really mean what we say about increasing productivity, we could spend the whole of the proceeds of North Sea oil on doing just this; but this would require a reversal of current exchange rate policy.

TECHNIQUES FOR REDUCING THE RATE

The Institute makes our point concerning the importance of the exchange rate when it identifies it as the key to the effects which North Sea oil will have on manufacturing industry. In arguing, though, that the oil makes inevitable an overvalued exchange rate, it falls victim to circular logic; it assumes that an overvalued exchange rate is desirable and inevitable and this leads the Institute to accept policies – tight money, high interest rates, underutilisation of capacity – which ensure not only that that outcome is achieved, but also that the continuing justification of exploiting North Sea oil through an overvalued currency – the low profitability of industry – is maintained. If we assume, however, that a lower exchange rate is both possible and desirable as a means of securing growth, the policies needed to stimulate growth will themselves bring about the more competitive exchange rate which is the precondition for their success.

The first essential is that the economy should be run at full capacity. This would stimulate increased manufacturing output, to meet the increased demand; and the benefit which the oil brings to our balance of payments would enable us to handle the increased demand without being constrained, as so often in the past, by balance of payments problems. Increased oil production would then constitute an additional element in a larger national output rather than a substitute for other elements of production in a static total. The relative fall in the size of manufacturing industry as a proportion of our total output, which North Sea oil makes likely, would not then mean a fall in its absolute size. North Sea oil would have brought us real benefits and greater output.

The technical problem of engineering a fall in the exchange

rate in these circumstances is far from insuperable. An economy which was run at full capacity, where public expenditure cuts were restored, monetary targets were abandoned in the interests of growth, and obstacles to expansion overcome by higher real wages in industry and an increased purchase of components and capital equipment from abroad, would also be one in which the exchange rate would fall. A policy for expansion would necessitate a lower exchange rate in order to pay for increased imports and would provoke such a 'loss of confidence' as to mean an outflow of 'hot money', which would in turn lead to rapid depreciaton.

A substantial fall in interest rates, permitted by the abandonment of monetary targets, would be an essential part of any strategy for growth, and an essential means of bringing down the rate of sterling. Footloose foreign money would then rapidly seek a more profitable home elsewhere. The government should reinforce the loss of income to foreign investors with the threat of a capital loss as well; this could be achieved by printing as many pounds as is necessary to reduce the value of the currency in the foreign exchange markets.

The real key to the achievement of a competitive exchange rate is, however, to identify a target level for sterling and announce it publicly. The mere fact that the authorities had publicly identified a target and were intent on moving the pound down would encourage the foreign exchange operators to run for cover. If the operators knew that the Bank were ready to intervene to sell sterling at any time, and that no floor would be placed under sterling until it had reached the desired level, they would be faced with a gamble which they could certainly lose and much less probably win.

If none of these measures succeeded in bringing the pound down to a competitive level, we could then try some of the positive measures which other countries such as West Germany and Switzerland have tried – measures such as negative interest rates and physical controls. It is a little unconvincing for the authorities to argue that they cannot get the rate down, when they have never tried any of the measures which would be required, and when all their efforts and public pronouncements are directed to the opposite objective. If nothing else, the supposed difficulties of bringing the rate down effectively dispose of the other factor which is sometimes thought to have inhibited a realistic approach to the exchange rate – the fear that a fall, once started, could not be stopped. This always was a totally unrealistic obstacle to depreciation; once the rate had dropped to the point where our goods were competitive enough to start making inroads into the markets of the surplus countries, there would be little danger of the foreign exchange markets allowing it to fall further.

A further obstacle to the consideration of devaluation as a policy objective has been that the authorities have consistently taken an overoptimistic view of our competitiveness at any given time. It is only in retrospect, as our share of world trade drops inexorably, that we are forced to accept that our competitiveness has not matched our needs. We consider in the next chapter the errors which have led to an overoptimistic assessment of our current level of competitiveness.

5 Measuring International Competitiveness

On 9 April 1976, the then Chancellor of the Exchequer, Denis Healey, authorised the Treasury to issue a statement declaring that there was 'no economic justification' for the sharp fall in the value of sterling in the previous days, which had taken the rate down from $2.02 in February to around $1.82. It was almost without precedent for the Treasury to make such a statement; but once the government had been committed to the view that the fall in the exchange rate was excessive, they had little option but to agree that the reserves should be used to prevent it falling any further. What evidence was available at the time about the competitiveness of the British economy?

We were quite certain at the time that sterling was not competitive. On 16 January 1976 we expressed the view that $1.60 would be a realistic exchange rate for sterling and on 5 May in the same year we explained in some detail why we considered that the equilibrium rate was not much more than $1.50, arguing that the action of the authorities in raising MLR by 1½ per cent to hold the pound above $1.80 could only be justified on the assumption that the government had abandoned its objective of export-led growth. We pointed out that export prices had risen a good deal faster than import prices and that the balance of trade in manufactures had deteriorated since 1970, despite the substantial increase in surplus capacity. We concluded, on the basis of the Treasury's estimate of the effect of a change in the exchange rate on imports and exports, that a devaluation of at least 14 per cent was required to restore the position to what it had been in 1970.[1]

DEFINING COMPETITIVENESS

The Treasury statement of 9 April did not say in so many words that our goods and services were competitive at home and overseas and it is possible that those who were given the task of preparing it were only too well aware that any such statement would be open to serious challenge. It is true, of course that competitiveness is not an absolute standard which can be readily tested and that an ideal level of competitiveness can be identified only in the context of other factors. The higher the price of oil, for example, the less we need to export to balance our overseas account and the more that countries like Japan and the United States have to export to balance theirs. The higher our contribution to the EEC budget and to the cost of maintaining troops in Germany, the more we have to export and the less other EEC countries need do so. The higher our rate of growth, the lower the exchange rate needs to be to balance our overseas accounts, all other things being equal. But, making all necessary allowances for variables of this sort, the general principle is that we can only regard our goods and services as competitive if the exchange rate enables us to balance our overseas accounts without imposing any constraint on our freedom of action to pursue policies at home and abroad which we believe to be in our own and the general interest and which enables us to maintain our share of world trade in manufactures. How relevant to this objective was the Treasury's assessment of our competitiveness?

It became clear in correspondence with the Chancellor in early 1977[2] that the Treasury were using not one but six measures of competitiveness, though they were reluctant that this should be generally known, and it was not until February 1978 that particulars were released in an article in *Economic Progress Report*. This argued that a comparison of relative export prices was unsatisfactory because it took no account of changes in profit margins, competition between imports and domestic production in our own and foreign markets, or unsuccessful quotations for exports. They had therefore added five other measures of competitiveness, as shown in Table 5.1.

The UK wholesale price index for manufactures excluding food etc., divided by the unit value of imports, was devised as a measure of import price competitiveness (col. 6). The UK wholesale price index was also divided by the unit value of exports of manufactures to provide a measure of the relative profitability of exports (col. 4). The fourth measure was the ratio of UK wholesale prices of manufactures to a weighted average of competitors' wholesale prices of manufactures (col. 5), the fifth made the same

TABLE 5.1　　*Indices of competitiveness, UK, 1963–80*

	Relative Unit Labour Costs	Relative Normal Unit Labour Costs	Relative Profitablity of Exports	Relative Wholesale Prices	Import Price Competi- tiveness	Relative Export Prices of Manufs.	Terms of Trade for Finished Manufs.
1963	110	111	94	117	na	106	99
1967		113	97	120	na	110	102
1968	110	99	101	107	na	104	97
1970	101	102	100	108	103	104	100
1971	104	105	96	113	107	106	102
1972	101	104	95	110	108	106	103
1973	88	92	98	96	101	97	96
1974	92	95	98	96	97	96	97
1975	100	100	100	100	100	100	100
1976	93	92	101	94	96	97	97
1977	91	87	103	100	97	102	102
1978	99	93	103	103	99	108	104
1979	114	107	100	114	103	116	109
1973 June–Dec.	85	88	98	91	98	94	93
1976 Oct.–Dec.	85	84	103	89	93	93	96
1979 Oct.–Dec.	120	112	98	117	104	117	110
1980 Jan.–Mar.	131	120	97	124	102E	123	110
1980 Apr.–June	138	128	97	–	110	127	114
1980 July–Sept.							117

SOURCES: MRETS Annual Supplement No. 1 (revised) 1980. Cols. 2 and 3 are the IMF series. Col. 3 is col. 2 adjusted for variations in productivity about its long-term trend. Col. 4 is the unit value of exports divided by a weighted index of wholesale prices. Col. 6 is the unit value of imports divided by a weighted index of wholesale prices, adjusted for tariffs. A downward movement in each series indicates greater competitiveness, except in the case of export profitability, where it is assumed that an increase in the unit value of exports relative to wholesale prices indicates increased competitiveness.

comparison for unit labour costs (col. 2), and the sixth was a comparison of 'normal' or 'cyclically adjusted' unit labour costs which had been worked out by the IMF to take account of the trend increases in productivity in each country on the assumption that actual unit labour costs do not reflect the potential when the economy is working at less than full capacity (col. 3). No use was made of the terms of trade for manufactures (col. 7), apparently on the grounds that imports were not comparable with exports.

RELATIVE NORMAL UNIT LABOUR COSTS

The Chancellor did not at first attach any great significance to the IMF figure for relative normal unit labour costs; he even said that the Treasury had not managed to compile a reliable series of this kind. It soon proved useful, however, because all the other series showed a marked reduction in our competitiveness in the first nine months of 1977, and the authorities were obviously keen to find a plausible defence against charges that letting sterling float upwards at the beginning of November 1977 would harm industry's prospects. The IMF index showed that in the last quarter of 1977, i.e. after the pound had been allowed to float upwards, the exchange rate was 14 per cent more competitive than in 1971!

The index of relative export prices on the other hand showed that we were 2 per cent less competitive than in 1971 and marginally less competitive than in 1967, based on the 1970 trade weights, though it should be emphasised that moving the weights forward to 1975 gives a more favourable, but quite misleading, comparison with 1967. It therefore comes as no surprise that the Treasury began to argue that, in most contexts, the IMF index provided the best measure of our international competitiveness.[3] The difference between the two indices, on the 1975 base, is brought out in Figure 5.1

The chart includes (for the quarterly figures) a second and new series of normalised unit labour costs which the Treasury have recently started using in preference to the IMF series. Even the Treasury presumably became embarrassed at the fact that the IMF index was still showing a lower figure in late 1979 than in the early and middle 1960s, and their new series, introduced without notice, is based on revised trade weights and a less optimistic view of the margin of spare capacity. We shall return to this point later, but in view of the importance which was long attached to the IMF figures and the key role which this index still plays in international discussion, we must first consider to what extent it is a valid measure of international competitiveness.

The Treasury justified their choice of the IMF index on the grounds that it was not affected by differences in pricing policies and that it gives equal weight to competitiveness at home and abroad. We accept these points and the general proposition that unit costs are affected by the level of capacity at which the

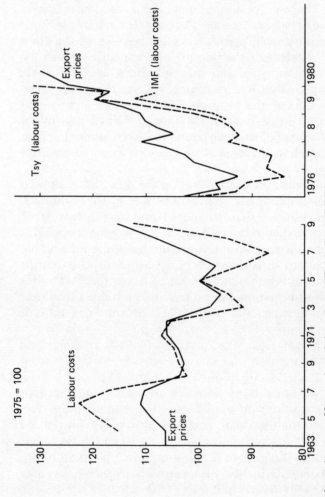

SOURCE: Written Answers, Hansard, 22 July 1980 and Table F3, MRETS June 1980 and *Annual Supplement*, no. 1 (1980). The 1980 figures for relative export prices are our estimates.

FIGURE 5.1 *Relative export prices and relative normal unit labour costs for manufactures, 1963–79 and quarterly 1976–80*

economy is working – this is indeed crucial to our own case that productivity improvements are most easily secured in conditions of expansion, and that expansion rather than contraction is the most effective counter-inflationary policy. We believe, however, that any indicator which, like the indices of relative actual and normal unit labour costs, fails to distinguish goods which are internationally tradeable from those which are not, is bound to be misleading. As we have argued earlier, exports are produced in each country by the most efficient firms in the most efficient industries and the cost curves of most of these firms will be, and indeed have to be – because of additional transport costs – more favourable than that of manufacturing industry generally. This will be particularly true where the firms in question have been able to expand to meet rising demand at home as well as from abroad. The converse is true of firms confronted with a decline in demand for their products. The assumption implicitly underlying the use of indices such as relative normal unit labour costs is that all manufactured goods are internationally tradeable, but this is manifestly not the case. One only has to walk round an industrial trading estate to see that many industrial activities are highly localised and do not depend for their competitiveness on significant economies of scale. International trade on the other hand consists largely of mass-produced consumer goods, capital-intensive materials such as steel, and science-based chemical and engineering products which are costly to develop. Economies of scale in such cases are very significant and affect both costs and prices.

The deficiencies of the index of relative normal unit costs on this account are common to all indices which relate to industry as a whole, rather than exclusively to the internationally traded goods sector. The Treasury measures of export profitability and import competitiveness likewise assume that the cost of producing internationally tradeable goods rises or falls in line with the movement of manufacturing costs generally.

It is true that a sharp rise in the overall level of costs and prices will affect the cost of producing goods for export because the increases in cost cannot be immediately absorbed. It is also true, however, that in economies such as our own, with a low rate of profit due to slow growth and a contracting share of world trade, such increases are more likely to be reflected in export prices than they would in an expanding, export-oriented economy, where the differences between export and domestic prices over a period can be and have been very considerable, much greater in fact than the unit margin of profit which a manufacturer requires to make new investment worthwhile in terms of raising new equity capital.

THE 'KALDOR PARADOX'

The Treasury have not of course been alone in accepting the validity of measures of international competitiveness which are, in effect, variants of the purchasing power parity theory and which fail to distinguish traded from non-traded goods. Professor Kaldor argued in a long letter to *The Times* on 9 November 1976 that devaluation had not worked; he based his argument on the fact that net Japanese exports to the United States had increased very rapidly, even though her labour costs had doubled relative to those of the USA between 1970 and 1975. This proposition – widely known as the Kaldor Paradox – is inherently improbable because it assumes that the price mechanism works in national but not in international markets (an assumption apparently but inexplicably made by most of those who are sceptical of devaluation's effectiveness), and its improbability should have been enough to warn economists that overall labour costs are not a reliable or relevant measurement in this context.

The paradox is of course resolved when account is taken of movements in export prices which can and do move at variance with costs and prices in the economy generally. The value and volume of net exports is then shown to be highly sensitive to price and exchange rate changes, as the Japanese example itself shows with unmistakeable clarity. In the fifteen years 1952–66 the unit value of Japanese exports of manufactures fell by over 20 per cent – on the 1958 base – compared to an increase of 23 per cent for the UK and 9 per cent for the main manufacturing countries. Not surprisingly, the Japanese share of world trade in manufactures increased from 4 per cent to 10 per cent. Their prices then rose in line with those of other countries, but with the introduction of floating exchange rates in mid-1972 they rose a little faster from 102 – on the 1970 base – to 104 in the third quarter of 1973, relative to the weighted average of the increase in other countries. In the next twelve months, Japanese export prices shot up to 113 compared to other countries and their share of world trade dropped equally sharply from 15.5 per cent in the second half of 1974 to 12.8 per cent in the first half of 1975. By the first quarter of 1976 relative prices had dropped back to 94 – on the 1970 base – and by the third quarter of 1976 the Japanese share of world trade had leapt to 15.8 per cent. This put an intolerable strain on the United States' balance of payments and in the first nine months of 1978 the value of the yen rose under pressure from the United States and pushed up Japanese export prices by more than 10 per cent relative to those of other countries. Exports then dropped by 5 per cent in volume in the second half of 1978 and by no less than 12 per cent in the first quarter of 1979, compared with a year earlier. The volume of world trade was rising by about 5 per cent during this period and the Japanese share must have fallen significantly from the peak of 16.8 per cent reached in the first quarter of 1978. The NIESR estimate for the third quarter of 1979 is 13.3 per cent. Fortunately for Japanese industry, the rise in oil prices then depressed the value of the yen and Japanese exports have again become highly competitive. This sequence of events not only provides no support for the Kaldor Paradox but shows conclusively that export prices are of great importance in determining market share.

EXPORT PROFITABILITY

The Treasury argued in the autumn of 1976, when exports were not increasing as fast as the public had been led to expect as a result of the fall in the nominal exchange rate, that the increase in the margin between wholesale and export prices showed that exporters had taken advantage of the fall to reap a windfall profit rather than increase volume. This was accepted by even the most reputable financial journalists and even encouraged *Tribune* to leap into the arena with a demand that the price of exports should be controlled to stop such profiteering. A proportion of exports is of course invoiced in foreign currency and in such cases the firms concerned may not have reduced their export prices to take account of the fall in the exchange rate. The pressure on margins which an overvalued currency imposes also means that an inadequate and belated devaluation is likely to be reflected in increased profitability rather than lower prices, but if the devaluation had been effective rather than nominal, firms would almost certainly have used a large part of the proceeds to expand their sales, e.g. by giving bigger discounts to foreign distributors and by investing more in sales and service. It should also be remembered that most firms had learnt from bitter experience that the Bank of England would take the first opportunity of raising the real exchange rate by not allowing the nominal exchange rate to fall as fast as required by our higher rate of inflation. The Chancellor was repeatedly saying that the pound was undervalued and no businessman worth his salt would have taken any risks on the uncertain assumption that our prices would remain as competitive as they were at that time.

In any case, to the best of our knowledge, no attempt has been made to test the proposition that the difference between the wholesale price index for manufactures less foodstuffs, etc. and the unit value index for exports of manufactures, on which the Treasury based its argument about profiteering, really reflects changes in profitability. The unit value of manufactured exports rose 13.5 per cent between 1963 and the devaluation of 1967, compared to 9 per cent for wholesale prices, but no one has dared argue that this showed that our profitability and competitiveness in export markets was actually increasing at that time! The increase of nearly 5 percentage points in our relative export prices reflected what was really happening. The National Economic Development Office nevertheless used the index of export profitability in their highly publicised paper on international price competitiveness, non-price competition and export performance to challenge the conventional wisdom about the effectiveness of devaluation. Their figures differed from those produced by the Treasury, but both series suggested that there was a very substantial increase in the relative profitability of exports between the end of 1972 and the end of 1976, amounting in the case of the NEDO figures to about 11 per cent on sales – of which about half occurred in the years 1973 and 1974 – following an equally sharp decline in the years 1971 and 1972.

Since the margin of profit on sales in manufacturing industry generally is of the order of 8 per cent before payment of interest charges and tax, firms which exported a high proportion of their output should, if these statistics were a reliable guide to profitability, have increased their margin of profit in 1973–4 by very much more than the firms which sold wholly or mainly to the home market. There is, however, no evidence that this is what happened. The figures collected by the Mechanical Engineering EDC for companies reporting in the year ending 31 March 1975, indeed, suggested that exports were less profitable than production for the home market. They showed that, while a minority of firms which had concentrated on the production of specialist lines, such as crawler tractors, had combined high exports with high profitability (this was particularly true of American subsidiaries, presumably because they had a ready-made market for their products overseas), the majority of British-controlled firms making a diversity of engineering products and exporting at least twice the sector average of 18 per cent of production earned only 7.5 per cent on sales compared to 10.1 per cent in the case of those which exported no more than half the sector average. A comparison with 1971 also shows that the profit of the leading exporters had declined from 8.2 per cent whereas that of the firms which had concentrated on the home market had risen from 8.5 per cent.

The fact is that there was no tangible evidence at the time that our exports were very competitive or very profitable, either relatively or absolutely. The CBI survey in July 1976 showed that 46 per cent of the respondent firms expected their prices to set a limit on their export orders and a year later this figure had risen to 56 per cent. Export prices had also been rising faster than import prices for a considerable period, which, though not conclusive, ought to have raised question marks about the validity of the argument. The fact that imports of manufactures were also rising much faster than exports, despite the huge margin of surplus capacity, should also have given the Treasury food for thought.

Anecdotal evidence will always throw up cases of firms which strike a rich vein of profitability overseas as well as at home, but very few firms reporting in the first half of 1977 on their operations in the second half or even the fourth quarter of 1976 – when the real exchange rate was much lower than in any subsequent year – were able to tell their shareholders that profit margins on exports had increased as a result of devaluation. The press had occasionally referred to export successes by particular firms, but references to increased profits on manufacture overseas were frequently more prominent. Since the removal of exchange controls in 1979, more and more companies are buying manufacturing capacity abroad to replace unprofitable production at home with profitable production overseas.

IMPORT PRICE COMPETITIVENESS AND RELATIVE WHOLESALE PRICES

The index of import price competitiveness is equally unreliable and has little to commend it. Again, the figures for 1963/67 should warn us against the accuracy of this indicator. The import prices of manufactures rose significantly faster than wholesale prices over that period, even though the landed price of imports was held down by the import surcharge, but it would be very rash to assume from this that imports were becoming steadily less competitive. One reason why import prices can rise relative to wholesale prices without impairing their competitiveness is that unit values are based on the landed price, excluding customs and excise duties. The reduction of tariffs in the Kennedy Round and their elimination on imports from the EEC gave importers an opportunity to raise their prices without detriment to their sales, but this is only an added complication because there is in any case no reason to believe that the cost of making import substitutes is any more likely to move in line with costs in manufacturing industry generally than in the case of exports.

The objections which can be made to the indices of relative unit labour costs, of export profitability and import price competitiveness apply with much greater force to the index of relative wholesale prices. Quite apart from the deficiencies specific to each and the problem of indirect taxes which is common to all, none deal exclusively with the internationally traded goods sector and cannot therefore be relied on to tell us anything of value about international competitiveness.

The only two indices which deal exclusively with goods entering into international trade are those covering relative export prices for manufacturers and the terms of trade for manufacturers. It should come as no surprise that, used with care, these two indices are better able than any others to explain what has actually happened to our trade.

RELATIVE EXPORT PRICES

The message spelt out by the index of relative export prices of manufactures in 1976 must have seriously embarrassed those who were anxious to see sterling rise again as soon as possible and who preferred deflation to devaluation as a means of improving competitiveness. This index showed that, on the 1970 base, our manufactures were less competitive in the first three-quarters of 1976 than in any quarter from June 1973 to April 1975. It is hardly surprising, therefore, that the Treasury professed to find relative export prices of manufactures an unreliable indicator of our competitive position. But while no measure of competitiveness is wholly satisfactory, the objections raised by the Treasury and the Bank of England to the use of the index of relative export prices appear to us relatively minor, if not misconceived, compared to the problems raised by their alternatives.

Our own objection to the index of relative export prices is that, while it correctly concentrates on the prices of goods which are being internationally traded, it seriously understates the loss of competitiveness. In the first place, it takes no account of goods which have been priced out of or into the market by changes in competitiveness. This is likely to be particularly important in the case of a country whose share of world trade is changing. Our share of world trade in manufactures fell by nearly two-thirds between 1950 and 1975 and it is obvious from this that a great many products were literally priced out of export markets and in many cases the home market too. It is impossible to quantify this, but it is of interest and in our view significant that the forward shift of the base period, from 1961 to 1970, and from 1970 to 1975, in both cases showed a significantly smaller increase in prices for the periods in which they overlapped with the previous series. The 1970 index showed an increase of 16 per cent in export prices between the first quarter of 1970 and the fourth quarter of 1972, compared to 24 per cent over the same period for the series using 1961 as the base year. The 1975 index showed a 56 per cent increase between the first quarter of 1975 and the fourth quarter of 1977, compared to 61 per cent for the same period in the case of the 1970 series.[4] The difference in this case was smaller, but the period was one in which we had regained some of the competitiveness we had lost, following the devaluation of late 1976. There are technical reasons why overlapping series can differ but, given the decline of our share of world trade, there must be a very strong presumption that the series based on more recent base years show a more favourable picture, at least in part, because they no longer take account of those goods whose price competitiveness has declined so far that they could no longer be sold at all.

The index of relative export prices may also understate our loss of competitiveness over a long period because it takes no account of changes in tariffs and quotas. We were able to charge a higher price in Commonwealth markets before we joined the EEC because we enjoyed a substantial tariff preference against our competitors, in addition to which our trade was protected in the 1950s by widespread quotas on imports from, in particular, Japan and the USA. The Board of Trade in 1965 estimated that our tariff preferences were worth 7 per cent on our total exports to the Commonwealth and as much as 12 per cent on the goods directly affected.[5] This meant that we could charge significantly higher prices than our competitors and still remain competitive. When we lost these preferences, we had to reduce our export prices just to stand still. The opposite was of course true of our exports to the Six after we joined the EEC, but even this was offset by the loss of our very valuable preferences in EFTA and the Irish Republic when they either joined or agreed to free trade with the EEC.

This is reflected in the trade figures. Our share of the market of the Six for manufactures increased by about 0.7 per cent to about 7.0 per cent between 1970 and 1979, but our share of the Danish and Irish markets fell by 4.5 and 10 percentage points, respectively, to about 11 per cent and 52 per cent. The Six's share of our market rose over the same period from 28 per cent to 47 per cent and it is significant that the imbalance of trade has been particularly marked in the case of motor cars and steel on which the effective protection conferred by the tariff had been very considerable. Over the same period, our share of the EFTA market fell from 13 per cent to 9.5 per cent and their share of our market from 22 per cent to 19 per cent. Changes in tariffs are effectively changes in the exchange rate and no index which overlooks such changes can be accurate. Despite its obvious advantages over other indices preferred by the Treasury, therefore, and its greater accuracy in tracking the actual course of our trading performance, the index of relative export prices is likely to err on the side of optimism. It suffers a further disadvantage in that there is a substantial delay in obtaining other countries' figures which are often not broken down into sectors which match our own.

THE TERMS OF TRADE INDEX

A further contender is a measure of competitiveness which successive governments have rejected as unsuitable – the terms of trade for manufactures; indeed, no index for this measure was published until it appeared for the first time in the February 1980 edition of the *Monthly Review of External Trade Statistics*. We agree that the series has certain limitations, which are discussed below, but we do not accept the argument that imports and exports of manufactures are either not comparable, or are less comparable than either of them are with the range of products covered by the wholesale price index for manufactures less foodstuffs etc, two of the indices which the Treasury prefer. The essential point about imports of manufactures is that they consist largely of goods which are subject to economies of scale and for which the demand is in most cases price-sensitive. This puts them on the same footing as most of our exports. The change in the relative volume of trade is therefore likely to be very sensitive to price as reflected in the terms of trade. That this is indeed the case is shown in Figure 5.2 which shows, on the basis of trade in 1975, the movement in the terms of trade and the relative volume of exports over imports of manufactures since 1955 and in more detail since the beginning of 1978.

There is a very close correlation after allowing a year for change in the terms of trade to be reflected in relative volume; the one exception to the general run of figures in fact proves the rule. The improvement in the trade balance in 1965–6 occurred despite an increase in the terms of trade, but only because the import surcharge forced overseas suppliers to cut their prices to enable them to retain a foothold in the market until the surcharge was lifted. This probably explains, too, why import prices rose so sharply after the devaluation of 1967, when the surcharge was removed. The import deposit scheme introduced in November 1968 undoubtedly helped to check the rise in imports in 1969, but the improvement in the trade balance in that year was mainly

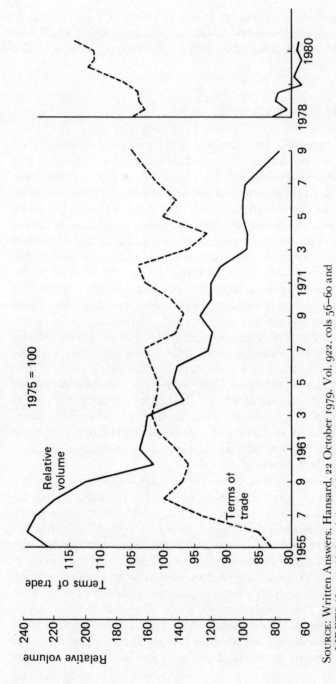

1975 = 100

FIGURE 5.2 *Terms of trade and relative volume: manufactures, 1955–79, and finished manufactures, quarterly, 1978–80*

SOURCE: Written Answers, Hansard, 22 October 1979, Vol. 922, cols 56–60 and MRETS (June 1980) and *Annual Supplement*, no. 1 (1980).

due to the rapid increase in exports. This was reflected in the 1961-based terms of trade which fell to a low of 89 per cent of the 1967 figure by the fourth quarter of 1969, compared to a high of 103 in 1963 and the figure of 102 just before the devaluation of 1967.

The terms of trade index has the very considerable advantage that it not only concentrates on the prices of internationally traded goods, but also focuses specifically on those goods which make up the trade of the UK, both as an exporter and importer, as opposed to goods being traded by and between other countries. Even so, it inevitably combines the defects of its components to the extent that these do not cancel each other out, and it has the same tendency as the index of relative export prices to reduce the difference between our own and our competitors' prices when the base date for the calculation is shifted forward, presumably because such changes take no account of goods which have meanwhile been priced into the market in the case of imports and out of the market in the case of exports. It also takes no account of changes in profit margins and changes due to changes in tariffs and quotas.

In September 1978, the Bank of England published an article[6] which attempted to cast doubt on the usefulness of the terms of trade as a measure of competitiveness. The article rightly emphasised that an index of unit values does not take account of changes in the composition of trade. The extent of such changes can be found by comparing average values with unit values and the article showed that such changes had been particularly marked in the case of finished manufactures in the period 1970–4 as well as in the period 1975 to the first quarter of 1978, the latest available date. This should not have been a cause for surprise. We have argued that changes in the real exchange rate have the most marked effect on industries which benefit from economies of scale and we would expect the pattern of trade in finished manufactures to reflect changes in the real exchange rate as well as changes in the general level of activity in this and other countries. What the authors of the article called the substitution effect may also have been greater in the case of items which have been, respectively, priced into imports and out of exports. They nevertheless concluded that, because the changes affected imports and exports about equally, the accuracy of the terms of trade index was not, in this respect, significantly affected.

The article noted in passing that the terms of trade for finished manufactures had been extraordinarily stable over time, with the exception of 1977. Although this was seized on by a number of commentators as evidence that devaluation does not alter the terms of trade, we do not share the view that a terms of trade index which fluctuated between 96 per cent and 104 per cent of the 1970 level in the period 1963 to 1976 can be described as extraordinarily stable, particularly in view of the low profit margins on our exports of mass-produced goods. The authors had in any case put down a warning marker when they added that the averages concealed – they thought rather puzzlingly – divergent trends and considerable fluctuations in the two SITC sections in question. The figures for engineering products fluctuated by nine percentage points, between 98 and 107, and that for miscellaneous manufactures by eighteen percentage points, from 83 to 101 – in both cases on the 1970 base. These fluctuations are more significant than, and are concealed by, the overall average figures for finished manufactures. They puzzled the Bank's economists, but as we shall see, they are easily explainable in terms of both different growth rates and commodity prices in different sectors, particularly in the case of semi-manufactures.

THE NEED FOR DISAGGREGATION

The extent to which the average conceals substantial differences in performance across the range of manufactured goods is shown in Table 5.2 on the 1975 base.

The figure for manufactures as a whole conceals what would appear on the face of it to be a very creditable performance for semi-manufactures, but this is misleading because it does not take account of a number of special factors. In the case of iron and steel, output and prices are more or less controlled by the European Coal and Steel Community, but all the producers are under very heavy pressure to cut prices to keep down the number of redundancies. The relatively low figure for textiles undoubtedly reflects the increasing severity of the restrictions on imports from the less-industrialised countries and the trading up which has taken place within the quotas in both price and product range. The figure for chemicals is also misleading because 39 per cent of imports and 58 per cent of exports of inorganic chemicals consist of nuclear materials whose prices are largely determined by government-sponsored and government agencies. The extraordinary price and volume figures for inorganics cannot therefore be regarded as representative. Trade in plastics is also influenced by the production and marketing policies of the multinationals, leading to changes in composition and transfer prices which may not always respond to changes in market prices in the short run.

TABLE 5.2 *UK terms of trade and relative volumes in 1979, manufactured goods*

Commodity	Terms of Trade	Relative Volume
Manufactures:	105:	76:
Semi	96	94
Finished	109	66
Semi manufactures:		
Chemicals:	90	83
Organic	114	91
Inorganic	55	177
Plastics	91	83
Textiles	100	74
Metal manufactures	126	67
Iron and steel	97	134
Finished manufactures		
Machinery:	116:	61:
Consumer	131	47
Intermediate	123	68
Captial	106	60
Road vehicles	89	44
Clothing and footwear	98	115

SOURCE: MRETS, *Annual Supplement* (1980), and Written Answers, Hansard, 1 April 1980.

There are fewer problems in the case of finished goods. An important exception is motor cars, where the unit value of imports has risen much faster than exports, in part because the Japanese have been trading up within their unofficial quotas, and in part because Ford, General Motors and Peugeot-Citroen have transferred production of their larger models to the Continent since 1975. There are also problems within the machinery field, as a result of technical developments and intense competition in microelectronics, which has led to a substantial reduction in the sterling price of imports of advanced data-processing machinery from the USA, France and Germany and of imports of TV, radio and audio equipment from Japan and Hong Kong. This is reflected in the figures for machinery consumer goods in Table 5.2 and for electrical machinery in Table 5.3. The terms of trade figure of 131 for the first group compares with a low of 82 in 1973, an increase of nearly 60 per cent. Imports in this group not surprisingly increased nearly five times faster than exports over the last decade. The corresponding figures for the second group – which includes traditional items such as power station equipment – were a 30 per cent increase in the terms of trade and a rate of increase in imports nearly double that of exports.

Despite their limitations, the figures for the terms of trade and relative volume are able, as the above figures show, to tell us what is actually happening in our trade. The overall average tends to understate the loss of competitiveness and so does a move forward in the base date, but the first difficulty can be overcome by disaggregation and the second can be estimated. We also know that the figures would look significantly worse if we were able to take into account changes in profit margins. Exporters are having to cut their margins to the bone and beyond, and there is plenty of evidence that importers are taking advantage of the increase in the real exchange rate to increase their margins, in many cases using the increase to strengthen their market share by promotional schemes and by improved servicing and other facilities.[7]

Taking account of all these points, we would select, as key indicators of trends in competitiveness, the terms of trade and relative volume of mechanical machinery, electrical machinery, metal manufactures and organic chemicals. These four accounted for 46 per cent of our exports and 36 per cent of our imports of manufactures, excluding erratic items in 1975, and the trend since 1970 is shown in Table 5.3.

This brings out very clearly how our trade responded to the substantial fall in the real exchange rate in 1973–4 and how the decline was resumed after 1975 because the fall in the nominal exchange rate was not much greater than was required to offset our higher rate of inflation. The chemical industry was alone in bucking the trend, both in terms of relative volume and price, but even so, the exception shows that there is a close correlation between price and performance. The message elsewhere is equally unmistakeable. An increase in the terms of trade between 20 per cent and 69 per cent (in the case of metal manufactures) must be without precedent for an advanced industrial country and it is hardly surprising that the effect on UK trade has been catastrophic.

TABLE 5.3 *Key indicators for the terms of trade*

Year	Mechanical Machinery		Electrical Machinery		Metal Manufactures		Organic Chemicals	
	T. of T.	Rel. Vol.	T. of T.	Rel. Vol.	T. of T.	Rel. Vol.	T. of T.	Rel. Vol.
1970	94	121	100	115	91	154	111	59
1971	93	127	105	117	93	149	114	68
1972	100	100	107	90	96	112	114	68
1973	94	88	94	80	84	102	92	88
1974	95	89	103	78	93	96	80	114
1975	100	100	100	100	100	100	100	100
1976	97	96	95	97	98	102	96	114
1977	100	90	101	87	107	100	93	112
1978	106	76	107	80	124	82	96	108
1979	110	67	122	60	126	67	114	91
1980 Q1	112	66	125	63	135	60	118	102
Q2	113	73	130	63	142	50	126	99
Q3	116	76	134	64	139	63	119	99

SOURCE: MRETS, June 1980.

It is evident from these figures that the measures of competitiveness which the Treasury were using at a crucial stage in our affairs were totally misleading. They preferred to use indicators which showed, incredibly, that our goods were much more competitive at home and overseas in 1978 than they had been in 1970; the index for the relative profitability of exports even showed that the situation in 1979 was no worse than it had been in 1970, despite the enormous contraction which had taken place in our trade over the intervening period. The index of relative normal unit labour costs may tell us something about the movement in the general level of costs and prices, but it was nothing short of mischievous to use it to imply that our export prices had fallen relative to those of our competitors by as much as 17 per cent compared to 1972 and 26 per cent compared to 1966. At the same time, the Treasury chose to ignore the very different and much starker message offered by the index of relative export prices and by the terms of trade index for manufactures, which has the advantage of being available within six weeks of the events to which it refers.

THE NEW TREASURY INDEX

The arguments which were used to justify the Treasury's curious preferences must now be an embarrassment to their authors, which is perhaps why we now hear so little of the IMF index of relative normal unit labour costs. The irony of the situation is that, as we mentioned earlier, the Treasury have recently stopped using the IMF index, although it is still published in the relevant government publications. The Treasury found through bitter experience that we were right in saying that this measure of competitiveness was unrealistic, but it seems that they nevertheless still believe that a measure based on the performance of manufacturing as a whole is a valid measure of international competitiveness. What seems to have happened is that the IMF assumed in estimating our potential output a trend growth in productivity which was considerably higher than has actually been achieved. The assumed rate was 3 per cent up to 1976 and 2.75 per cent thereafter, but the cumulative effect meant that, by 1979, the potential output assumed by the IMF was no less than 21 per cent higher than actual output, compared with 1973.[8] It is a measure of the failure of successive British governments that this gap between assumption and actual performance should have opened up.

What the Treasury appear to have done for the purpose of normalising relative unit labour costs, is to reduce the figure for potential output by reducing the assumed trend rate of productivity to 2.5 per cent in 1976, 1.75 per cent in 1977 and 1.5 per cent in 1979. They have also devised a different system of weights for the trade of other countries. These changes have had a dramatic effect on this particular index of competitiveness, as shown in Table 5.4.

The dreadful significance of the 1980 figure of 131 in the new Treasury index, which has to be compared with a low of 92 in 1973 on the same basis, is that it is almost unprecedented for any country to move even as much as 10 per cent from the mean, at least since 1964, the date from which the IMF calculations begin. While it is true, as we have argued, that labour costs could be significantly reduced if output were to be increased to take up the huge margin of slack in the economy, there is no way short of devaluation that British industry can overcome the handicap revealed by this index.

TABLE 5.4   *IMF and treasury indices of relative normal unit labour costs*

		IMF Index	Treasury Index	Export Prices	Terms* Trade
1978		93	94	108	104
1979	Q1	98	101	111	106
	Q2	106	111	115	109
	Q3	112	119	120	112
	Q4	108	118	117	110
1980	Q1	n.a.	131	123	110
	Q2	n.a.	n.a.	127	114

*Terms for finished manufactures.
SOURCE: MRETS, June 1980 and Written Answers, Hansard, 3 July 1980.

SHARE OF WORLD TRADE

While the new Treasury index adds grist to our mill, the best and most conclusive test of our international competitiveness in the long term must be the change in our share of world trade in manufactures and the change in our balance of trade in manufactures – particularly finished goods – in conditions of full employment and the maximum sustainable rate of growth. These changes reflect the real judgement of the market place, which is in the end the only judgement that matters. They enable us to dispense with nice arguments about the statistical accuracy of particular measurements and give us incontrovertible evidence as to what is actually happening to our trade compared to that of other countries. They both show a steady deterioration over a long period and it is against this background that we must consider the special pleading of the Treasury and others, based on statistical indices of doubtful validity.

Our share of world trade in manufactures – as measured by the exports of the main manufacturing countries – fell by more than half between 1956 and 1976 to 8.7 per cent, but this was only the most recent instalment of a decline which has gone on with little relief for over a century. There had been a steady decline to 30 per cent in 1913 and a further decline to 22 per cent in 1938, a little less than the figure for Germany. In 1950 our share had recovered to 25.5 per cent compared to 27.3 per cent for the USA and only 7.3 per cent for Germany. But since 1950, there have in fact been only three years when our share of world trade did not fall.

In 1971, it increased by 0.3 per cent to 10.9 per cent, mainly as a result of a contraction of the home market following the measures introduced by Roy Jenkins in the 1969 and 1970 Budgets, but also because of a fall in American competitiveness which reduced the American share of world trade by 1.6 per cent to 17.0 per cent before the devaluation of the dollar in December 1971. In 1975, our share increased by 0.5 per cent to 9.3 per cent, mainly as a result of the very substantial devaluation of the pound in real terms in the twelve months to June 1974 which greatly helped our exports to the expanding OPEC countries at a time when trade elsewhere was receding. Our exports were also helped by the reduction of the EEC tariff. In 1977, our share recovered to 9.3 per cent (after falling 0.6 per cent in 1976) mainly as a result of the fall in the real exchange rate in the second half of 1976, but also helped by a further increase in our margin of preference in the EEC.

The increase in the real exchange rate since 1977 has been so great that our share of world trade in terms of value has increased slightly in 1978 and possibly in 1979 as well. We have benefited from an inverted J-curve. As we have already noted, however, our share in terms of volume must have fallen because while our volume remained more or less static, the volume of world trade went on increasing. The future trend in volume, given the lags involved, must be sharply downward.

The picture looks much worse if one considers the ratio of imports to exports of manufactures. There is of course a natural tendency for the ratio to increase because international trade in manufactures is increasing faster than output, but in our case the process has gone further and faster than that of any other industrialised country. In the period 1950–9, imports of semi-manufactures rose from 86 on the 1954 base to 135 and imports of finished manufactures from 74 to 201, but exports of manufactures generally at first declined from 106 to 96 in 1953 before recovering to no more than 117 in 1959. The next decade was little better. Imports of semi-manufactures rose from 96 on the 1963 base to 158, and imports of finished manufactures from 84 to 242, though exports did rather better, rising from 91 to 145. In the 1970s, imports of semi-manufactures nearly doubled from 75 – on the 1975 base – to 147 and imports of finished manufactures nearly trebled from 56 to 164, but exports of manufactures generally rose by little more than half, from 77 to 119.

By 1979 the landed value of imported manufactures was equal to no less than 96 per cent of the f.o.b. value of exports, despite the fact that export prices had risen much faster than those of imports. The volume of imports may fall in 1980 as a result of the recession, but in the absence of a change in government policy on the exchange rate, it cannot be long before we become, for the first time in perhaps 300 years, if not since Roman times, a net importer of manufactured goods. This is intolerable, given the huge margin of unemployed labour and capital and the prospect that production from North Sea oil will decline in the next decade.

The impact of these coldly compelling statistics, with their inescapable message that our international competitiveness has been declining for a very long time, was for long obscured by the very long-term nature of that decline. It is difficult to find a point in our economic history over the past century when our competitiveness was not in decline; the norm has therefore become one of continuing loss of competitiveness and current performance is constantly measured against this unsatisfactory norm. There is not much point in congratulating ourselves on being as competitive as we were, say, in 1962 or 1972, when these were years in which we were losing ground. Yet all too often, the deficiencies and over-optimism of the indices of competitiveness on which most reliance has been placed have been compounded by reference to trading performances which were themselves unsatisfactory and which were sustained only by the most severe of deflationary policies.

Those who are suspicious of or confused by trade statistics can turn to recent survey evidence and to the forecasts of the major computer models of the economy. The CBI survey showed that, even when the Treasury was insisting in April 1977 that British goods were unprecedentedly competitive, the number of firms believing that a loss of price competitiveness would inhibit the securing of export orders had risen to 56 per cent and was on a rising trend. Since then, and not surprisingly, the CBI survey has shown a steadily worsening picture. In fact, the situation is now so bad that no one is prepared to argue that our goods are competitive.

The question now is how much damage will be done. The

Treasury forecast at the time of the 1980 Budget that exports in 1980 would be only 0.5 per cent higher than in 1979, compared to 2.5 per cent in the case of imports, but this conceals a substantial improvement in the balance of trade in oil and the implication is that they expect manufactured exports to fall. This seems also to be the view of Cambridge Econometrics and of the St James' Group whose forecast is published in the *Economist*.

Only policy-makers who have resolutely insisted on deceiving themselves, by inventing indices which match their prejudices, could honestly have persisted with a policy which has for so long been totally at variance with the needs of our situation. There can be little doubt that endemic errors in measuring our competitiveness have allowed the managers of our economy to ignore the reality of our position and to pursue policies which are diametrically opposed to what is required.

6 False Trails

The policies now being applied in Britain have been pursued with varying degrees of emphasis for the greater part of the past century. The current combination of monetarist deflation and an overvalued currency is of course most closely paralleled by the return to the Gold Standard from 1925–31, but it has been the mainspring of economic policy over much of the period since it first came to prominence in the aftermath of the Napoleonic Wars.

We have already explained in detail, in Chapters 2 and 4, the defects of these twin pillars of current economic policy. There are, however, other aspects of current orthodoxy which also have a long and dishonourable history and which require some attention. These elements – a reduction in public spending, an attack on the power of the trade unions, and the use of planning and exhortation to improve productivity – are considered in turn, before we assess the alternative to current policy which is at present most widely canvassed.

PUBLIC SPENDING

There has been a sustained attack in recent years on the level of public expenditure both nationally and locally. Since 1976, successive governments have given way to pressure, mostly from the City, to cut down on the public services, particularly education and the social services, on the grounds that the economy cannot 'afford' the expenditure involved. The argument has been that the high level of taxation required to finance the public sector has reduced the will to work and that the public sector has pre-empted the resources needed for the expansion of the private sector. This 'crowding out' is held responsible for our poor economic performance and is also said to be the explanation for such detailed aspects of current policy as high interest rates. The inevitable conclusion is that the level of public spending has to be reduced.

The attack on public spending is not of course confined to this country. It is very evident in the United States, and most Western European governments have reacted to the slowing down in economic activity by cutting government expenditure, usually under pressure from their central banks. It is indeed an old song. It was the reaction of most governments to the onset of the great depression in 1930–1 and if we go back ten years further we find the British government reacting in exactly the same way to the recession produced by the overvaluation of sterling. The pressure, of course, comes from those who believe that they have more to gain from a reduction in taxation than they would lose as a result of the reduction in the services provided by the public sector, and it is part of the strength of those who are opposed to public expenditure on doctrinaire grounds that people can very easily be persuaded into thinking that they can get something for nothing as a result of reductions in taxation at national or local level.

We are not concerned here with the essentially political choice between the public and private sectors or with the question of whether the level of taxation has destroyed the will to work. Our concern is whether the growth of the public sector has starved the private sector of the labour and/or capital required for expansion. The first point to make is that there is no evidence that the general level of taxation in this country is excessive compared to that of other countries, or that the rate of economic growth is higher in countries where taxation is lower.

Comparisons are of course difficult. Social security contributions are often treated differently in national statistics and differences in economic and financial structure have an effect on both the total and on the form of taxation; the figures for one country may differ from another simply because the one gives assistance in the form of cash grants for, for example, new machinery or medical expenses, and the other allows the expenditure to be deducted before assessment to tax. The general picture is, however, well established in Table 6.1, derived from an article published in the December 1979 edition of *Economic Trends*.

This brings out very clearly that the total weight of taxation, including social security charges, is not particularly high in the

TABLE 6.1   *Taxes in 1977 showing (a) per cent of GNP at factor cost, (b) origin of tax, (c) impact on personal incomes and (d) growth since 1970*

		UK	Germany	USA	Italy	France	Japan
Taxes as % of GNP: factor cost							
(1) Excluding soc. security	(a)	33	29	25	23	25	18
	(d)	−4	+29	−1	+3	−1	+1
(2) Including soc. security	(a)	40	45	33	38	44	25
	(d)	−3	+6	0	+5	+3	+4
Share of (2) from: household							
income	(b)	36	29	35	22	15	22
	(d)	+4	+3	−1	+7	+1	+2
expenditure	(b)	39	31	28	34	36	30
	(d)	−4	−6	−4	−7	−7	−6
corporate income	(b)	6	5	12	5	6	18
	(d)	−3	0	0	0	−1	−3
social security	(b)	19	35	24	39	42	30
	(d)	+5	+3	+4	0	+6	+8
Share of personal income							
(1) Including employer contr.	(c)	22.8	(22.4)*	20.7	19.6	23.3	13.2
	(d)	+2.0		+1.4	+2.7	+3.4	+2.4
(2) Excluding employer contr.	(c)	19.0	(17.0)	16.7	10.2	12.7	9.6
	(d)	+0.8		+0.5	+2.2	+2.2	+1.5

*1970 only.
SOURCE: Derived from tables in *Economic Trends* (December 1979).

UK. Japan is rather a special case, in view of the paternalistic role of the employer in the system, and the United States is not nowadays classed as one of the successful countries in the monetarist roll of honour. Germany and France both take a bigger share of GNP than we do and the Italians only a little less. The picture is less favourable when social security charges are excluded, particularly if taxation excluding the employer's contribution is calculated as a proportion of personal income, but the figures for Germany and for the USA are not substantially lower than for the UK and could be rather higher if account is taken of the fact that in this country the health service is financed out of direct taxation. The other point to note is that the weight of taxation dropped quite considerably in the UK between 1970 and 1977, at the same time as it rose in other countries, with the sole exception of the USA. The preliminary figures for 1978 suggest that, in most countries, taxation fell slightly compared to

1977, but that the fall was particularly marked in the UK. The decline in the case of the UK is likely to have continued in 1979 as a result of cuts in government expenditure and it could well have continued in 1980 despite the fall in the Gross National Product.

Money which cannot be raised by taxation can however be borrowed at home and abroad and to that extent the figures in Table 6.1 may understate the public sector's claim on the available resources. Table 6.2 shows expenditure by government on goods and services in terms of 1975 prices and exchange rates as a percentage of GDP in 1978 together with the average annual increase in government expenditure and in GDP over the period 1969–78.

TABLE 6.2   *Government final consumption expenditure as per cent of GDP in 1978 at 1975 prices and exchange rates, and growth, 1969–78*

	UK	Germany	USA	Italy	France	Japan
Share of GDP 1978	21.1	19.9	17.6	15.7	14.4	9.6
Annual increase exp. 1969–78	2.1	4.1	1.1	3.4	3.5	5.1
Annual increase GDP 1969–78	2.1	3.2	2.0	2.7	3.7	5.3
Per capita expenditure, 1978 ($)	936	1518	1440	489	1028	500

SOURCE: Derived from tables in *National Accounts of OECD Countries* (1950–1978).

This shows that in the case of the UK, the claims made by central and local government on the available resources are rather larger than in competing countries, but the difference is again largely accounted for by the fact that health services are publicly financed in this country. Again, there is nothing to suggest that anything which has happened in the past ten years has added to our difficulties. The average annual increase in government expenditure has been exactly the same as the increase in GDP. In Italy and Germany, the ratio has increased significantly and in France and Japan it has fallen slightly. Only in the United States has the increase in public expenditure fallen well behind the increase in GDP. The variable in each case tends not surprisingly to be the movement in GDP. In 1969–70, GDP in most countries was rising rapidly and the increase in government expenditure lagged well behind. In 1975, GDP fell sharply everywhere and public expenditure ratios rose equally sharply. Only in the UK and the USA do there appear to have been attempts to reduce the significance of the public sector in the economy, though this has not yet been reflected in the UK figures because of involuntary expenditure by government as a result of the increase in unemployment.

In any case, the fact that the UK spends a slightly higher proportion of total output on public services does not establish a causal connection between government expenditure and the rate of economic growth. It is, after all, eminently predictable that, in an economy where manufacturing is in decline, the attempt to maintain public services at a level greater than could be justified by the wealth-producing activities of the economy will produce an imbalance between the two; the failure here, however, is that of manufacturing industry rather than that of excessive public spending. More efficient economies are able to sustain a high level of public spending, proportionately as well as absolutely, because their manufacturing industry is functioning well and producing the necessary resources.

There has, nevertheless, been increasing pressure over recent years to reduce public expenditure in this country. It is argued that the public sector borrowing requirement (the difference between taxation and expenditure to which we have already drawn attention) is excessive, that the excessive borrowing requirement is responsible for the high rate of interest, and that the high rate of interest is responsible for the high exchange rate. The effect of this is said to be twofold. Our goods are being priced out of home and overseas markets by foreign competition, and manufacturers are unable to raise long-term finance in the bond and equity markets to finance investment in stocks and productive assets.[1]

Whether the authorities believe this is questionable, but it would not be out of character with the muddled thinking that has characterised the management of economic and monetary policy since the government rediscovered Bank Rate in 1951. What determines the amount of capital available to industry is the pressure on real resources. If industry is short of capital at a time when there are idle resources, the fault must lie with monetary policy rather than with the supposed competition for funds between the public and private sectors. Investment in industry is inadequate, not because there is a shortage of capital available, or because the public sector is pre-empting more than its share – the clearing banks have had ample funds for lending to industry

for many years – but because monetary and exchange rate policies destroy the conditions in which it makes sense to invest in
industry. Interest rates are being forced up, not because there is
too great an overall demand for finance, but because the
government is attempting, in the interests of a quite unnecessary
and misplaced monetary discipline, to restrain bank lending to
the private sector, despite the amount of slack in the economy,
and insists on funding the whole of its own borrowing requirement through the gilt-edged market.

The muddled thinking – if it is not indeed deliberate – arises
initially from an assumption that a reduction in government
expenditure will of itself lead to a reduction in interest rates. A
reduction achieved simply by raising charges to the public would
reduce saving by the private sector by as much or almost as
much as the increase in saving by the public sector. The effect on
the supply and demand for loanable funds would be negligible;
the demand for credit (or the reduction in saving) would simply
have been transferred from the public to the private sector. If the
reduction in expenditure was offset by a reduction in taxation
which would allow persons – including companies – to meet the
increased charges, the PSBR would be unchanged.

The only escape from this dilemma is to reduce the total expenditure, both public and private, on the level of services, but
this means simply a contraction in the real economy rather than
a diminution of inflationary pressures. In other words, the
assumption which lies behind the call for a reduction in government expenditure is that it would reduce the demand for money
relative to the supply, but it could only do so by reducing the
corresponding demand for goods and services. It is difficult to see
how this would encourage the investment which is supposed to
have been crowded out by the public sector, or how it would
reduce inflation, since the ratio of money to goods and services
would not improve and may worsen. The better alternative, particularly when the economy is operating at less than full capacity,
is surely to increase the supply of money relative to the demand.
The money would then either be spent, in which case there
would be a reduction in the amount which industry would need
to borrow, or it would be saved, in which case interest rates
would fall. Provided it was spent on the provision of new goods
and services, it would not be inflationary, and it could not be
inflationary if it were saved.

The government, and particularly Nigel Lawson, Financial Secretary to the Treasury, have nevertheless argued that there is a close relationship between the PSBR, the growth in the money supply and the level of interest rates. This is because, they say, the PSBR has either to be financed by the banks, through the market for Treasury bills, which increases the money supply, or by the sale of debt to individuals and institutions at ever-increasing rates of interest. Lord Kaldor has shown conclusively[2] that the first part of this proposition is, as he put it, no better than a fairy tale. In the three years ending in the financial year 1979/80, the total amount of unfunded debt was only £390m compared to an increase in Sterling M3 over the same period of £18 billion. In the preceding three years, when the PSBR averaged 9.5 per cent of GDP compared to 5.5 per cent in the later period, the unfunded debt was a massive £10.4 billion, compared to the increase in the money supply of £8.1 billion. In other words, the growth of the money stock was actually very much lower when the amount of unfunded debt was very high and vice versa. When the increase in Sterling M3 was only 7.0 per cent, the unfunded PSBR was over twice the increase in the money stock, so defined, and when it reached a high of 15.5 per cent in 1977/8 the unfunded PSBR was actually negative. The real problem was bank lending to the private sector and, according to Lord Kaldor, this was the explanation, in terms of regression analysis, of no less than 83 per cent of the increase in the money supply between 1966 and 1979. The second part of the proposition, concerning interest rates, was equally misleading because the long-term rate of interest had actually fallen significantly since 1975, despite the increase in short-term rates.

The damage which was being inflicted on the real economy in the summer of 1980 by the Bank of England's operations in the gilt-edged market had very little to do in any case with the financing of the PSBR. The government, as Gordon Pepper pointed out at the time, was not merely raising long-dated rather than short-dated finance, but was actually borrowing long and re-paying short-dated debt. In six months, it had sold almost £5000m worth of long-dated gilt-edged stock to the non-bank private sector, an amount which exceeded the central government borrowing requirement by some £2000m. The justification for this was the alleged need to compensate for the growth in bank lending, but the growth in bank lending was in large part a result of the monetary squeeze and so the government had in effect trapped itself in a vicious circle. Allowing interest rates to be determined by bank lending to the private sector is to confuse a lagging with a leading indicator and can only magnify the down-swing in the business cycle[3]. In other words, as we have argued, credit was far too tight.

There is nothing in the government's stance on the PSBR that can be justified even in terms of monetarist theory. Professor Milton Friedman confirmed this in an article in the *Observer* of 6 July 1980, in which he roundly condemned what he described as the key role assigned to targets for the borrowing requirement. He described them as unwise for several reasons. First, that the numbers produced in the Financial Statement and Budget Report for 1980–1 were highly misleading because they failed to take into account the effect of inflation. Second, that there is no necessary relationship between the size of the PSBR and monetary growth and that the current relationship held only because of the undesirable techniques used to control the money supply, by which he appears to mean, as we ourselves believe on more pragmatic grounds, that the high interest rates generated by the Bank to enable them to fund the borrowing requirement by the issue of long-term debt are themselves inflationary. Third, although the size of the PSBR does affect the level of interest rates, the major effect is from the real and not the nominal PSBR: and that interest rates should in any case be left to the market to determine. Fourth, and here we see how monetarism becomes no more than the economic rationalisation of political prejudice, emphasis on the PSBR diverts attention from the total of government spending, which Professor Friedman regards as excessive. He even claims that a cut in both expenditure and taxation which led to an increase in the PSBR could reduce the pressure on interest rates because it might be more than offset by an increase in saving, a possibility which we have already noted.

CROWDING OUT

This brings us to a rather older and perhaps already and deservedly discredited account of how the public sector has crowded out the private sector to the disadvantage of the public at large. This was given exceptional prominence in a series of articles by Walter Eltis and Robert Bacon in the *Sunday Times* which was subsequently reproduced in book form. They drew a distinction between the 'marketed' sector, which financed itself, and the 'non-marketed' sector whose output was sold at less than cost or provided free of charge. They argued that government spending on non-marketed activities (health, education and transfers such as unemployment benefit) had taken resources from other areas where they would have been used to better advantage, and that the rise in the share of GNP going to the non-marketed sector had increased the burden on the marketed sector. As a consequence, wage and salary earners had only been able to maintain their incomes at the expense of the corporate sector, whose profits as a proportion of GNP had fallen from 16 per cent in 1961 to 9 per cent in 1974.[4]

What is the evidence for this thesis? The OECD figures of final consumption expenditure referred to in Table 6.2 suggest that the government share actually fell from 21.9 per cent of GDP in 1960 to 20.8 per cent in 1974. This was in terms of 1975 prices and rates of exchange, but even if this is somewhat misleading, there is little evidence of a major shift which would justify sweeping reductions in the public services of a kind which are now in train. It is true that the growth in public expenditure is considerably larger if transfer payments are included, but what we are concerned with here is the distribution of real resources and not the distribution of income. The proportion of GDP going into investment over the same period actually increased significantly from 16.8 per cent to 19.7 per cent.

In our view, the squeeze on the marketed sector is the consequence rather than the cause of our decline, and so far as it is a cause, it is the inevitable outcome of policies designed to bear specifically on manufacturing industry. It was the lack of competitiveness in internationally traded goods, and hence slow economic growth in Britain, which caused the shift to the non-marketed sector rather than the other way round. Bacon and Eltis perhaps unwittingly conceded this by remarking (page 11): 'it must be emphasised that it is not the rate of growth or productivity which has let Britain down. What has let Britain down is that it has been allowed to produce growing numbers of redundancies instead of the increases in employment, and growth in the availability of real resources, which should have resulted.' They go on to say (page 15): 'the extra workers were therefore drawn into the public sector because all wanted improved social services, and because to increase public sector employment appeared a cheap and socially desirable way of achieving full employment in times of recession.' This we believe was the correct order of causation.

International comparisons also provide some reason for treating the Bacon and Eltis theory with caution. All developed countries have seen marked shifts towards the non-marketed sector in recent years. In particular, as Bacon and Eltis themselves admit (page 32), 'the shift [into public services] in the Scandinavian economies, Sweden, Norway and Denmark, has been even faster. These countries have not suffered from Britain's difficulties.' If this is so, it certainly does not suggest that the shift from the marketed to the non-marketed sector is the factor, unique to Britain, which explains our poor economic performance.

Bacon and Eltis again concede the point. They show (page 99) that if GNP were to rise as fast as it has done in other West European countries, the shift which has taken place in the British economy from the marketed to the non-marketed sector could be accommodated within an overall rise in private consumption. The peculiarity of the British experience has been that GNP has not grown fast enough to allow the shift to take place without a markedly slower increase in private consumption than in other countries. If it is indeed possible, as other countries show, to achieve a high overall growth rate, which ensures that net investment is kept up in the marketed sector and that demand for labour from manufacturing industry makes the creation of unemployment in the non-marketed sector unnecessary, what is then left of the Bacon and Eltis thesis?

The truth of the matter is that the supposed high level of public spending, or in the alternative formulation, the high proportion of the GNP being taken up by non-marketable output, is a symptom rather than a cause of our economic decline. It has achieved prominence largely for political reasons. A great deal of public spending could be saved, for example, by abolishing the National Health Service and requiring people to buy health care privately; this would be a change of considerable importance in political terms, but, so far as it had any economic effect, would, on the evidence of other countries, be likely to increase spending on health services without adding to the sum of human welfare.

The argument that our problems are caused by 'crowding out' seems unlikely to survive the point at which cuts in public expenditure make their contribution to a total of more than two million unemployed. The cuts will then be seen to have failed in their supposed aim of releasing resources for the marketed sector. Their main impact will be to have added to the problems which misguided monetary and exchange rate policies have heaped upon British industry and to have substantially increased, through a fall in tax revenues and a rise in benefit for the unemployed, the very government expenditure they were supposed to have reduced.

THE TRADE UNIONS

A further explanation of Britain's economic decline which has been assiduously promoted by the media is that British trade unions – represented as uniquely powerful in terms of both membership and political conviction – have achieved a monopoly position and used it to frustrate the normal operation of market forces, thereby creating both unemployment and inflation. Once this analysis is accepted, as it is by many unthinking people, the obvious remedy is to reduce the bargaining power of trade unions through legislation or political action.

Again, comparative and historical facts should induce a sense of caution in accepting this thesis. Britain's economic problems, as we have argued earlier, go back well into the middle part of the nineteenth century, long before the trade unions became a powerful force. In 1879, the US Secretary of State reported to Congress 'that the British working man had at last brought himself face to face with the inevitable and that British manufactures could go no further unless their workmen, by accepting less wages, assisted them to maintain the foreign markets already being contested for by other nations'. The belief that the excessive level of real wages was at the root of our economic problems was clearly well entrenched long before most workers had organised themselves into unions or had anything approaching their present bargaining power.

The lie is given to the notion that it is the trade unions that inhibit growth in Britain when we consider those periods, all too brief, when the economy has expanded quickly. We noted earlier that production had increased very rapidly in the 1930s and that manufacturing output per head increased by almost 18 per cent between the first quarter of 1971 and the third quarter of 1973; are we to believe that the trade unions were so enamoured of Heath's government during this period that they lifted all their restrictive practices only to clamp down again under Wilson? The explanation, both for this short burst of growth and for the longer periods of stagnation, must surely lie elsewhere.

While there is very little evidence that it is the influence of trade unions which has caused Britain to grow so slowly, there is conversely plenty to show that trade unions have been affected by our relatively unsuccessful performance. British trade unionists have had a markedly different and less satisfactory economic experience than their colleagues in Germany or France over the last quarter of a century. It is this, we believe, that is the key to understanding the role of trade unions in the British economy, particularly their attitude to wage claims, technical innovation and unemployment.

The crucial difference between the experience of trade unionists in most countries of Western Europe, on the one hand, and in Britain on the other, is that for the former the mixed economy has worked extremely well, producing increases in real incomes well beyond what many would have dreamed possible only a few years back. In these successful countries, support for the mixed economy is in consequence widespread – even among its nominal opponents – and attitudes to wages, technical change and unemployment are framed broadly speaking in ways which keep the system working.

In Britain, by contrast, increases in real income, especially post-tax, have been much lower, and now look like having stopped altogether. In this environment, a different set of imperatives comes to the fore. Trade unionists understand as well as everyone else that large money wage increases, unfunded by any conceivable increases in productivity, are bound to be inflationary. However, in an economy with static total output where expectations are still rising, the interests of the economy as a whole take second place to the problems of defending and improving living standards in the only way which is then possible – at the expense of other groups in the economy, and through the pursuit of high money wage claims.

There is also a very important political dimension to this process. The attitude of trade unionists to wage increases is coloured not only by personal considerations but also by more general perspectives about how the economy should be run. There has been a shift away from general support for the mixed economy, in the light of its failure to deliver rising living standards, in favour of other solutions, particularly among the politically involved shop-floor leadership. As trade unionists generally, and those in key negotiating positions in particular, become more and more disillusioned with the liberal capitalist system, so it becomes harder and harder to maintain the restraint which is essential if the system is to work successfully.

For similar reasons, there is a significantly different attitude to both technical change and unemployment in Britain compared to elsewhere. All changes in technology involve some upheaval for the labour force involved and, in the nature of things, any new equipment or process which increases productivity threatens at first sight to put jobs at risk. Provided there is enough confidence that productivity increases will lead to more output and not just fewer jobs, it is possible to persuade people on the shop floor to go along with technical changes. However, if increasing scepticism about the consequences of innovation for output and jobs begins to creep in, the situation becomes much more difficult. Opposing change becomes a much more rational course of action, at least for each individual group of workers involved. The trade unions in consequence become increasingly defensive. Restrictive practices grow, overmanning becomes more prevalent, and increases in productivity become more and more difficult to achieve. Such restrictive practices are not, however, peculiar to the trade unions. Employers, too, have frequently had recourse to price maintenance and other monopolistic practices, and doctors, lawyers, architects and other professional men are expert practitioners when it comes to defending their livelihoods.

Of course, the problem is that these actions on wages, technical changes and employment make no sense for the country as a whole, however reasonable they may appear in individual circumstances, and in this sense there is a very real problem with trade union attitudes in Britain. Big money wage rises without any corresponding productivity increases lead to inflation. Unwillingness to accept changes in technology makes the whole economy less competitive and increases unemployment across the board. Trade unions understand this as clearly as anyone else, but they also know that they cannot carry their members with them in dealing with individual negotiations over pay, work practices, etc. unless what is required for the country as a whole also makes sense at the local level.

The problem is that, the worse the overall performance of the economy, the more difficult it is to get any congruence between local settlements and the national interest. Nothing illustrates this more clearly than the recent tangled history of incomes policy. The long-standing support given by the trade unions to repeated attempts to secure wage restraint – including a voluntary wage freeze in 1948 – surely gives the lie to the myth of union irresponsibility; but the eventual failure of each attempt shows how difficult it is to obtain such co-operation when the development of the economy as a whole provides little incentive to workers to subordinate their sectional interests to the general good. In the end, workers will quite understandably resist a reduction in their real wages.

There is in any case a misunderstanding of the role of the trade unions in the management of the economy as a whole – a misunderstanding which is exploited by and perhaps shared by the proponents of monetarism. It is an essential element of monetarist theory that for each economy there is a minimum sustainable rate of unemployment. Just how this minimum sustainable rate is to be identified is never explained but its significance is that it enables the blame for unemployment to be placed on the trade unions. The argument runs that if the government should succumb to trade union pressure, and should try to raise demand and therefore reduce unemployment below the minimum sustainable rate, the only outcome will be inflation and, in the end, higher unemployment. It is then the trade unions which are to blame, rather than the rigidities of monetary policy.

The man in the street is not in a position to refute the argument that it is the trade unions which are responsible for pricing their members out of jobs. The truth is, nevertheless, that the trade unions are not in a position to determine the demand for labour overall. They can use their monopoly power to restrict employment in a given industry, either by restricting entry or by raising the price of labour to a level which makes it uneconomic for employers to use as much of it as they otherwise would, but the demand for labour generally is determined by the demand for the product of labour and this in turn is a function of government policy. Only the government can prevent employers from passing

on increases in wage costs in the form of higher prices; the practical means of doing this is by manipulating the exchange rate.
Current exchange rate policy not only refuses to accommodate
any increase in wage costs, but has actually imposed on British
industry over the past year or two a burden, reflected in the
unemployment levels, which is greater than that resulting from
the inflationary effect of wage settlements.

In any case, how can it be argued that real wages are too high
when, at the same time, the exchange rate is rising? Either we
can afford the loss of competitiveness implicit in an appreciating
exchange rate, in which case there is no good reason why trade
unions should not take their share of the available margin of
competitiveness; or we cannot afford the smaller loss of competitiveness which arises because of higher wage costs, in which case
we have no business in imposing on industry an even greater loss
of competitiveness through the upward movement of sterling.

The truth is that unemployment is at present far above its
minimum sustainable rate and could be substantially reduced if
money were made cheaper and more plentiful, if demand were
raised and if proper attention were paid to international
competitiveness. Current rates of unemployment owe virtually
nothing to supposed union militancy and a great deal to the
application of monetarist theories whose solution to the problem
can only make matters worse.

It is one of the most astonishing and perverse aspects of our
economic decline, which is almost entirely due to the mis-
management of our economy by the financial establishment over
many years, that they have not only inflicted this unnecessary
damage to the living standards of working people but have
saddled them with the blame as well. It is a sad triumph for the
efforts of an establishment-dominated press that large numbers
of working people should now be convinced that our national
failings are due to the supposed laziness and bloody-mindedness
of the British working man and woman. Such a prejudice is only
to be expected from those whose ignorance of working life means
that they know no better; but for working people, the shouldering
of a quite unjustified moral burden can only exacerbate their
sense of economic failure, a failure for which they have little or no
responsibility.

PLANNING FOR PRODUCTIVITY

Much attention has been paid in Britain to questions of efficiency and productivity; perhaps it is only to be expected that the less satisfactory the performance, the greater the volume of words on the subject. Particularly since the end of the war, successive governments have made sustained efforts to 'talk up' productivity through study tours to America, national plans, sector working parties and an endless series of ministerial speeches and exhortations. Labour governments have been particularly prone to this form of activity but both Heath and Thatcher have done their share of exhortation. While there is no evidence that these efforts have been actually counterproductive – productivity in Britain has continued to rise, albeit slowly – there is equally little evidence to suggest that planning for and talking about productivity do any good.

What is remarkable about our problems of lower than average productivity is that they are of such long standing. As we have remarked earlier, lower levels of productivity in British industry, compared with their American counterparts, have been a source of concern since the middle of the nineteenth century. Early attention was paid to the textile industry;[5] and in 1878 the American Consul in Newcastle, reporting on seamen's wages[6] and Representative Wheeler of Alabama, commenting on the shoe industry in 1888,[7] identified low productivity as the major problem. Two American historians writing in 1928 commented that 'greatly increased productivity in British industry cannot come until there is more adequate use of modern technology and labour-saving devices'.[8] In 1947 the President's Scientific Research Board noted that British industry had fallen behind since the turn of the century and that the modernisation of industrial facilities was one of the most serious long-term problems facing the British government.[9] Teams of experts were sent to the United States to study the means by which they achieved their high levels of productivity.

When ministers and others currently lay emphasis, therefore, on the need to improve our productivity, they are not saying anything new; to identify low productivity as the cause for our economic problems is not to advance the matter very much. The difficulty is not in stating the problem but in resolving it, and our long and unsuccessful history of attempting to do so suggests that if talking about it were indeed a solution it would have been solved long ago.

It is natural that those with little understanding of the economic process might believe that an overnight improvement in productivity requires only the application of goodwill and effort. If, indeed, productivity could be increased rapidly by 20 per cent or 30 per cent many of our economic problems would disappear. The desirability of this objective is not in doubt; the question is whether it can be achieved in the context of current financial and fiscal policies.

Gains in productivity at the microeconomic level are achieved through a myriad of small changes and improvements leading to cost-cutting, greater efficiency in particular processes, the better interchange of knowledge and so on. These changes depend on experimentation on the ground and on the incentives provided by the prospect of greater profitability and market share. As we pointed out in Chapter 1, many of these changes are unplannable because unforeseeable, and occur almost fortuitously at various parts of the productive process. It is therefore intrinsically unlikely that substantial productivity increases can be produced by administrative action at national or even industry level. An industrial strategy may have an important role to play in tackling the problems of particular regions or industries, and ensuring that public agencies work with rather than against the interests of manufacturing industry. But in terms of bringing about an improvement in the overall level of productivity, all that those responsible for economic policy can hope to do is to establish the macroeconomic conditions in which innovation will be encouraged.

The major error of the ministerial speech-makers, industrial strategists, and economic planners is to believe that improvements in productivity come about in a vacuum and are completely divorced from other aspects of industrial activity, such as the prospects for growth and profitability. As we have pointed out earlier, there is a great deal of evidence to suggest that productivity improvements depend on the rate of growth, rather than vice versa, as is so often assumed by British policy-makers. There is also, as we have explained, a misunderstanding as to the role of productivity in establishing international competitiveness. If the general level of productivity improvements falls short of the international average, this is simply another way of saying that we have failed to remain price competitive at the prevailing exchange rate and that we have therefore saddled our industry with an overvalued currency. If the real point of the continuing governmental emphasis on productivity is to try to improve international competitiveness, there is a much simpler, more direct and more effective means of achieving this – through the exchange rate. Once our international competitiveness is established by means of a competitive exchange rate, the growth generated by that competitiveness will establish the conditions in which productivity can be expected to improve.

One of the obstacles to a rational approach to this issue is the element of moral judgement which is permitted, perhaps unconsciously, to influence policy. The British have become accustomed for so long to being told that the failures of the policy-makers are in fact their failures, that they seem to take a masochistic pleasure in believing that Britain's economic performance is declining because the British working man is lazy, strike-prone and bone-headed. This belief has become so deeply ingrained that it is now one of the mainsprings of government economic policy. Confronted with evidence that British industry is closing down through rapidly declining international competitiveness, the Prime Minister and other ministers are apt to reply that firms are in difficulties because they are too inefficient and because the workers do not work hard enough. Even if this were true, the consequence would be a lower standard of living rather than, if financial and exchange rate policies were correctly applied, declining international competitiveness. But the depth of confusion that exists on this issue is shown by the fact that lower productivity and higher inflation, as elements in reducing international competitiveness, are exacerbated rather than diminished by the government's own policies on exchange rates and interest rates.

It is this incongruence between what ministers say and what ministers do which makes a policy based on exhortation so futile. The lesson from a hundred years of declining international competitiveness is that talking about the problem is not good enough. No amount of talking or planning can succeed if industry is denied the macroeconomic conditions which will allow it to grow, innovate and prosper.

AN IMPORT CONTROL STRATEGY

As Britain's economic performance, compared with that of other countries, has deteriorated, so alternative policies for reviving our economy have proliferated. Even in the relatively prosperous 1950s, when the 'Butskellite' post-war consensus was still very much to the fore, there was growing unease at the relatively slow growth of the British economy. As the deep-seated nature of the British economic problem has become more pronounced, with high rates of unemployment and inflation added to slow growth, so the search for alternative strategies has become more wide-spread.

Perhaps the most important of these is the strategy for limiting imports, advocated by the University of Cambridge Department of Applied Economics. Since 1972, and regularly each year since 1975, the Cambridge Economic Policy Group, headed by Wynne Godley, has produced a biting analysis of the failings of the British economy in their Cambridge Economic Policy Review.[10]

We agree with much that they have to say. We entirely share their view that the monetary policies pursued since 1976 are incoherent and that they 'will rapidly depress the economy and weaken British industry without necessarily reducing inflation'. We agree that a fundamental change of policy is required. Nor are we opposed to some use being made of tariffs as a way of helping to deal with Britain's economic problems. Their insistence that it is Britain's weakness in foreign trade which is at the root of our economic malaise is a proposition which we wholly endorse.

The seven-fold increase in the volume of world trade in manu-factures during the past quarter of a century has been very much a mixed blessing. While the welfare gains from the international exchange of goods and services are very large if there are large variances in relative costs between different countries, the gains are much less and the disadvantages potentially much greater if the variances are smaller, as has in fact been the case. The variances in cost required to make international trade worthwhile have fallen as mass production has become increasingly impor-tant and as transport costs have gone down in real terms; and these variances in costs increasingly depend, not on unchange-able factors such as geography or geology, but on the economies of scale available.

The growing importance of marginal cost advantages has meant that some countries have been able to dominate the market in those areas where the variances in production costs are most favourable to them. Thus, the most competitive countries experience very large increases in exports of manufactured goods, where productivity growth is potentially very great, while other countries are left to export services and raw materials where the scope for productivity increases is much less. As a result, the successful manufacturing countries achieve very high growth rates, and build up balance of payments surpluses. The weaker economies necessarily develop corresponding deficits and are then forced into deflationary policies to contain their balance of payments problems. However, as deflation spreads and international demand falls, those countries whose driving force is increased exports are also affected and the whole world moves towards slower growth. The loss of welfare from growth foregone must, in these conditions, far outweigh any possible gain from the extra trade which brought the deflationary conditions in train; there is then a strong case for erecting artificial barriers to trade, such as import tariffs or quotas, to bring the destabilising effects of concentrated export success under control and to spread a more even and sustainable rate of growth throughout the world economy. There is, therefore, a powerful argument, on international as well as national grounds, for preferring some interruption of free trade to the competitive deflation which most countries now feel obliged to pursue.

Since we are not opposed to import restrictions on grounds of principle, the only question in our view is whether import controls are to be preferred to other strategies as being more effective in raising the standard of living than any practical alternative, and, if so, whether this advantage would be offset by any detriment, including the detriment to other countries. The calculation must be reduced to one of gain and loss. There is nothing sacrosanct about 'free trade'.

The supposed evils of protection are in any case more apparent than real. The rise of American and German industry in the period 1870–1914 took place behind a very high tariff and contrasted with the decline of British industry in conditions of free trade. This did not pass unnoticed by the Royal Commission on Depression of Trade and Industry which reported in 1887 and concluded that, as a result of the tariff, producers were 'placed in secure possession of a great and steady home trade' and were thus able to 'enter with confidence and spirit upon an enlarged scale of operations, and in so doing bring into play every invention and improvement that can contribute to the perfection and economy of his work'. They also argued that the fuller and more regular output enabled the producers to 'reduce the cost of manufactures in the most healthful manner, by the distribution of fixed charges over a larger annual production'.

The experience of other countries since the Second World War also shows that free trade is not necessarily beneficial to those countries which pursue it. The greatest post-war success story is that of Japan, which has mastered every device for restricting competition from imports as well as for keeping control of Japanese industry in Japanese hands. The Germans were no less protectionist in the early 1950s in the case of any industry which they thought might be damaged by foreign competition in the home market. Spain. Austria and Norway have flourished behind high tariffs, as have Australia, Canada and Brazil. All these countries have prospered, in marked contrast to the USA and the UK, which have been the leading advocates of free trade and which have probably gone further than any other countries in dismantling the protection afforded to domestic industry.

The advocates of import controls correctly identify the reason for our poor trade performance as being the loss of price competitiveness of our manufacturing output both at home and abroad. The only way of resolving this problem is to make the output of home industry more competitive – i.e. cheaper than manufactures from abroad – in both the home and export markets. The import control strategy however seeks to do this by concentrating entirely on the home market, while ignoring the export market. As a comprehensive strategy, this exposes it to fatal weaknesses.

In the first place, whereas a devaluation makes all goods and services from abroad more expensive and therefore less competitive on the home market, import controls, whether tariffs or quotas, cannot do this. One quarter of our purchases from abroad are in the form of services, and the scope for imposing controls on many of them, certainly at high rates, is very limited. However, even with visible trade, where in principle a substantial uniform tariff could be applied, the pressure for exemptions is in practice always very great. Food, fuel, raw materials and capital equipment are obvious candidates for special treatment. So are imports from Third World countries. The result is that the scope for limiting imports is substantially reduced.

The CEPG studies recognise these difficulties and suggest, in their Report of April 1980, a variety of tariff rates; 20 per cent for semi-manufactures, 30 per cent for finished manufactures, 15 per cent for services (foreign travel, shipping, etc.), and zero for food, oil and raw materials. Leaving aside the practicality of some of these proposals – particularly in the case of some services where we do not believe it would be feasible to have charges at all – we would emphasise that the top rates of tariffs are very high compared to, for example, the EEC tariffs of 4 to 7 per cent for most machinery, 11 per cent for cars and 13 to 18 per cent for textiles and clothing.

Moreover, tariff levels which might be adequate at the beginning of an import control strategy would become increasingly ineffective as the strategy ran its course. A policy which restrains imports but does nothing to expand exports is likely to mean that a progressive increase in the level of protection is required. This is because, if export volume stays static but domestic demand expands behind the protective barrier, the ratio of exports to domestic product must fall. If imports are to remain stable in proportion to domestic demand, there will be an unavoidable tendency for imports to increase in relation to exports, whatever the prevailing level of import restraint. The only way out would then be to raise the level of the tariffs or to make import quotas progressively more restrictive.

The problem is likely to be exacerbated because exports would almost certainly fall under an import control strategy. The restriction of imports would increase the demand for domestically-produced goods and services. This would raise the margin of profit on home sales relative to exports and direct goods from export to the home market. The demand for our exports would also fall because, quite apart from the possibility of retaliation, the effect of the tariff on costs and prices is bound to make our exports less competitive. The result is that within a relatively short time the import control strategy either has to be accompanied by a substantial devaluation to retain enough world market share to make the policy work at all, or else the tariffs or quotas imposed reach totally unmanageable proportions.

The CEPG Report in 1980 accepts this. They admit (page 15)

that 'The results of very tentative calculations . . . are that by 1990 the highest tariff rate, that on finished manufactures, might have to reach about 70% to sustain growth of business output at 4% per year . . .' But with tariffs at this level the British economy would be almost totally isolated. If a 70 per cent tariff were required to keep out foreign manufactures, this would imply that British industrial costs were at about 170 per cent of the world level. In these circumstances, British industry could hardly be expected to export anything at all. Indeed, it is doubtful whether, if we were in this predicament, we could even afford to buy in the food, fuel and raw materials essential to keep the economy operating.

Furthermore, we cannot rule out, although we should not overstate, the possibility of retaliation. The CEPG accept that their strategy would mean leaving the EEC; however much this might be welcomed on other grounds, it might mean a fall in our exports to EEC countries. The CEPG put this potential loss at 5 per cent of our total exports of goods and services. Our other international obligations, particularly under GATT, allow for some departures from established free trade, especially if they are designed to deal with temporary disequilibria; but tariffs running to 70 per cent and beyond are precisely what GATT is designed to avoid. Furthermore, if rising domestic costs mean falling exports, the argument that protection will not reduce Britain's imports in total but merely as a proportion of the national income becomes unsound. If Britain's exports fall, our imports will have to fall too, and the risk of retaliation must then add a further twist to the spiral.

There is a further difficulty in practical terms. There would be so much pressure at home and abroad to get rid of the controls that users would not be convinced that it was in their long-term interest to switch their purchases from foreign to domestic suppliers. Importers and their customers, backed in many cases by their employees, would be continually pressing for larger quotas on grounds of cost, performance, export requirements, lack of availability in the home market, the threat to jobs, etc. Domestic suppliers would be equally reluctant to expand their capacity, since they would know that their new customers would take the business abroad again as soon as opportunity offered; and because of the international implications, the government would find it difficult to offer them any assurance on this score and certainly not beyond the lifetime of a single Parliament. The shortfall in supplies would therefore be made up to a very considerable extent by switching production from unprofitable exports to the more profitable home market, making our position from an employment and balance of payments point of view little better than before. There would be little incentive to adapt our economy to the ever-changing pattern of world trade, and the problem of eventual re-entry into a competitive trading system would be even more difficult.

The advantage of devaluation over import controls in dealing with a weak trading position is that it acts comprehensively across all purchases to make them more expensive for home consumers, while at the same time increasing the attraction in price terms of British goods and services overseas. There are thus benefits to be secured not only from reducing imports but from increasing exports as well. These latter benefits, depending crucially on the economies of scale and falling unit costs available only from expanding export markets, are totally ignored by an import control strategy; the advantages it offers are the much smaller ones of a larger home market and they are in any case offset by the loss of markets abroad which seems an unavoidable consequence of the strategy. Why then do the Cambridge Group reject devaluation, which alone guarantees an across-the-board improvement in our international competitiveness, in favour of import controls, which are, in effect, only half a devaluation and the less effective half at that?

Some guide as to the CEPG reasoning on this point can be gained from their 1978 Report where they compared their import strategy with a devaluation strategy. We are, however, extremely critical of the assumptions on which their hypothetical devaluation strategy was based. They provided for an improvement in cost competitiveness of only 4 per cent a year from mid-1978. Our view in 1978 was that a reduction of 15 to 20 per cent was required in the real exchange rate to promote export-led growth. We were therefore not greatly surprised at their conclusion that, in the short run, output and employment would increase faster as a result of the imposition of quantitative restrictions on imports than in the case of the devaluation they proposed. The devaluation horse was effectively nobbled from the start.

This seems to have been due, at least in part, to a failure to distinguish between changes in the nominal and in the real exchange rate, and in part to the use of the index of relative normal unit labour costs to measure competitiveness, errors shared in common with the Treasury and the London Business School. It is nevertheless of interest that their calculations showed that the growth in GDP in the longer run would not be much less in the case of their limited devaluation than that which was predicted in the case of import controls; and we would argue that the much higher figure shown for exports in the case of devaluation was of particular importance because of the dependence of the regions and the unskilled on employment in manufacturing and because economies of scale in the export and import-competing industries help to reduce the rate of inflation as well as stimulate export-led growth.

In their Report of April 1980, however, the CEPG substantially shifted their ground and in doing so implicitly accepted the force of much of our criticisms of their earlier proposals. Without publicity and unnoticed by almost all their followers, the CEPG totally abandoned the idea of import quotas, presumably because of the administrative problems in applying them; what they proposed instead was very substantial tariff protection on top of a reduction in the exchange rate of no less than 25 per cent. This is a very considerable volte-face, not so much because it includes a substantial devaluation – which could be reasonably defended as doing no more than offsetting the contrived appreciation of sterling over the past two years – but because it relies on the price mechanism to restore the balance between home production and imports and to that extent avoids some of the distortions inherent in their previous proposals. The question is not whether the new strategy could be made to work, but whether the combination of a high tariff with a measure of devaluation is as effective as devaluation on its own.

The CEPG took considerable pains to provide the answer. They calculated that, after only four years, GDP would be 22 per cent higher under their strategy than it would be in the case of devaluation alone and 34 per cent higher than under present policies. Consumers' expenditure would be only 15 per cent higher and the increase in real wage settlements would actually be the same as it would be in the case of the devaluation strategy, though post-tax real earnings would be some 6 per cent higher. The other significant factor, and the one which accounts for most of the difference between the increase in GDP and the smaller increase in post-tax earnings, is the difference in employment. In the case of devaluation alone, the numbers employed would drop from 23.1m in 1979 to 21.3m in 1985, still better than the 20.3m predicted under present policies. Unemployment would rise from 1.3m to 3.6m compared to 4.4m if present policies were unchanged. The corresponding figures for the tariff plus devaluation solution are 23.6m for employment and 1.8m for unemployment.

The CEPG rightly say that, in present circumstances, when we are operating in uncharted territory, any predictions must be uncertain. We are nevertheless entitled to point out that their predictions, which seem so favourable to the devaluation plus tariffs strategy, as opposed to devaluation alone, are based on a number of very doubtful assumptions. In the first place, the so-called devaluation strategy involves a slightly smaller devaluation – 22 per cent compared to 25 per cent – than is the case with their alternative. It cannot be legitimately argued that, in the case of devaluation alone, a reduction of 22 per cent in the exchange rate is the most the economy could stand, when they are prepared to recommend a 25 per cent devaluation when accompanied by tariffs. Secondly, because the proposed tariff would be contrary to the Treaty of Rome, they assume that in their case, and their case alone, we would leave the EEC and would thus obtain our food supplies at world prices. The assumption that we would leave the EEC is a perfectly reasonable one, but it seems to us inadmissible to claim the benefit in one case and not to consider it in the other.

The assumption is, of course, crucial to forecasts of movements in prices and, consequentially, movements in real earnings. We have always accepted that devaluation will raise prices as must any strategy designed to reduce the competitiveness of imports. Manufactures have been crucified by a 40 per cent increase in the real exchange rate since 1976 and, in present circumstances, we would expect the increase to be quite sharp, despite falling unit costs made possible by rising output. The CEPG predict that, under devaluation alone, consumer prices in the first year would rise by 17.8 per cent compared to 12.6 per cent under present policies. They would then fall for two years to 10 to 12 per cent compared to 10 to 11 per cent under present policies, but would then take off to 20 per cent or more, compared to only 8 to 9 per cent if the policy was unchanged. This is in strong contrast to their preferred alternative, where prices would rise in the first year by only 9.8 per cent, rising to 11.3 per cent in the second year, but falling again in the third year to only 6.6 per cent before taking off to 14.2 per cent and 20.4 per cent in the fourth and fifth years.

The increase in the rate of inflation is due, in the case of both strategies, to wage inflation, following the end of a short-term incomes policy which the CEPG assume would be necessary to soften the impact of devaluation, either alone or accompanied by tariffs. That is as may be. Our concern is to question the astonishing assumption that the increase in prices in the first year would be 8 percentage points less if the tariff plus devaluation solution were to be adopted rather than devaluation alone. We do not know how the figure was reached, but we are quite certain that it cannot be right.

The tariff proposal, as we have seen, puts a tariff of 30 per cent on manufactures, 20 per cent on semi-manufactures and 15 per cent on services. Food, oil and raw materials would be admitted duty-free. The impact of the tariff would of course be very great and while we do not doubt that it would have a dramatic effect on output and employment, it must have an equally telling effect on prices. It would come on top of the devaluation and would raise the price of imports, finished manufactures by no less than 72 per cent, less any reduction the supplier agreed to make in his margin of profit. The corresponding increase in the price of semi-manufactures would be 59 per cent. It would need a devaluation of 42 per cent and 37 per cent respectively to achieve the same result, which compares with the 22 per cent allowed for under the devaluation alone strategy.

What must then be explained is how a much larger increase in the cost of imported manufactures and services, in the case of the tariff plus devaluation strategy, can be reconciled with a much smaller increase in consumer prices than that which they predict for devaluation alone. This is particularly puzzling since the devaluation element is actually greater under the tariff solution than with devaluation alone. The answer cannot lie in the absence of a tariff on imports of oil and raw materials, since there is no tariff on oil and the tariff on most raw materials is nil or negligible. We are therefore driven back to the fact that, under the CEPG's preferred strategy, agricultural products would be relieved of the burden of the CAP: but this is certainly tantamount to cooking the books, given that the option of leaving the EEC is available in both cases.

We are in any case doubtful whether unrestricted entry for foodstuffs would have such a far-reaching effect on the cost of living as the CEPG postulate. Although we have never accepted the Whitehall view that increases in CAP prices have a negligible effect on the cost of living, we find it impossible to accept that the retail price index would fall by 7 to 8 per cent simply on account of the drop in the food component, which accounts for only a quarter of the total. In fact, the postulated change must be greater than this because, if it were not for the difference in the treatment of foodstuffs, the tariff solution on the CEPG's figures must result in a bigger increase in the cost of living than that shown for devaluation only.

This is not to say that an argument based solely on the cost of living should necessarily be conclusive; what matters ultimately is the standard of living. The higher cost of imports under both the CEPG and devaluation strategies would lead to an increase in output and employment and this would enable living standards to be raised as well as provide resources for increased investment. The advantage of devaluation alone, however, is that it operates on both sides of the account; by raising the demand for goods and services, both at home and in expanding markets abroad, it would help to increase output and employment by substantially more than would be possible under a tariff solution which, on the CEPG's own reckoning, would still leave us with 1.8 million unemployed. Thus, living standards would rise even further. It would also help to reduce costs because the producers of internationally tradeable goods would in most cases benefit from much larger economies of scale than would be possible under an import control strategy. There would also be less scope for evasion and less distortion to normal channels of trade.

The CEPG case seems to rest on the hope – but the point does not come out very clearly – that the revenue from the tariff could be used to cushion the impact of price rises through tax reductions. We believe this argument is altogether too simple. A tariff solution, because it would stimulate production for the home market only and not for export as well, would require a bigger increase in import prices than in the case of a devaluation alone to achieve a given increase in output and employment; and this higher price level would apply to all prices, domestic as well as imports, since the tariff would not only raise the price of imports but would also permit (indeed this would be its purpose) domestic prices to rise behind the tariff wall. Even if all the revenues which are raised on imports alone were returned to the consumer through VAT reductions, therefore, this would offset only a part of the overall price increases generated by the tariffs, which are already greater than in the case of devaluation alone.

In other words, the CEPG are caught in a cleft stick on this point. Either tariffs rising to 70 per cent would be prohibitive of imports, in which case there would be no revenue available to reduce domestic prices, or else they would not be prohibitive because even with tariffs at that level, domestic prices would have risen so far that imports remained competitive and continued to come in despite the tariff. In either case, the inflationary consequences of the tariffs could not be avoided, would be substantially higher for a given improvement in output and employment than in the case of devaluation alone, and could only be partially offset by the revenue they produced.

The additional margin of devaluation possible in place of the CEPG's tariff would be 12 to 15 per cent, and the effect of this on the profitability and growth prospects of British industry would be dramatic in terms of both volume and price. The increase in revenue from incomes of all kinds and from expenditure taxes would be very substantial and would go a long way towards matching the revenue from the CEPG's tariffs. Because everyone would know where they stood – a not unimportant consideration in the real world – the response to the opportunities offered would in our view be much greater than would be likely if the CEPG proposals were to be adopted.

There are some proponents of an import control strategy who regret that the CEPG has abandoned quotas in favour of tariffs. Such people correctly identify the CEPG's general import controls as a market-oriented strategy, like devaluation; and would prefer, perhaps on political rather than on economic grounds, a strategy which was more interventionist in flavour. For this reason, they advocate selective import controls, based on quotas, in an attempt to escape the dominance of the market.

The difficulty here is that any strategy which attempted to ignore the fact, however palatable or unpalatable it may be in domestic political terms, that international markets are still overwhelmingly dominated by the price mechanism is quite unnecessarily stacking the odds against success. In any case, the CEPG gave up the idea of quotas for good reason. There is no escape from the inflationary consequences of import controls through the use of quotas rather than tariffs – quotas would allow British suppliers, freed from cheaper foreign competition, to raise their own prices, and the shortages created would inevitably lead to a system of rationing by price, both officially and unofficially, through the black market – but more importantly, quotas would mean an administrative nightmare. Either the quotas would be imposed across the board (or at least would apply to most manufactured goods since no one argues that they should be imposed in respect of food, fuel and basic materials) or they would be imposed selectively. In the latter case, a huge infrastructure of licences, application procedures and appeals would have to be put into place; in the former, the only way of creating a non-discriminatory system of quotas would be to auction all licences, regardless of end use, to the highest bidder. It would be possible to do this by having separate auctions for specified import headings, but the greater the number of headings the greater the confusion; at the end of the day, there would be howls of rage from those who had failed to get a licence, either because they could not afford the price or because they had discovered after the event that they had not foreseen the whole or a part of their requirement. The earlier the stage of production, the worse the problem. Clothing manufacturers using imported cloth would be outbid by retailers who wanted to buy imported clothing, unless there were separate auctions for cloth and clothing, but in that case importers of grey cloth for finishing would be outbid by clothing manufacturers who wanted to import finished cloth: and so on and so on. The higher the import content, the greater the potential profit to the importer and the easier it would be for him to outbid manufacturers relying on imports of materials and components at an earlier stage of production. The effects would be quite arbitrary, production schedules would be adversely affected and expansion plans based on the use of imported machinery and/or components would often have to be modified or abandoned. The consequent impact on the general level of prices, which would then be determined by the least, rather than the most, cost-conscious firms, would be far from negligible.

This is not to say that free trade is the answer to all our

problems, even with a competitive exchange rate. The combination of a 30 per cent devaluation, 10 per cent tariff and increased tariff preferences in the Commonwealth put us far ahead of other countries in the growth league in the 1930s. We would likewise see nothing but advantage in resuming tariff protection against imports from the EEC. Some industries have been so run down as a result of the overvaluation of the pound that special measures will be needed to get them back on their feet. We see no objection in practice or principle to the use of selective import controls in these circumstances.

Our problem with general import controls is that, while we are entirely in agreement with the CEPG analysis of the problems which confront us, we believe that they have been led down the wrong road by their failure to recognise the importance of economies of scale in generating export-led growth. Their import tariff strategy would deal partially with the symptoms but not with the causes of our declining international competitiveness. It would concentrate exclusively on the progressive raising of the prices of competing imports rather than on the reduction of our prices *vis-à-vis* foreign competition in our own and in export markets. It is in short, only half a solution, and could not, as the keystone of a strategy for growth, bear the weight which would be placed upon it.

7 Monetarism or Prosperity

THE HISTORY OF FAILURE

British economic management over the past century or more has been dominated by the preoccupation with 'sound money'. The pre-eminence of financial interests in our economy, the importance of the City as a financial centre and the universality of sterling as a medium of exchange have meant that the interests of the real economy – of manufacturing industry – have been subordinated to the money economy and to the international role of sterling. The whole thrust of economic policy has been directed towards financial orthodoxy so as to preserve the value of sterling, irrespective of the consequences for internal growth. This has meant a constant recourse to deflation in the attempt to hold down costs and thereby maintain competitiveness; but because an overvalued pound and the deflationary policies needed to support it have been entirely destructive of our international competitiveness, we have found ourselves in a vicious downward spiral which has not only denied to manufacturing industry the conditions essential to its expansion and prosperity but which has also, in the long term, negated the objective of 'sound money' itself.

There is little sign that the current managers of our economy recognise that their policies have such a long history of failure. Nor are they (apparently) aware that the earlier occasions in our economic history when strict monetarist disciplines and an overvalued exchange rate were jointly pressed to their logical extremes led in each case to disaster. In the aftermath of the Napoleonic Wars, economic policies were framed on the basis of principles which would gladden a modern monetarist heart; those policies led inexorably to economic misery, social unrest and the massacre of Peterloo. A similar set of consequences accompanied the return to the Gold Standard in 1925. The attempt to force costs down in order to justify a new and higher parity for sterling led to the General Strike, to the industrial stagnation which Britain alone endured during the 1920s and to the swollen unemployment totals which reached their peak in the early 1930s. For those with a sense of history, these earlier episodes offer an ominous parallel with the damage being inflicted on our economy by a similar combination of policies in the 1980s.

THE CURRENT EXPERIMENT

Undeterred by the history of prolonged and repeated failure whenever monetarist doctrines have been put into practice, monetarist theorists are currently conducting yet another experiment on the hapless British economy. Already the high hopes with which that experiment was ushered in have dimmed. As monetarist prescriptions fail to produce the desired results, the proponents of the doctrine, like religious fanatics, are splitting into sects. The purists maintain that success has so far eluded them because the doctrine has not been applied rigorously enough. Others say that patience and faith are required – that only a few more months will see the policies bear fruit. Yet others, government ministers included, adopt the posture of early converts to Christianity; while ostentatiously worshipping at the altar of the new monetarist god, they also take out a form of insurance by offering prayers to the old pagan gods of wage control and exhortation.

The reasons for this growing disarray amongst monetarist opinion are not hard to find. The monetarist experiment is now in deep trouble. It is not so much that output is falling, unemployment is rocketing upwards and insolvencies are at record levels; these are the penalties which monetarists warned us we would have to pay. It is not even that inflation doubled in little more than a year; a true monetarist regards a rise in the retail price index as a delayed response to past events and as such irrelevant to the real battle against inflation. The central failure of the monetarist experiment is one which, while of little significance to most of us, is absolutely destructive in terms of monetarism itself. It is, quite simply, the abject and comprehensive failure to control the money supply.

The extent of that failure has meant that, by the autumn of 1980, not only was Sterling M3, the government's chosen measurement of the money supply, rising substantially beyond the limits set for it, but no one could tell how far it was out of control. The figure on which the government had based its whole policy was thus rendered devoid of any meaning. The futility of trying to define money, measure it and control it, as the only objective of government policy, was thus amply demonstrated.

The failure was explained on the grounds that the lifting of the 'corset' had distorted the Sterling M3 figure. This is more an admission than an explanation of failure; but accepting that the unwinding of the 'corset' was a major factor in the sharp rise in the Sterling M3 figure in July and August 1980, there are other factors which will also render difficult, if not impossible, any attempt to control the money supply in the rigorous way which monetarists postulate as necessary to the success of their policy. The removal of exchange controls, for example, has meant that what cannot be borrowed at home can be borrowed abroad. In any case, the Bank of England does not, at bottom, attempt to control the money supply. It stands permanently as a lender of last resort to the banking system as a whole and its main instrument for controlling the money supply is to ration it through its price. It is in effect trying to limit the demand for money, through the manipulation of interest rates, rather than control its supply.

All of this means that while monetarist theory may produce neat and simple results when tested on computer models of the economy, it breaks down in a real economy where, for example, companies have to borrow, at whatever the interest rate, simply in order to survive. Distress borrowing, caused directly by the monetarist squeeze, renders ineffective the attempt to control bank lending through high interest rates.

Monetarist theory is also invalidated in practice when it comes to the other main element in the government's attempt to control the money supply – the reduction of the public sector borrowing requirement. As the government squeeze drives more and more firms into bankruptcy and more and more workers into the dole queue, it is inevitable that the pressure on the public sector borrowing requirement will be upwards rather than downwards; it is estimated that each additional 100 000 unemployed will mean an additional £500 million on the borrowing requirement, through increased unemployment and unemployment-related payments and reduced revenue.[1] Not only, therefore, is the difficulty of controlling the money supply much greater than ministers had supposed – the fiasco over the 'corset' shows how easily even the banks can avoid control – but the very attempt to control the money supply can increase the difficulties.

The manifest failure of the authorities to control the money supply, which means that whether or not the rest of monetarist theory is a proper basis for policy-making is at best a hypothetical question, has led some monetarist theorists to suggest that the attempt should be abandoned in favour of a control over a wider measure of economic activity. Writing in the *Financial Times* on 31 July 1980, Sam Brittan expressed belated doubts about the merits of trying to control the quantity of money (M) alone and recommended that government policy be directed instead towards the control of MV – the nominal national product. In other words, attention should be directed to the flow of money rather than merely to its quantity.

This is a welcome recantation of the simple-minded monetarist view that it is the quantity of money alone which matters; but it is doubtful whether Sam Brittan realises how closely what he is now advocating approximates to the old-fashioned demand management which monetarists affect to despise. MV is a measure of total economic activity in monetary terms and it could be effectively controlled only through restricting the demand for credit. This would require a shift of emphasis – difficult to accommodate within monetarist theory – from the attempt to control the money supply in any direct sense to the use of familiar deflationary instruments, such as high interest rates and fiscal policy, to hold down demand. In practice, it is precisely these measures which are being pursued by the authorities in the name of monetarism, as the Green Paper on Monetary Control openly concedes. The authorities, while happy to use monetarist jargon in order to please their political masters, are clearly content to pursue an old-fashioned deflationary squeeze under cover of the new fashion. Sam Brittan has belatedly, and perhaps unwittingly, come to recognise this.

Even if the attempt to control the money supply had been successful – even if ministers had succeeded in producing a universally acceptable definition of money which could be properly measured, which bore a stable relationship to the real economy, and which could be brought under adequate control – it is still the case that the effort to do so would have been misconceived. The exercise could only be worthwhile if, as monetarists suppose, the demand for money is for all practical purposes constant; in that case, controlling the supply of money would not affect the level of economic activity in real terms and could only affect the level of prices. If, however, as is in fact the case, the demand for money varies according to 'the needs of trade', then any attempt to keep the supply of money stable will, when labour and capital are underemployed, have its first and most important effect on the real economy rather than on prices.

The monetarist error, as we pointed out in Chapter 2, is to assume that there is a stable relationship between MV and PT, such that an increase in M necessarily results in an equivalent increase in P. There is nothing in the Fisher Equation, however, to suggest that action concentrated on M will necessarily affect only P. The equation would remain intact if changes in M were offset by changes in the velocity of circulation (V) or in the number of transactions (T). In other words, even as a matter of theory, a change in the quantity of money is likely to mean a change in the velocity of circulation and/or a change in real output, both of which are likely to precede and outweigh in importance any changes in the level of prices. The current monetarist experiment demonstrates that this is in fact what happens; not only does the velocity of circulation change substantially in order to meet changes in the quantity of money, as we showed in Chapter 2, but the attempt to control the money supply, when there is less than full employment of capital and labour, has a much greater and more direct effect on the level of economic activity than it does on the level of prices.

The theoretical deficiencies of monetarism in this respect are exacerbated by the inability of monetarist theorists to show by what transmission mechanism control of the money supply is actually translated into changes in the level of prices. The best explanation on offer seems to be that, so far as monetarist controls eventually do bring the inflation rate down temporarily, they are indistinguishable in their operation from old-fashioned deflationary demand management. In other words, the quasi-scientific monetarist theory depends for its practical effect on the crude deflationary sledgehammer.

Nor is there any empirical evidence to make good these theoretical deficiencies. As we showed in Chapter 2, there is nothing in our own or in other countries' experience to suggest that control of the money supply has the mechanistic and causal relationship with the level of prices which monetarists postulate. The available evidence points strongly to the absence of such a relationship, as does our current experience of four years of monetarist disciplines. Even if it could be shown that there was a correlation between the money supply and the level of prices, it would by no means follow that it is the money supply which determines the level of prices. It would be at least equally plausible, and a good deal more consonant with practical experience, to argue that the supply of money responds to the level of prices, rather than the other way round.

OLD-FASHIONED DEFLATION

The theoretical deficiencies and technical difficulties of monetarism mean that its true significance lies, not in offering a theoretical basis or a practical guide for a new economic policy, but in providing camouflage for the policies of deflation and squeeze which the authorities wish to pursue anyway and to which they have always had recourse in circumstances where, through an appreciating exchange rate or otherwise, our international competitiveness had declined sharply. The impact of monetarism is twofold; first, by providing a spurious theoretical framework for these old-fashioned policies, it will encourage ministers and others to push them far beyond the point when the damage they do to the economy demands a change of course; and secondly, monetarist policy, or what passes for it when applied by the Bank of England, will encourage the authorities to eschew fiscal measures, the more usual means of restraining demand, in favour of high interest rates. The significance of this is that it imposes a deflationary squeeze in the form which is most damaging to manufacturing industry. A fiscal squeeze transfers money from the personal sector to the public sector; high interest rates, on the other hand, transfer resources from borrowers to lenders – from manufacturing industry, which needs capital in order to provide jobs and invest in new plant, to those who hold assets and deal in money.

This is the century-old bias of British economic policy at work again. It is no accident that the high interest rates which have accompanied and implemented monetarist policy in this country have meant that, while manufacturing industry nosedives into an unprecedented recession, bank profits have soared.[2] Little wonder that the City of London is the last beleagured citadel of monetarism.

None of this would matter so much if deflation was in any case the appropriate policy to follow in our present circumstances. The futile attempts to control the money supply could be tolerated if they were merely a harmless means of keeping ministers occupied while the economy responded to the correct level of demand. Unfortunately, while the more arcane aspects of monetarist theory are now seen to have little substance, the deflationary squeeze carried out in their name is real enough. It is this squeeze which is doing its familiar damage, reducing output, increasing unemployment and providing only a brief and unsustainable check to price rises which must resume again as soon as a weakened real economy has to deal with an increased level of demand and attempts are made to restore wage levels and profit margins.

The difficulty with deflation is, and always has been, that it may be appropriate in some circumstances, but it is clearly inappropriate and damaging in others. It is usually pressed into service as a means of countering inflation – still best defined as too much money chasing too few goods. But the problem of inflation admits of two solutions. We can either reduce the money supply in relation to goods, or we can increase the supply of goods in relation to money. The choice as to which course to follow depends crucially on whether the economy is operating at full capacity or not.

If the production of goods cannot be increased, then any increases in the supply of money will of course be inflationary unless the velocity of circulation falls and the additional money is saved. In the past, however, we have assumed too easily that the limit to capacity has been reached and at the first sign of shortage of labour and materials the government has been persuaded to take measures which have been quite literally counter-productive. We have consistently failed to appreciate that an economy in which there are no shortages is an economy in which there is no growth and that productivity can only be significantly increased by attracting labour from industries in which it is being prodigally used to industries which can use it more sparingly. It is only when the economy is operating at or near full capacity that resources of labour and capital will readily be persuaded to

move to areas where they can be used more efficiently. The
lesson of other countries and of Britain in the 1930s shows that in
an expanding environment the limits to capacity can be raised
very substantially.

   If the economy is operating substantially below capacity, as
our economy is at present, it is even more obvious that the solution to the inflation problem is to increase the supply of goods by
allowing the economy to use fully the resources available. A
deflationary reduction in the supply of money is not only inappropriate; it will in all probability reduce the supply of goods at
the same time, thereby inflicting great damage on the real
economy and negating the counter-inflationary objective. The
supply of money and of goods will both fall; the supply of money
will then have to fall a very long way before it eventually out-
strips the fall in the supply of goods and achieves its counter-
inflationary effect. It is considerations of this sort which explain
what must appear to a monetarist to be a puzzling phenomenon;
that four years of fixing and applying monetary targets have led,
not to the predicted fall in prices, but to an inflation rate which
has become entrenched at a level much higher than the world
average.

THE OVERVALUED POUND

The damage that deflation has inflicted on the economy has been
gravely exacerbated by the other pillar of monetarist orthodoxy –
the overvalued rate for sterling. It is the 'strong pound' which is
the instrument of recession. It has burdened British industry
with an unprecedented loss of competitiveness – which has
destroyed markets abroad, turned the flow of imports into a flood
and forced companies to sell, when they can, at a loss. The
pound's overvaluation has in effect imposed a tax of at least 45
per cent on exports and provided a subsidy of more than 30 per
cent to imports.[3] If this had been done directly, through fiscal
measures, the CBI and the public generally would have been
outraged; but because it is done through the exchange rate, we
are told that we 'must live with it'. The effect of this 'hidden tax
on industry' is catastrophic; as one industry follows another to
extinction, each will have been pushed over the precipice by

specific factors – high energy costs, unfair foreign competition and so on – but the precipice is there because of the overvalued pound.

The connection between monetarism and an overvalued currency is not accidental. The government's chosen instrument for conducting its monetary policy – high interest rates – has intended and inevitable consequences for the exchange rate. Underpinned by our North Sea oil reserves, sterling has become an attractive investment for the world's 'hot money' and this attractiveness is considerably enhanced by the extremely high return which foreign investors are offered. As long as the government regards high interest rates as a necessary part of domestic monetary policy, it is an inevitable corollary of that policy that sterling will remain at an overvalued level. We would go further; we maintain that it is the exchange rate which is and is intended to be the mainspring of the government's economic policy and interest rates merely the lever.

Professor Marcus Miller of the University of Warwick has made the same point in a different way. He has argued that it is the tightness of monetary policy, rather than North Sea oil, which is the main reason for the appreciation of sterling. His calculation is that, to achieve a 1 per cent reduction in the rate of monetary growth, interest rates will have to remain 2½ per cent higher than they would otherwise have been over a period of two years. This in turn would mean a 5 per cent rise in the exchange rate for every 1 per cent reduction in the rate of monetary growth. According to this calculation, the tightness of monetary policy could be responsible for a 20 per cent loss of competitiveness.[4]

The overvalued currency may be seen by some as a simple by-product of monetary policy; but unless the Bank of England is even more incompetent than is generally supposed, the rise of 45 per cent and 35 per cent respectively, in the real and nominal exchange rates which has occurred since November 1976 must have been a deliberate act of policy, intended to operate as an integral element of the overall strategy. A 'strong pound' is the anvil against which the government hopes to beat inflation out of the economy. Their willingness to allow, and indeed encourage, the currency to appreciate, even in conditions of declining international competitiveness, is meant to reinforce the message to industry that the government is not to be deflected from its course. What they do not seem to realise is that industries which are caught between the twin jaws of falling domestic demand and a decline in international competitiveness – exacerbated this time by an appreciating exchange rate – are likely to be squeezed out of existence. Only those industries to whom international competitiveness does not matter will escape the squeeze. The effect of the government's policy is therefore to tilt the balance of the economy decisively in favour of those sectors which do not need to compete; those sectors which have to compete in order to survive, and which are by definition the most efficient and productive, are those which are likely to be extinguished altogether by the combination of tight money and an overvalued currency.

The government's attachment to an appreciating exchange rate is reinforced by the argument by the Institute of Fiscal Studies to the effect that an appreciating currency is the only practicable means of enjoying the benefits of North Sea oil. We dealt with this argument in Chapter 4; it rests on the belief that the comparative decline in the share of our national wealth produced by manufacturing, which is made inevitable by the increased share provided by North Sea oil, necessarily means an absolute decline in the size of our manufacturing industry. The reverse is in fact true; North Sea oil should enable us to run the economy at a much higher level of output and demand and allow manufacturing industry to expand without running into the limits of capacity and the consequent balance of payments problems which have inhibited us in the past.

Traditionally, the level of domestic economic activity has been severely pruned back in order to produce improvements in a balance of payments which has perennially threatened to lurch into substantial deficit and has usually managed to make good the threat. If North Sea oil is able to resolve this problem for us without the necessity to cut domestic demand, the boost to manufacturing industry should be substantial. If we were prepared to run the economy at full capacity, the technical problems which are emphasised by the Institute of Fiscal Studies would decline in importance. A higher level of economic activity would require the exchange rate to fall as a greater volume of exports was needed to match the increase in imports; with a lower exchange rate and increased output, an expanding and newly profitable manufacturing industry would then provide an attractive investment opportunity for North Sea oil revenues.

The government are prevented from pursuing this obvious and common-sense course because they are caught in a vicious circle of their own making. Because they insist that it is necessary to restrain the money supply and thereby restrict demand in order to reduce inflation, the economy is condemned to operate at much below capacity. Manufacturing industry is thereby denied the conditions in which it might expand. The situation is exacerbated by the overvaluation of sterling which is itself the product of the high interest rates which the monetary policy requires. Because manufacturing industry is declining and unprofitable, there is no way in which it can absorb the revenues produced by North Sea oil. The only way then in which we can take advantage of those revenues is through an appreciating exchange rate, thus completing the vicious circle and providing a further reinforcement for the decline, both absolute and comparative, of manufacturing industry. This sequence of cause and effect could of course be unwound and reversed by policies which deliberately set out to achieve a virtuous circle of rising output, growing competitiveness, lower interest rates and a lower exchange rate. We set out the basis of these policies later in this chapter.

As we saw in Chapter 3, the exchange rate has assumed such an important role in monetarist theory because of the influence of one school of monetarist economists – the international monetarists – who believe that the exchange rate is the elusive transmission mechanism by which changes in the money supply are translated into changes in the level of prices. According to this theory, an appreciating currency will mean a rate of domestic inflation which is lower than the world average. Not only has this view been entirely falsified by our own recent experience of four years of currency appreciation, but it is also contradicted by the experience of other countries. Those countries which have succeeded in running large and sustained balance of payments surpluses have not found that those surpluses spill over substantially into the domestic money supply; and even to the extent that they have done so, the surpluses have not had the inflationary consequences which monetarists postulate. International monetarism depends in the end on the accuracy of the so-called Law of One Price; but as we showed in Chapter 3, the Law of One Price is not only contradicted by the available evidence, but is unable to explain, because it overlooks, the centrally important changes in a given country's share of world trade in manufactures.

An essential element in the monetarist approach is the view that money is 'neutral', i.e. that all prices rise by the same amount when the value of money falls and that changes in the exchange rate do not and cannot affect the level of activity in anything but the short term. Lord Kaldor has asked why, in that case, the elimination of inflation should be such an objective of government as to be given 'overriding priority'. In what way is a community better off with constant prices than with constantly rising (or falling) prices?[5] Keynes asked the same question in his *Tract on Monetary Reform*. The answer of course is that inflation causes serious distortions and leads to a deterioration in economic performance, but this makes the basic monetarist proposition – that the behaviour of the real economy is neutral with respect to monetary disturbances – untenable. As we have repeatedly emphasised, changes in the exchange rate are de-stabilising because the changes in market share which result confer additional benefits on those who gain and impose additional penalties on those who lose. The Law of Continuous Causation – as we have called it – is the mainspring of both the virtuous circle of export-led growth and the vicious circle of import-led contraction.

For all these reasons, the credibility of international monetarism has declined substantially over the last year or so. Nevertheless, it remains a seminal influence on government policy, and a leading international monetarist, Professor Terry Burns, has been appointed as the Chief Economic Adviser to the Treasury. While ministers may no longer have as much confidence as they did in the efficacy of an appreciating exchange rate as a means of reducing inflation, the influence of international monetarism no doubt remains as a reinforcement of the traditional preference of our policy-makers for the highest possible parity, irrespective of its appropriateness to our industrial circumstances.

REAL WAGES

Although an appreciating currency is undoubtedly an integral part of the government's monetarist strategy, this is not to say that there is not some lack of congruence between the continuing rise in the exchange rate and the other elements of their policy. An appreciating currency is clear evidence that either credit is too tight or wages are too low. The government is, however, unwilling to concede that either of these two propositions is true.

So far as wages are concerned, the government argument that they are too high and must be reduced if workers are to protect themselves against further unemployment is difficult to accept if, at the same time, the currency is allowed to appreciate. It is a necessary implication of such a policy that the economy enjoys a margin of competitiveness; and the government should not be surprised if wage earners engage in a race with the exchange rate to take advantage of the competitiveness which is assumed to exist.

There is certainly nothing in the government's current support for an appreciating currency to suggest that any reduction in the level of real wages, whether voluntary or involuntary, would improve our international competitiveness. Since a fall in real wages would lead to renewed confidence on the part of foreign investors in the stability of sterling as a place for parking their 'hot money', any gain to competitiveness would be eliminated by a further rise in the value of sterling which the government would presumably encourage.

It is in any case difficult to argue that a reduction of real wages is the key to success. Not only are British wages near the bottom of the league table of Western industrialised countries, but whole industries are being destroyed in circumstances where, irrespective of what happens to labour costs, the overvalued pound ensures that those industries are substantially less competitive than they were only a year earlier. The newsprint industry is a typical example; labour costs are less than 15 per cent of total costs, and workers could work for nothing, eliminating labour costs altogether, and still leave the industry less competitive in the autumn of 1980 than it was a year earlier. It is the exchange rate, not wage levels, which is pricing workers out of jobs.

A reduction in real wages, accompanied by a rise in the exchange rate, would be nothing more than a compulsory transfer of incomes from the real economy to the money economy. The only economic justification for a fall in real wages would be to transfer resources into investment or exports; but exchange rate appreciation ensures that those resources, obtained from the productive sector through unemployment and cuts in real wages, will be transferred to the unproductive sector – from those who earn wages and profits in manufacturing industry to those who hold wealth.

Even if a reduction in real wages could be secured, it would be immensely damaging to the economy. Not only would it intensify the declining attractiveness of industry to skilled labour and to our brightest talents; it would also ensure that any incentive to improve productivity, through increased investment in capital equipment, would be removed. We would encourage the reverse of the high-wage, high-profit economy which we must develop in order to compete.

A low-wage, low-profit policy is bound to fail in the longer term. If growth is to be resumed, profitability must be restored so that firms can afford to pay higher real wages in manufacturing industry. The workers, too, will insist on recovering lost ground as soon as growth is attempted through a relaxation of monetarist rigidity; there is no reason to suppose that a fall in real wages enforced by monetarist unemployment is any less likely to end in a wages explosion than has been the case with wage restraint secured by incomes policies.

A STRATEGY FOR GROWTH

The combination of monetarist deflation and an overvalued exchange rate is entirely destructive of the conditions which are required for growth and improved productivity. As we have repeatedly argued, British policy-makers have consistently denied to British industry the essential conditions which have allowed other economies to grow. A deflationary squeeze reduces the level of demand at home while an overvalued currency ensures that our international competitiveness continually declines and that an increasing share of the reduced demand goes to imports. We are thus launched into the very reverse of the virtuous circle we seek; manufacturing industry is neither profitable enough nor growing fast enough to attract the investment of capital or the skilled labour which are required, or to take advantage of the economies of scale which have enabled more successful economies to combine rising labour costs and standards of living with increasing competitiveness in the internationally traded goods sector. In those more successful economies, increasing competitiveness permits and encourages those parts of the economy where productivity increases are most easily secured to flourish and to grow in relation to the rest of the economy; in our own case, the reverse is the case.

Any strategy for growth must therefore take as its starting point the reversal of the policies which have been so consistently unsuccessful. These policies, in their current extreme form, are now defended only by the argument that there is no alternative. As a matter of logic, this must be nonsense; the logical alternatives to the present policies of contraction and worsening competitiveness are policies which give priority to establishing international competitiveness and the conditions which make growth possible.

These policies are not in themselves novel or untried; they have after all been the foundation of the success which other countries have enjoyed. They have been eschewed in Britain because it is thought that the British economy suffers inhibitions – the balance of payments, inflation, 'supply side' problems – which other economies do not. We must consider whether those obstacles are indeed truly insuperable or whether they are simply the consequence of erroneous policies; do they loom so large only because the combination of policies needed to overcome them has never been pursued comprehensively and for a long enough period?

In the past, attempts at domestic reflation have been brought to nought because an expanding economy has run into balance of payments problems. Domestic growth has been impossible to achieve in conditions of external equilibrium because insufficient attention has been paid to our international competitiveness. On the rare occasions when the exchange rate has permitted export-led growth, the authorities have bent all their efforts to reversing these conditions as quickly as possible. Even under a regime of floating rates, the pound has been managed to prevent it from falling, as the failure to fulfil the undertaking to the IMF on a competitive exchange rate dramatically shows; the longer-term benefits of a competitive exchange rate have therefore never had time to materialise.

The essence of the strategy which we recommend is that the economy should be run at full capacity and that the exchange rate should be set at such a level as to enable this to be done without running into the balance of payments problems which have inhibited us in the past. Whatever else may or may not be claimed for devaluation, there can be no doubt of its effectiveness in correcting a deficit.

The establishment of a competitive exchange rate would do more than remove a major obstacle to growth; it would also provide a powerful incentive, in terms of both expanding demand and increased profitability, to a sustained investment in new export capacity. The whole balance of the economy would be tilted in favour of those sectors which offer the greatest chance of expansion and improved productivity.

A competitive exchange rate would also deal successfully with the group of difficulties which are sometimes described as 'supply side' problems. Just as the increased profitability generated by a correctly positioned exchange rate would offer sufficient rewards to both capital and labour to enable a skilled, well-rewarded and therefore more co-operative workforce to be developed in the internationally traded goods sector, so it would also allow improvements in servicing, promotion, delivery, spare parts and the purchase of necessary components and semi-manufactures – from foreign suppliers if necessary – so that any bottlenecks could be quickly overcome. The shortages and overheating which have obstructed expansion in the past simply need not exist, since the supply of foreign-made components is to all intents and purposes inexhaustible. All that is necessary to the solution of these problems is that industry should be profitable enough and confident enough of expansion to be able to buy in what is needed. It is no accident that Germany is the world's biggest importer of manufactures as well as the biggest exporter.

A further objection to a wholehearted policy for expansion has always been that the economy would inevitably run into inflationary pressures. This objection has been thought to be particularly powerful in respect of a strategy which depends on devaluation to provide the stimulus to growth. We dealt with the arguments concerning the supposedly inflationary effect of devaluation in Chapter 4; but it is worth re-emphasising that, as a matter of common sense, economic expansion resulting from a reduction in the exchange rate and a relaxation of the monetarist squeeze must be less inflationary in the long run than are present policies, because GNP in real terms would be a great deal higher. While some part of this higher output would go to pay for those imports which devaluation made more expensive, the strategy for growth would enable us to produce a great deal of what is now imported. What is not generally realised is the enormous amount of spare capacity, not only in the idle factories and in the one-or two-day weeks now currently worked in industry, but also in power generation, road and rail transport, and a host of other services which have grown up to serve the needs of manufacturing industry. In many of these, output could be increased substantially at very little extra cost in either real or money terms.

The potential for greater output is enormous. In 1973, the number of registered unemployed was just over 600, 000, only about a quarter of the figure in late 1980, and if allowance is made for the numbers changing jobs, the number of involuntarily unemployed was less than one-fifth of what it is now. Yet GDP rose in that year by a record 8 per cent; how much greater now is the margin of unused resources, both human and material, and how much more easily now could output be raised with beneficial effects, through falling unit costs, on the inflation rate!

Our forefathers had grasped as long ago as 1887 that import-led contraction raised our unit costs faster than those of our competitors.[6] It is for this reason that we are quite sure that a policy of devaluation which allowed the full utilisation of our human and capital resources would be less inflationary than the present policies. A case in point is that of the nationalised industries. Their sales have fallen in real terms as economic activity has slowed down, but the government insists that they should produce the same return as before, with the result that they have had to raise their prices; this in turn has led to a further contraction in sales. There can be no clearer example of a policy which is literally counterproductive and therefore inflationary.

A policy of exchange rate depreciation would also be counter-inflationary in the sense that it would reduce the government's borrowing requirement. This may sound curious in view of the government's insistence that expansion cannot be allowed until the PSBR has been reduced, but the plain fact is that maintaining people in idleness is a very expensive undertaking; it is already leading the government, predictably enough, to cut the real value of benefits. Putting them to work at no cost to the Exchequer is quite clearly the most effective way of reducing inflation – the same amount of money would be chasing substantially more goods. As we noted earlier, it has been estimated that the cost to the National Insurance Fund of an extra 100 000 unemployed is £180m in extra benefits and lost contributions, and that the immediate loss of tax revenue and the second-round effects on income means that the total cost could be as high as £500m. This means that if unemployment could be reduced to 500 000 – far higher than at any time from 1951 to 1963 – the PSBR could be reduced by something like £7000m – £8000m. A reduction of this size would save in turn an extra £1000m which now has to be found each year to finance interest payments on the debt incurred in the previous year; this in turn would mean a further saving of £150m in interest payments on the interest!

As with balance of payments and 'supply side' problems, therefore, inflation is exacerbated by slow growth; what have been traditionally regarded as obstacles to a policy for growth are in fact the inevitable consequences of failing to achieve growth. The measures which are needed to secure growth and, in particular, to establish the essential precondition for growth – international competitiveness – are themselves the most effective means of overcoming the obstacles which have always loomed so large in our thinking. An economy which is deliberately set on a course in which growth and competitiveness reinforce each other will also be an economy which is no longer inhibited by fears of balance of payments crises, 'supply side' problems and inflationary excesses.

The contribution which a competitive exchange rate can make to a policy for growth must of course be supported by domestic economic and monetary policy. It is essential that manufacturing industry should be able to rely on a sustained level of demand at home as the basis for its expansionary plans. It is no part of our purpose to argue that money is not important; it is for this reason that we believe that the current emphasis on monetary restriction is so damaging. In the conditions of underutilised capacity we suffer at the moment, it is important that money should be cheap and plentiful so that the money supply can accommodate the expansion of industry on which further improvements in growth and productivity depend. We reject the view that it is no longer possible to spend our way out of a recession. When Callaghan made his statement to this effect in 1976 to the Labour Party Conference, he was clearly not aware of its illogicality. Since a recession is by definition a condition in which there is a deficiency of spending power, it follows that the only possible escape from the recession is to increase spending. If it is objected that the attempt to increase spending will lead to further and more difficult problems – our familiar bogeys of inflation, balance of payments problems and so on – the answer must be that the difficulty lies not in the increased spending but in the conditions of falling international competitiveness in which the economy is then expected to accommodate the increased purchasing power.

As a matter of logic, there can be no possible reason for allowing resources of men and capital to lie idle, other than the fact that the extra goods which could be produced in the internationally traded goods sector are so uncompetitive that satisfactory markets cannot be found for them. It is, in other words, the economy's lack of competitiveness which is responsible for our falling output and idle resources and, since that lack of competitiveness is in turn a function of the exchange rate, it is to the exchange rate that we must turn our attention. Just as an overvalued pound is at present the engine of deflation, so a competitive exchange rate, by permitting the economy to operate at full capacity, would be the engine of recovery.

It may be objected that our problems lie too deep for solution in this way because we are saddled with an outmoded industrial structure, because the increase in energy costs and the development of microtechnology must lead to a worldwide contraction in the market for the kind of goods we produce, and because we cannot hope to compete with the developing countries in many of the areas in which we are currently engaged. We agree of course that our problems are of very long standing; this is indeed our own constant theme. Where we part company from those who believe that our difficulties are caused by 'structural' problems is in our conviction that this confuses cause and effect. Our industrial structure is necessarily determined by the international division of labour; but if the real exchange rate rises as a result of changes in the money economy which are not reflected in underlying changes in the real economy, then our increasing costs in international terms will mean a growing structural imbalance. There will be a widening disparity between the actual distribution of capital and labour and the pattern which a growing loss of price competitiveness renders appropriate. But these structural problems would largely disappear with a competitive exchange rate, because the lower price of labour in international terms would then enable us to make profitable use of our less productive capital assets. The whole thrust of a devaluation-based policy of expansion would be designed to increase the profitability and therefore the appropriateness of existing investment, and also to encourage resources of capital and labour into new areas of high technology and productivity.

POLICY RECOMMENDATIONS

The current orthodoxies have led to the adoption of policies which operate as successive notches on a ratchet of increasing contraction, deflation and loss of competitiveness. A tight monetary policy requires high interest rates; these in turn drive up the exchange rate; foreign capital is attracted by the high interest rates and the appreciating currency, and the recession means an inevitable rise in the government's borrowing requirement and in distress borrowing by industry; the money supply therefore increases faster than intended; still higher interest rates are required, leading to a higher exchange rate; and so the destructive process continues.

There is no escape from our increasingly desperate dilemma unless a decisive break is made with these damaging orthodoxies. The ratchet can and must be reversed. The interaction of the exchange rate, interest rates and the money supply can be changed so that they reinforce each other in a beneficial, rather than a destructive direction, producing a lower exchange rate, lower interest rates and money to finance expansion. The following specific recommendations, applied as part of a comprehensive and radical strategy, will reverse the contractionary ratchet and provide a powerful stimulus to growth, productivity and competitiveness.

Devaluation

Our first recommendation is that, in order to establish the key condition of international competitiveness from which all else will flow, the value of sterling must be reduced very substantially. The index for the terms of trade for manufactures (which we identified in Chapter 5 as the most accurate index of competitiveness) must be brought down to the level of late 1973 and late

1976. This is not an unduly ambitious target; it is in effect the one
set by the IMF in 1976. The achievement of this target would
restore our competitiveness to a level which would give us a
chance of maintaining, and in the longer term improving, our
share of world trade in manufactures.

The depreciation required to achieve this would be substantial – a minimum initially of 35 per cent – and since it would
inevitably raise the cost of some imports, the second and third
round effects would have to be taken into account, through a
readiness to reduce the rate further so that the index was maintained at the required level. The total depreciation from the
initial starting point may approach 50 per cent. A devaluation of
these proportions may sound enormous, but it should not be
forgotten that the nominal rate for sterling appreciated by over
50 per cent against the yen in the 18 months to February 1980,
and that by late October 1980 the real exchange rate had risen
overall by at least 45 per cent and against Germany and the USA
by at least 50 per cent since 1976. Nor should we overlook the
fact that other countries – Japan and the United States – have
recently devalued by substantial amounts and that we have ourselves done likewise twice within living memory – in 1931 and
1949.

There is of course an instinctive resistance to devaluation on
the part of most of our policy-makers. The traditional attachment to a 'strong pound' is now reinforced by the popular myth
that devaluation has been tried and found wanting, whereas the
truth is that, because of a failure to distinguish an effective from a
nominal devaluation, it has not been tried at all. It is important
to stress, therefore, that a devaluation of these proportions would
be the first attempt made in modern British economic management to use the exchange rate as a deliberate instrument of
policy. It would be quite different in purpose and effect from past
devaluations which were reluctantly conceded in the face of
overwhelming market pressures and a pre-existing loss of competitiveness. For the first time, we should be choosing a level for
sterling which would serve the interests of manufacturing
industry as opposed to those of the financial establishment.

We do not accept that a depreciation of this size would be
difficult to achieve. The other major elements in our devaluation-
based strategy for growth would themselves be a powerful
stimulus towards depreciation, as we explain in the following

pages; and as we pointed out in Chapter 4, where we considered the techniques for bringing down the rate, protestations about the difficulty of doing so would be more credible if any real attempt had been made to that end. The mere fact that this argument is advanced and that, with North Sea oil, sterling's natural tendency is upwards shows, though, how unfounded is the conventional fear that, once moving downwards, sterling would 'fall through the floor'. Even without the underpinning of North Sea oil, the rate would tend to rise as soon as our new-found competitiveness meant that we began to eat into markets hitherto dominated by others and the real economy began to strengthen. The price-sensitiveness of international markets would ensure that sterling could not fall too far; our international competitors could not afford to allow it to do so.

Lower Interest Rates

The principal means of engineering a fall in the rate for sterling would be a rapid, substantial and sustained reduction in interest rates to eliminate and, if necessary, to reverse the difference between UK and international interest rates. The flow of 'hot money' into London would then be reversed, at the same time forcing down the exchange rate. The process would be encouraged by withdrawing the exemption from withholding tax at the basic rate which is now granted to non-resident investors in gilt-edged securities, an exemption which cannot now be defended on grounds of principle or of expediency. The shock to 'confidence' would probably be sufficient to achieve the exchange rate objective, but if not, steps could be taken as necessary to repay in advance the $20 bn of foreign debt incurred by the public sector and falling due for repayment over the next ten years. If this, too, was insufficient for the purpose, we could introduce (1) measures of the kind which have been used by the Swiss and Germans to discourage the inflow of foreign funds, including a negative interest tax and (2) a two-tier exchange rate which would ensure that, pending a reduction in the market rate to the target level, British goods would be competitively priced at home and overseas.

We envisage that the rate of interest would have to be brought down to not more than 5–6 per cent, the level to which it fell briefly in the autumn of 1977 and which it very seldom exceeded before 1968. The inflation rate was of course much lower than it is now; and interest rates as low as this might therefore provoke the kind of asset speculation which was experienced in 1972/3 and which more than any other factor contributed to the disastrous inflation of 1974/5. The mad scramble which took place then would not have occurred, however, if the quantitative controls over bank credit had not been replaced by the free-for-all which was dignified by the description 'Competition and Credit Control'. Banking, as Lord Kaldor has pointed out, is far too responsible and risky a business to be left to be regulated by competition alone, and indeed the Bank of England had to step in to save many of the secondary banks from the consequences of their own folly when the boom collapsed in 1974.

What is now required to avoid a repetition of this episode is a selective control of credit using a variety of instruments. This would take the form of directions to licensed deposit-takers and other financial intermediaries, but it would need to be reinforced by financial and fiscal measures to discourage less productive uses of capital, including differential reserve requirements, hire-purchase restrictions and other credit controls. A tax on borrowing for other than specified purposes or by specified classes of borrower might need to be introduced.

These measures would encourage capital to find its way into productive industry, but industrial investment has been unattractive for so long and the chances of a reversal of the strategy in the face of hostility from the financial establishment might look so great that investors might need some assurance of stability before committing themselves to the massive programme of investment required. The quickest and most certain way of providing such an assurance would undoubtedly be for the government to underwrite a high percentage of bank and other loans to manufacturers for investment in new plant and machinery and for other specified purposes, and to rediscount this percentage at a preferential rate of interest of, say, 6 per cent for periods of up to ten years. The rest of the money would be provided by the bank concerned at its own risk and at a market rate of interest. There would be a minimum of delay in providing the cheap finance which would be required to enable manufacturers to take advantage of the opportunities created by the competitive exchange rate, and the government would also have provided an earnest of its determination to give priority to the manufacturing sector on which our future depends.

There would of course also have to be massive additional incentives for development areas and for industries confronted with special problems as a result of the monetary and exchange rate policies pursued by successive governments in recent years.

The selective controls over credit would be bitterly attacked by those whose interests would be adversely affected, but the management of credit is a public trust and there is no case in equity for allowing the banking system in the name of competition to lend to the highest bidder to the detriment of the public interest. The present non-discriminatory form of control through credit contraction punishes the just more than the unjust. In the fifteen months ending in the first quarter of 1980, the note issue rose by only 8.6 per cent, suggesting that the half of the population who do not have a bank account were not responsible for the spending spree that persuaded the government to raise MLR to 17 per cent and yet it is principally these people who are required by the current policy to pay the price for profligacy in the form of lost jobs.

Increased Money Supply

Interest rates could only be reduced if the government were, at least implicitly, to abandon its attempt to restrict the money supply. We accept that it is not possible to control the level of sterling, the level of interest rates and the money supply all at the same time. The government has accepted the monetarist view that it is the restriction of the money supply which must take precedence; but we believe that, in conditions of less than full employment, appropriate levels for sterling and interest rates are overwhelmingly more important. It would be a necessary part of the drive to get the value of sterling down that the government should increase its supply so that its price fell to the required level.

The abandonment of money supply targets would not only be an essential element in reducing the value of sterling – reinforcing, through a 'loss of confidence', the outflow of foreign money which the fall in interest rates would provoke; it would also be beneficial in its own right. Cheap and plentiful money would provide British industry with every encouragement and opportunity to expand. The object would be to ensure that money is available to finance expansion; this policy should be maintained until the economy is fully utilising the resources available to it. This point would be reached only after a very substantial expansion had taken place; as we pointed out earlier, the limits to capacity would be substantially higher than have traditionally been the case, given that a profitable and expanding industry would be able to overcome bottlenecks more easily.

So far as monetary policy is concerned, the increased output from industry would mean that, although the total money supply would expand relatively quickly, the 'excess' money supply (the increase in the supply of money less the increase in output) would rise more slowly. Our monetary policy would then bear a marked similarity to that of more successful countries, like Germany, where the money supply is allowed to accommodate the rate of growth. In any case, monetarists cannot have it both ways. If they were right in pressing for the uncapping of sterling in 1977 because they feared that the money supply would increase as a result of an inflow of foreign capital, they should welcome a reduction in the exchange rate on the grounds that the outflow of capital which would accompany and help to engineer it would reduce the money supply.

Full Employment and Increased Public Expenditure

A lower exchange rate, lower interest rates and more plentiful money would raise the output and profitability of manufacturing industry; and the increased buoyancy of the manufacturing sector would mean less need for government spending in order to maintain the level of demand. As an expanding and profitable industrial sector began to spend rather than save, the public sector need no longer remain in deficit; we have already noted that the public sector borrowing requirement could be expected to fall.

Initially, however, a raising of the level of demand through the restoration of cuts in public expenditure would be an important element in getting the economy moving. Priority should be given to quick-acting stimulants to demand – raising the child benefit, for example, reducing or stabilising public sector charges such as fares and the charge for school meals, and restraining the rise in nationalised industry prices. Improvements in housing, education and health services would be slower acting but would also have important social and political benefits. Reductions in VAT on goods and in employers' National Insurance contributions in manufacturing industry would also raise demand and reduce cost and price levels. This increased level of demand could be safely undertaken in the conditions of competitiveness guaranteed by the new rate for sterling.

Improved Real Wages in Manufacturing

It is generally thought that a devaluation-based strategy would depend crucially for its success on the extent to which the rise in wages could be restrained to take advantage of the improved competitiveness which devaluation had made available. To the extent that this is the case, it is true of any strategy designed to make room for growth, including the import control strategy proposed by the Cambridge Economic Policy Group.

In this country, however, wage restraint has not generally been used as an element in a strategy for growth. On the contrary, it has usually been applied in circumstances where, because the main object has been to deflate the economy, no quid pro quo in terms of rising living standards and employment could be offered. Not surprisingly, real wage resistance has eventually undermined every attempt to sustain a wages policy in a deflationary climate and the notion that wage restraint could have a valuable role has been substantially discredited in trade union circles. While an agreed overall restraint in wages would certainly be beneficial and would be more easily obtained in a climate of growth, we do not however, see a formal or rigid incomes policy as a necessary or even desirable element in our strategy. Indeed, we would expect and encourage real wages to rise, particularly in manufacturing industry. A rigid wages policy would, by freezing the *status quo*, frustrate the shift of talent and skill into manufacturing industry which is the object of our strategy and confirm the damaging trend towards falling real wages in manufacturing relative to the rest of the economy. The nature and extent of that trend can be seen from the fact that, in the first half of 1980, earnings in the vehicle manufacturing industry rose by only 5 per cent, the economy as a whole by 11.8 per cent and insurance, banking and finance by 17.3 per cent. This is the very reverse of what is needed – within a climate of rising real wages generally, the room for manoeuvre which would allow wages in manufacturing industry to rise relative to all other incomes.

There is no reason to suppose that a policy for growth would be more likely to provoke higher wage claims than has been the case in periods of deflation. Table 7.1 in fact suggests that the reverse may be the case.

TABLE 7.1   *Percentage change in wages and salaries per unit of output, 1953–75*

	Stop		Go
1956–58	5.4	1953–55	2.2
1960–62	4.4	1959–60	0.0
1965–66	5.0	1963–64	−0.6
1970–71	10.7	1967–69	2.2
1974–75	28.9	1972–73	4.9
1977–79	13.5	1976	13.8

SOURCE: Figures derived from Written Answers, Hansard, 27 November 1979.

There are of course time lags between deflationary measures and the effect, if any, on wages; and the figures from 1966 onwards are distorted by various mandatory incomes policies, but even so it is difficult to believe on the basis of these figures that the combined efforts at the Treasury of Messrs Thorneycroft, Selwyn Lloyd, Callaghan, Jenkins and Healey to deflate the economy did much to reduce the rate of inflation.

Selective Import Controls

While devaluation is superior to general import controls as a comprehensive stimulus to the economy – as we explained in Chapter 6, import controls would be merely half a devaluation and the less effective and more problematical half at that – this is not to say that there is no place for import controls in a strategy for growth. Particular industries – those gravely weakened by current policies and those whose survival is crucial to the economy – may need the protection of selective import controls and we would have no hesitation in putting these in place where necessary. We also recommend that, where appropriate, more effective governmental action be taken to counteract unfair trading practices and dumping. Direct intervention of this sort would be used to supplement the market forces which devaluation would bring to bear in support of industry as a whole.

The EEC

Import controls outside the agricultural sector would almost certainly be condemned under the Treaty of Rome, even though our proposals for devaluation and selective controls would be less damaging to other member states than the general import control strategy proposed by the Cambridge Economic Policy Group. It is also true that, under the strategy we suggest, a smaller devaluation would be required if withdrawal from the EEC permitted us to reintroduce the tariffs on manufactured imports which were removed when we joined. We see nothing but advantage, too, in recovering the power, currently exercised by the EEC, of negotiating our own trade arrangements and of acting promptly to deal with dumping and unfair trading. Similarly, it would be easier to pursue an industrial and regional policy to stimulate growth outside the confines of the Treaty of Rome. As in the case of the Cambridge strategy, substantial benefits would arise, too, if relief could be obtained from the burdens of the Common Agricultural Policy.

Control over the Banking System

A strategy based on a massive devaluation, low interest rates and the abandonment of monetary targets would be opposed by the whole of the financial establishment, not least because it would hurt their pockets as well as confound their deepest prejudices. This raises the question of the status and attitude of the Bank of England. The Bank of England Act, 1946 – as the Bank itself has pointed out – did little more than formalise the Bank's position as a public institution by vesting the Bank's stock in the ownership of the Treasury. The Act does empower the Treasury, after consultation with the Governor, to give such directions to the Bank as it thinks necessary in the public interest, but this was only to be used in 'exceptional and unusual cases' and because, according to the Bank, no occasion for its use has yet arisen, the power has never been exercised.[7]

The fundamental question remains, therefore, whether it is appropriate for an organisation which in practice is responsible to no one but itself, and which so closely identifies itself with the interest of those whose activities it is meant to control, to exercise such a considerable power over the direction of the economy. Our view is that the nominal nationalisation of the Bank should now be made a reality by placing it under the operational control of ministers. This would ensure that the strategy would not be frustrated by non-co-operation and indifferent execution. It would mean that the UK would be represented at meetings of central bankers by a member of the Treasury. The subordination of the Bank to political control would also mean that the UK must reject any further proposal that we should join the European Monetary System, since this could only mean that the primary responsibility for monetary policy would remain in the hands of central bankers, but at a European, and not just a British level.

As Fred Hirsch, a former Financial Editor of the *Economist*, noted in 1965:

> Britain, through the teachings of Keynes, understands better than most countries, that money can be made a servant and not a master; the trouble is that among the people who manage money there is a constant feeling that the master, the political and electoral master, is too immature to be trusted: it is part of the wise servant's deepest duty to stop him from running amok. That ultimately, is the root of the central banker's reluctance to let the exchange rate be altered, even when it is clear that it is no longer appropriate. They fear that if the discipline is lifted; if politicians get to understand that they can change the monetary measure rather than having to contain themselves within it – then the floodgates to ruinous self-indulgence are open. This doctrine is about as unproven as most presumptions of original sin in other people, and about as intolerable too.

The central bankers have never been slow to find means of containing politicians within the 'monetary measure'. In the 1920s, it was the Gold Standard; in the post-war period, it was the parity of sterling; and now, with the advent of floating exchange rates, the bankers have been quick to fasten on the supposedly overriding importance of the money supply as a means of exercising control over the politicians. The politicians themselves have only rarely broken free from the dead hand of financial orthodoxy; even the most radical of our political leaders have been surprisingly timid when it comes to rejecting the advice consistently offered by the bankers and the civil servants. That advice has repeatedly led them to apply the very policies of deflation and overvaluation which have frustrated their radical objectives. There is not much point in proposing a wholesale restructuring of the ownership and control of British industry, while at the same time succumbing meekly to policy advice which guarantees the continuing primacy of the vested financial interests in our economy.

A RADICAL STRATEGY

The strategy we put forward is a radical one, in the sense that it requires a decisive break with the conventional wisdom which has been embraced by the political and financial establishment in this country for so long. Under our strategy, money would become the servant and not the master of the real economy, more importance would be attached to real factors such as the standard of living and the level of employment than to indicators of financial orthodoxy, and greater priority would be given to the interests of people whose standards of living depend on the success of manufacturing industry – principally industrial workers – rather than those of people who hold and deal in money and assets.

There can be little doubt that the strategy would succeed in promoting a rate of growth which is currently regarded as being beyond the reach of the British economy. On the only other occasion when a similar combination of policies was applied, from 1932 to 1937, manufacturing output rose by 59 per cent, and without the reinforcement which this spurt of growth provided to our industrial base, we may not have had the capacity needed to win the Second World War. Unfortunately, however, we had lapsed back into the old errors even before the decade ended; and since the war, while domestic reflation has been tried from time to time, it has never been accompanied by the competitive exchange rate which is necessary if expansion is to be sustained.

We believe that the failures of the British economy have been the failures of those who have dominated policy-making for so long. When the time comes for even the most purblind of monetarists to call a halt to the destructive policies pursued at present – and let us hope that that moment is not long delayed – it is essential that we should not lapse back into a muddled version of the orthodoxies which have done so much damage. What is needed is a coherent strategy which will enable us to break decisively with the failures of the past. The strategy we put forward would, we believe, free the British people from that legacy of failure and enable them to reach their full potential.

Postscript

The course of the British economy since this book was substantially completed in mid-1980 has largely confirmed our view that counter-inflationary policies which depend on a contraction of our industrial base combine the worst of all possible economic worlds. By the end of 1980, manufacturing output was 17 per cent less than in 1973, a fall greater than that which occurred between the peak of 1929 and the low of 1932. Unemployment, at 2.25 million, was moving sharply upwards, insolvencies were at record levels, investment was falling rapidly and further public expenditure cuts were planned.

It is true that the rate of inflation was lower than had been forecast in the spring of 1980. This clearly had nothing to do with controlling the money supply since sterling M3, by the end of 1980, was rising at roughly twice the rate of the upper end of the Chancellor's target range. The fall in the inflation rate owed much more to the massive reduction in the profitability of UK manufacturing industry and to the relative decline in incomes in the industrial sector. Neither of these trends can be sustained for very long and both will have to be reversed if economic recovery is to occur.

Ministers have attributed part of the blame for our economic collapse to the slowing down of world trade. In fact, world trade was rising considerably faster in 1980 than in recent years. There has been nothing in the world trading situation to prevent us from increasing our share of world trade in manufactures, if it were not for the massive loss of competitiveness British industry has endured as a result of the appreciating rate for sterling.

This loss of competitiveness has had its expected consequences for employment, investment and profitability; but it has not yet produced the downturn in our trade balance which many would have forecast. This is largely because of increased exports of North Sea oil combined with a fall in imports as a result of de-stocking. Exports of manufactures, which had marked time in

1978 and 1979, began to fall in the autumn of 1980. This has almost certainly meant a further decline in our share of world trade in manufactures.

A Treasury press notice issued on 24 November 1980 put the increase in the real exchange rate – based on relative labour costs – at 40–50 per cent since 1978. The 1978 figure was itself 15 per cent higher than it had been in the fourth quarter of 1976. The effect on costs and output of the inevitable contraction of domestic industry has been disastrous; output per head in manufacturing fell by no less than 6.5 per cent between May 1979 and the end of 1980. This figure shows dramatically that policies of deflation and over-valuation not only produce their inevitable effects in terms of total output but also make it quite impossible to secure the improvements in productivity which an expansionary economic policy would permit and has permitted in the case of our more successful rivals.

The contrast between the British decline and the success of other economies, and the extent to which that success depends on export-led growth, is shown conclusively in an answer to a Parliamentary Question, published in Hansard on 19 December 1980. This showed that consumer prices in Japan rose by 364 per cent between 1952 and 1979 compared to 442 per cent in the United Kingdom, but that over the same period, export unit values rose only 33 per cent compared to 380 per cent in the UK. The Treasury attributed the Japanese success in holding down their export prices to technological developments and to economies of scale made possible by a near fortyfold increase in the volume of exports over this period, mainly in electrical and other machinery.

The danger is that the clear lesson concerning the destructiveness of an over-valued exchange rate will be only partially learned. There will remain a strong body of opinion which will welcome as satisfactory a reduction in the nominal exchange rate of, say, 10 per cent, when what is required is an adjustment in the real exchange rate so as to achieve the level of domestic and international competitiveness of 1973 and late 1976. The aim must be to reduce the terms of trade for manufactures to the level obtaining at that time. Nothing less will suffice.

Further Reading

Readers interested in monetary theory and its implications for international trade should read Jacob Viner's *Studies in the Theory of International Trade* (New York: Harper, 1937) and R. S. Sayers's 'Monetary Thought and Monetary Policy in England', *Economic Journal* (December 1960). The Report in 1810 of the Select Committee on the High Price of Gold Bullion contains the seeds of the present controversy and a photocopy of its 33 pages can be obtained from the Reference Division of the British Library (Official Publications) for a moderate fee. The Final Report of the Royal Commission on Gold and Silver in 1889 is of interest, together with the Additional Note by Sir Louis Mallet; the oral evidence of Sauerbeck and Alfred Marshall – the one on 8 December 1886 and the other on 19 December 1887 and 16 January 1888; the statistical material supplied by Giffen (App. III) and Sauerbeck (App. IV); and Memorandum VII in App. XVI. Some of the papers presented to the Paris Monetary Conference of 1881 are also of interest, particularly Sections VIII and IX of the Appendix to the UK Record, which includes the paper read by Giffen to the Royal Statistical Society on 21 January 1879 on the fall in the price of commodities. A more up-to-date and very readable account of the working of the Gold Standard is to be found in the 1928 edition of the Cambridge Economic Handbook on *Money*, written by D. H. Robertson, and in R. G. Hawtrey's *Bretton Woods – for better or worse* (London: Longman, 1946). The Radcliffe Committee Report on the Working of the Monetary System (Cmnd. 827) sets the scene in 1958–9, following the earlier Report of the Macmillan Committee (Cmd. 3897, 1931).

Evidence of the long-standing nature of our economic problems can be found in the 19 consular reports from the UK in the volume referred to in note 2 to Chapter 1. These were principally concerned with wages and working conditions, but also cover the state of trade and industry. The foreword by the US Secretary of State might have been written in Fleet St today! The Royal

Commission on Depression of Trade and Industry, 1887, was almost evenly divided in its recommendations and the Majority and Minority Reports both have a familiar ring. The Additional Notes are also of interest. The numerous and very informative memoranda of the Board of Trade on British and Foreign Trade and Industrial Conditions in the opening years of this century are to be found in Cd. 1761 and Cd. 2336. Statistics up to 1910 are provided in Cd. 4954 and up to 1930 in Cmd. 3737. The state of the British economy during and after the First World War is described in the Final Report of the Committee on Commercial and Industrial Policy after the War (Cd. 9035) and in the Reports of the Balfour Committee on Industry and Trade dealing with, respectively, overseas markets, industrial relations, industrial and commercial efficiency, the textile industries and the metal industries. An authoritative account of the collapse of 1929 is L. Robbins, *The Great Depression* (London: Macmillan, 1934), and the views of Keynes and other eminent men on the problem are contained in a collection of lectures entitled *The World's Economic Crisis – and the Way of Escape* (London: Allen and Unwin, 1932). The monthly Bulletins of the London and Cambridge Economic Service between 1921 and 1939 are invaluable, as are the quarterly publications thereafter to 1967, when they ceased publication.

Notes and References

CHAPTER 1: GROWTH AND PRODUCTIVITY

1. Commission from the Ordnance Department to study the manufacture of small arms in the United States, 1855.
2. Reports of the United States Consuls in Europe on the State of Labor in Europe: 1878. Executive Document No. 5, 46th Congress, 1st Session. (See in British Library of Political and Economic Science, Congressional Papers, Vol. 1875, entitled Statistical Abstract Etc. 1878, HED 46/1 1879).

CHAPTER 2: THE MONETARIST CUL-DE-SAC

1. Taken from J. K. Galbraith, *Money: Whence it Came, Where it Went* (London: Pelican Books, 1976) p. 294n, adapted from James Tobin, *The New Economics One Decade Older* (Princeton University Press, 1974) pp. 58–9.
2. This paragraph is taken in an abridged form from R. S. Sayers 'Monetary Thought and Monetary Policy in England', *Economic Journal* (December 1960) pp. 711–13. Professor Sayers was a member of the Radcliffe Committee, had practical experience at the Board of Trade in the Second World War, and has written the definitive history of the Bank of England.
3. The Bank have recently published two series for Private Sector Liquidity (PSL 1 and 2) which broadly correspond to M4 and M5. An article introducing and explaining them appeared in the Bank's *Quarterly Bulletin* (September 1979).
4. Mais Lecture, City University, 9 February 1978, published in *Bank of England Quarterly Bulletin* (March 1978).
5. Lombard Column, *Financial Times*, 17 April 1979.
6. See W. Greenwell & Co., *Monetary Bulletins 81 and 83–5 of 1978*. We are greatly indebted to the firm for copies of the Bulletin.
7. Mais Lecture, *Bank of England Quarterly Bulletin* (March 1978).
8. W. Greenwell & Co., *Monetary Bulletins*.
9. Cmnd 7858, Chapter 6.1.
10. Cmnd 7858, Chapter 4.
11. Ibid.
12. R. G. Hawtrey, 'The Trade Cycle', *De Economist* (Rotterdam, 1926) and repeated in *Trade and Credit* (London: Longmans, 1928) and *Readings in Business Cycle Theory* (Philadelphia: Blakiston, 1944).
13. Mervyn Lewis, 'Rethinking Monetary Policy', *Lloyds Bank Review* (July 1980).

14. Ibid.

15. W. Greenwell & Co., *Monetary Bulletin No. 99* (1979) and *Lloyds Bank Economic Bulletin* (January 1980).

16. See *The Times*, 16 December 1976, p. 7.

17. R. Lomax and C. Mowl, 'Balance of Payments Flows and the Monetary Aggregates in the UK', Treasury Working Paper No. 5, HM Treasury, 1978.

18. D. Smith, 'The Demand for Alternative Monies in the UK: 1924–77', *National Westminster Bank Review* (November 1978).

19. A. J. Brown, 'Inflation and the British Sickness', *Economic Journal* (March 1979).

20. Sam Brittan, Economic Viewpoint, *Financial Times*, 30 August 1979.

21. R. Tarling and F. Wilkinson, 'Inflation and Money Supply', *Economic Policy Review*, No. 3 (March 1977) Department of Applied Economics, Cambridge University.

22. The IMF figures in col. 2 exclude quasi-money. The London and Cambridge Economic Service figure in col. 3 includes cash and not deposits of the clearing banks. The GDP figures in col. 5 were originally based on 1975.

23. Cols 2 and 5 from Table 138; col. 6 from Table 16 and col. 7 from Table 111 of the 1979 edition. Col. 3 from Table 12 of 1972 edn and col. 4 from Table 142 of 1973/4 edn.

24. *Lloyds Bank Review* (April and July 1976).

CHAPTER 3: INTERNATIONAL MONETARISM

1. R. J. Ball, T. Burns and J. S. E. Laury, 'The Role of Exchange Rate Changes in Balance of Payments Adjustment: the UK Case', *Economic Journal* (March 1977).

2. Ibid.

3. D. A. Currie, 'Some Criticisms of the Monetary Analysis of Balance of Payments Correction', *Economic Journal* (September 1976).

4. H. G. Johnson, 'Monetary Approach to Balance of Payments Theory and Policy', *Economica* (August 1977).

5. P. W. Robinson, T. R. Webb and M. A. Townsend, 'The Influence of Exchange Rate Changes on Prices: a Study of 18 Industrial Countries', *Economica* (January 1979).

6. Currie, 'Some Criticisms of the Monetary Analysis'.

7. Robinson *et al.*, 'The Influence of Exchange Rate Changes'.

8. Ball *et al.*, 'The Role of Exchange Rate Changes'.

9. Robinson *et al.*, 'The Influence of Exchange Rate Changes'.

10. Quote by Peter Vinter in 'Public Expenditure – The Next Steps on the Road to Reform', *Lloyds Bank Review* (October 1978).

11. J. M. Keynes, Essay in *The World's Economic Crisis* (London: Allen and Unwin, 1932).

12. H. G. Johnson, 'The Monetary Approach to Balance of Payments Theory' in *Further Essays in Monetary Economics* (London: Allen and Unwin, 1972).

13. Ottmar Emminger, 'The Exchange Rate as an Instrument of Policy', *Lloyds Bank Review* (July 1979).

14. Ottmar Issing, 'Foreign Assets and the Income Balance of the Federal German Republic', *German Economic Review*, No. 1 (1974).
15. Currie, 'Some Criticisms of the Monetary Analysis'.
16. Johnson, 'Monetary Approach to Balance of Payment Theory and Policy'.
17. L. H. Officer, 'The Purchasing-Power-Parity Theory of Exchange Rates – a Review Article', *IMF Staff Papers* (March 1976).
18. Jacob Viner, *Studies in the Theory of International Trade* (New York: Harper, 1937) p. 385.
19. Bela Balassa, 'The Purchasing-Power-Parity Doctrine – A Reappraisal', *Journal of Political Economy* (December 1964).
20. P. Isard, 'How Far Can We Push the "Law of One Price"', *American Economic Review* (December 1977).
21. The UN have a number of different series for wholesale prices in most cases and these have changed over the years. The following are the series – UK and Holland – Finished Goods; Germany – Industrial Goods; France – Domestic Goods; Rest – General. The series are arithmetically linked in 1958 and 1972.
22. The Annual and Quarterly Reports of The United States High Commission in Germany in the years 1949–52 make it clear that German exports were very competitive on price before 1952. These reports are to be found in the British Library for Political and Economic Science under reference S5955 and S6638.
23. Ball *et al.*, 'The Role of Exchange Rate Changes'.
24. Robinson *et al.*, 'The Influence of Exchange Rate Changes'.

CHAPTER 4: THE EXCHANGE RATE

1. Sources. Wages etc. from A. L. Bowley, 'Wages, Earnings and Hours of Work 1914–47', Special Memorandum No. 50, London and Cambridge Economic Service. Trade figures from UK Submission to the International Economic Conference, Geneva, May 1927. Prices from 'Memorandum on Currency and Central Banks 1913–25' and 'Balance of Payments 1913–27' (League of Nations). Production from OEEC Industrial Statistics 1900–1959. Unemployment from UK Submission and from the LCES Bulletin.
2. See Economic Commission for Europe, *Economic Survey of Europe in 1948* (Paris: UN).
3. R. M. Stern, J. Francis and B. Schumacher, *Price Elasticities in International Trade*, for the Trade Policy Research Centre (London: Macmillan, 1976).
4. Written Answer No. 215, Hansard, Vol. 908, 24 March 1976.
5. J. R. Artus, 'The 1967 Devaluation of the Pound Sterling', *IMF Staff Papers* (November 1975).
6. *The Times*, 11 July 1977.
7. D. Ricardo, 'Notes on Malthus' in *Principles of Political Economy*, ed. J. H. Hollander and T. E. Gregory (Baltimore, 1928).
8. A. J. Brown, 'Inflation and the British Sickness'.
9. H. G. Johnson, 'The Monetary Approach to Balance of Payments Theory'.

10. W. Godley, 'Large Scale Devaluation is not the Answer', *The Times*, 18 July 1977.
11. See Reports of United States High Commission referred to in Chapter 3, note 22.
12. P. J. Forsyth and J. A. Kay, 'The Economic Implications of North Sea Oil Revenues', *Fiscal Studies* (July 1980).
13. S. Stewart, 'The International Competitiveness of Sterling and the UK Exchange Rate – a Note', *Journal of Economic Studies* (November 1976).
14. Samuel Brittan, 'Sterling and the Dutch Disease', *Financial Times*, 28 April 1977 and 'What the Dutch Do About Their Disease', *Financial Times*, 19 April 1979.
15. See OECD, *Economic Outlook*, no. 27 (July 1980) p. 56 and the *Monthly Review of External Trade Statistics* (June 1980). The latter excludes the UK and a number of smaller industrial countries from the denominator, which may account for a rather greater variation.
16. Prof. T. P. Hill, *Profits and Rates of Return* (OECD, 1979).
17. Speech by Dr A. H. E. M. Wellink, Treasurer-General, Netherlands Ministry of Finance, 25 January 1978.
18. OECD, *Economic Outlook*, no. 27 (July 1980) p. 56; *Monthly Review of External Trade Statistics* (June 1980).
19. Stewart, 'The International Competitiveness of Sterling'.
20. D. W. Jorgenson and M. Nishimizu, 'US and Japanese Economic Growth, 1952–74; an International Comparison', *Economic Journal* (December 1978).

CHAPTER 5: MEASURING INTERNATIONAL COMPETITIVENESS

1. Correspondence columns, Business News, *The Times*, 16 January and 5 May 1976.
2. Bryan Gould MP to the Chancellor – 29 December 1976 and 26 January, 8 March and 17 March 1977. One measure – the index of relative unit labour costs – has been quietly buried; presumably because the figures would have been embarrassing.
3. See the Treasury's *Economic Progress Report*, February 1978.
4. Written Answer, Hansard, 27 November 1978.
5. R. W. Green, 'Commonwealth Preference: UK Customs Duties and Tariff Preferences on Imports from the Preference Area', *Board of Trade Journal* (31 December 1965).
6. R. A. Allen and R. N. Brown, 'The Terms of Trade', *Bank of England Quarterly Bulletin* (September 1978).
7. D. Marsh, 'Import Prices Start to Level Off', *Financial Times*, 4 August 1980.
8. Written Answers, Hansard, 3 and 22 July 1980.

CHAPTER 6: FALSE TRAILS

1. OECD, *Financial Statistics*, vol. 1 (1979) p. 534.
2. Lord Kaldor, 'Money Supply and PSBR; Are We Worshipping False Gods?', *The Times*, 6 August 1980.
3. W. Greenwell & Co., *Monetary Bulletin No. 105* (1980).
4. R. Bacon and W. Eltis, *Britain's Economic Problems – Too Few Producers* (London: Macmillan, 1976).
5. F. W. Taussig, *Tariff History of the United States* (New York: Putnam, 1888; 8th edn, 1932).
6. Chapter 1, note 2.
7. Congressional Record, 4–5 May 1888 from privately bound speeches on tariff legislation in the Senate and House of Representatives in April–May 1888. 50th Congress, 1st Session.
8. F. A. Ogg and W. R. Sharp, *Economic Development of Modern Europe* (New York: Macmillan, 1928) p. 685.
9. Quoted in *Technological Stagnation in Great Britain* (Chicago: Machinery and Allied Products Institute). The teams were subsequently despatched by the Anglo-American Council on Productivity.
10. *Economic Policy Reviews* (Gower Publishing, Farnborough, Hants).

CHAPTER 7: MONETARISM OR PROSPERITY

1. Melvyn Westlake, 'The Rising Cost of Unemployment', *The Times*, 14 August 1980.
2. Pre-tax profits of the London clearing banks rose from £218m in 1969 to £1610m in 1979.
3. We estimate that the index of relative export prices stood at 135 in October 1980 (at an effective exchange rate of 79.9) compared to 93 in the fourth quarter of 1976. This takes no account of the fall in profit margins.
4. Professor Marcus Miller, *Guardian*, 18 August 1980.
5. Memorandum by Lord Kaldor to the Treasury and Civil Service Select Committee, Session 1979/80.
6. The Minority Report of the Royal Commission on Depression of Trade and Industry, 1887.
7. Memorandum by the Bank of England in 'Memoranda on Monetary Policy', Treasury and Civil Service Select Committee, Session 1979/80.

Index

References to tables and figures are given in *italic*.